The Cooking of Germany

LIFE WORLD LIBRARY
LIFE NATURE LIBRARY
TIME READING PROGRAM
THE LIFE HISTORY OF THE UNITED STATES
LIFE SCIENCE LIBRARY
INTERNATIONAL BOOK SOCIETY
GREAT AGES OF MAN
TIME-LIFE LIBRARY OF ART
TIME-LIFE LIBRARY OF AMERICA
FOODS OF THE WORLD
THIS FABULOUS CENTURY

Foods of the World

The Cooking of Germany

by

Nika Standen Hazelton

and the Editors of

TIME-LIFE BOOKS

photographed by Ralph Crane

and Henry Groskinsky

TIME-LIFE BOOKS, NEW YORK

THE AUTHOR: Daughter of a German diplomat, Nika Standen Hazelton spent much of her childhood in European capitals, with her home base remaining in Germany. She wrote for the *New Statesman* in London before moving to New York and joining the staff of FORTUNE in 1934. Her books on food include *The Best of Italian Cooking, Continental Flavor* and *The Art of Scandinavian Cooking.*

THE FIELD PHOTOGRAPHER: Ralph Crane, shown chatting with the author in a German café *(left),* was born and raised in Germany and left in 1935, working for *The New York Times.* A LIFE staff photographer since 1951, he makes his home in Los Angeles. To make the pictures for this book, Crane and his crew made a rambling 5,000-mile tour of his native country in a Volkswagen bus.

THE CONSULTING EDITOR: Michael Field, one of America's leading culinary experts, supervised the testing, adapting and writing of recipes for this book and is responsible for food presentation in the entire series. His books include *Michael Field's Cooking School* and *Michael Field's Culinary Classics and Improvisations.*

THE TEST KITCHEN PHOTOGRAPHER: Henry Groskinsky *(far left)* planned and photographed the pictures made in the test kitchen of FOODS OF THE WORLD. He began his career in the photography department of LIFE magazine, and is now a LIFE staff photographer.

THE CONSULTANT: Berlin-born Irma Rhode *(left)* first studied cooking under the tutelage of the Grand Duchess of Baden. After earning a Ph.D. in chemistry at Kiel, she moved in 1928 to New York, where she ran a gourmet shop and later worked as a dietitian. She has written *The Viennese Cookbook.*

THE COVER: A gingerbread house makes a fine family holiday project. The directions for making the basic structure are on pages 196 and 197.

TIME-LIFE BOOKS

EDITOR: Maitland A. Edey
Executive Editor: Jerry Korn
Text Director: Martin Mann
Art Director: Sheldon Cotler
Chief of Research: Beatrice T. Dobie
Picture Editor: Robert G. Mason
Assistant Text Directors: Harold C. Field, Ogden Tanner
Assistant Art Director: Arnold C. Holeywell
Assistant Chief of Research: Martha T. Goolrick

PUBLISHER: Rhett Austell
Associate Publisher: Walter C. Rohrer
Assistant Publisher: Carter Smith
General Manager: Joseph C. Hazen Jr.
Business Manager: John D. McSweeney
Production Manager: Louis Bronzo

Sales Director: Joan D. Manley
Promotion Director: Beatrice K. Tolleris
Managing Director, International: John A. Millington

FOODS OF THE WORLD

SERIES EDITOR: Richard L. Williams
EDITORIAL STAFF FOR THE COOKING OF GERMANY:
Associate Editors: Jay Brennan, William Frankel
Picture Editor: Donald Hinkle
Designer: Albert Sherman
Assistant to Designer: Elise Hilpert
Staff Writers: Geraldine Schremp, Ethel Strainchamps, Carolyn Tasker
Chief Researcher: Helen Fennell
Researchers: Sarah B. Brash, Wendy Afton, Val Chu, Monica Suder, Audry Weintrob, Arlene Zuckerman
Art Assistant: Gloria duBouchet
Test Kitchen Chef: John W. Clancy
Test Kitchen Staff: Fifi Bergman, Sally Darr, Leola Spencer

EDITORIAL PRODUCTION
Color Director: Robert L. Young
Assistant: James J. Cox
Copy Staff: Rosalind Stubenberg, Eleanore Karsten, Grace Hawthorne, Florence Keith
Picture Department: Dolores A. Littles, Joan Lynch
Traffic: Arthur A. Goldberger

The text for this book was written by Nika Standen Hazelton, the recipe instructions by Michael Field, the picture essays and appendix material by members of the staff. Valuable assistance was provided by the following individuals and departments of Time Inc.: Editorial Production, Robert W. Boyd Jr.; Editorial Reference, Peter Draz; Picture Collection, Doris O'Neil; Photographic Laboratory, George Karas; TIME-LIFE News Service, Richard M. Clurman; Correspondent Elisabeth Kraemer (Bonn).

Contents

Introduction   6

I   Surprises of the German Table   8

II   How to Eat Five Meals a Day   28

III   The Pleasures of Dining Out   44

IV   Old and New Ways of Party Giving   66

V   A Cooking History 2,000 Years Old   88

VI   The Northern Style: Cold-Climate Cuisine   104

VII   The Central Style: Rich and Filling   124

VIII   The Southern Style: A Lighter Touch   142

IX   Baking Raised to a Fine Art   166

X   Festive Revelry and Nostalgic Holidays   184

Appendix   *Glossary*   198

Recipe Index   200

General Index   202

Credits and Acknowledgments   208

The Recipe Booklet that accompanies this volume has been designed for use in the kitchen. It contains all of the 74 recipes included here plus 30 others. It also has a wipe-clean cover and a spiral binding so that it can either stand up or lie flat when open.

Introduction: Ways to Approach a Great Cuisine

When I first began to think about this book, I was puzzled. Here I was, ready to give the world a message about German cooking. But what German cooking? Should the book be about the cooking of present-day Germany? Should it be about the cooking I grew up with between World Wars I and II? Or should it be about the cooking of an even earlier time, the time of Imperial Germany before World War I? Each approach could be illuminating—and each had its drawbacks.

Anybody who has had a pleasant childhood and adolescence, as I did, hankers at times for the past. But among the many branches that grow upon the sturdy trunk of old nostalgia, few are so misleading as the memory of the food of once-upon-a-time. Ah, those glorious dishes that delighted us when we were young! Surely, nothing today could measure up to them. But were they really all that good—or did I think so because I was happy when I first ate them? Besides, I was to write a book about the food of Germany, not a personal memoir. My early life was lived within a small circle, and small circles are just that: their ways are not the ways of a whole people.

Then I considered leaving myself out of the book altogether, simply reporting on the food of present-day Germany. But reporting facts does not necessarily make them interesting. Foreign dishes are meaningless unless their background and setting are explained. I thought of all the foreign cookbooks that come to me for review every year, listing foreign dishes that run together in the mind as the colors of a bad print run in the wash. Such books make me react with the enthusiasm of an apathetic camel, and I felt sure that my readers would have the same reaction if I followed that approach.

Looking at the cuisine of pre-World War I Germany as a sort of prototype of German cooking is an approach that has its appeal, and it is reflected to some extent in Chapters 6, 7 and 8 of this book. But this approach has its limitations, too. Why write about a bygone age? The Germany of those days is gone forever—and good riddance to it.

Slowly, as the book took form in my mind, I began to realize that my choices among these approaches would have to depend upon my personal taste. Every cookbook reflects the taste of its author, if only by what is included and what is omitted. There really is no such thing as impersonality in matters of food. All one can do is stick to the narrow path of fairness as closely as one knows how. Finally and inevitably, I put a little of all three of my possible approaches into this book, hoping that together they will give the reader a reasonable picture of the food and the life of a great nation.

During the last 50 years that nation has changed more than any other in Western Europe. Yet it has remained German, because everything that happens to a nation or a people happens because of what went on before. Physically, much of Germany no longer looks as it did as recently as 1939, because of the destruction of war and the reconstruction that followed. Time and again I have found myself lost in such once-familiar cities as Hamburg, Berlin or Mainz. Yet these cities, built and rebuilt at the same time and with the same materials as cities in Scandinavia, look German, not Scandinavian, because they were built by Germans with German traditions.

The same historical continuity applies to food. The foods of modern Germany are produced in much the same manner as modern foods anywhere, but even a frozen German vegetable tastes different from its American counterpart. In the first place, it is grown on different soils and in a different climate. Secondly, it is not nearly so heavily sprayed in the field as American vegetables are. Finally, it is frozen with fewer (if any) preservatives, because the Germans mistrust chemicals in their foods. Differences of this kind are all to the good in a world fast sailing into uniformity, and they must be understood to make an unfamiliar cuisine come to life.

A word about the recipes in this book. Any country as complex as Germany will produce a great variety of representative recipes. The ones chosen for this book by the editors aim to exhibit the very diversity of German food that I have tried to describe in the text. The recipes have been written by Michael Field, who, with his staff, tested and adapted them for American cooks and kitchens. As in any cookbook, some readers will miss their own favorites, or question the ingredients or techniques that went into making a typical dish. I can only remind them that no book is all-inclusive, and that most of the traditional dishes of any country come in almost as many versions as there are cooks. This is an asset rather than a fault, for it gives room to pleasant speculation on the whys and wherefores of a dish—pleasant speculation, because food and cooking are pleasant and comforting in themselves. To quote the great Munich chef Alfred Walterspiel: "Die Kochkunst ist wie die Musik dazu angetan, Freude zu bereiten und den Menschen über sorgenvolle Zeiten hinwegzuhelfen"—"The art of cooking, like music, is meant to give pleasure and to tide people over troublesome times."

Nika Standen Hazelton

7

I

Surprises of the German Table

An American tourist planning a trip to Germany is likely to have some very clear ideas of what he will see and hear. The air will be filled with the strains of Bach and Beethoven. There will be castles perched high over the Rhine, and Hansel-and-Gretel towns nestled in dark forests. And there will, of course, be cuckoo clocks, Christmas trees and Volkswagens.

The tourist will have some ideas of what he will be eating, too. Most of us think of German food as an endless succession of sausages and sauerkraut, working up to a grand climax of *Sauerbraten* and dumplings, with every dish washed down by great steins of beer hoisted by hefty maidens while the band plays *oom-pa-pa*.

When this American actually reaches Germany, he is in for some surprises. Everything he anticipates is there—but with a difference. The Rhine castles tower over cloverleafed superhighways. The Gretels are miniskirted, the Hansels long-haired, and they sway to transistorized rock 'n' roll in the automobile-choked streets of their age-old towns. Cuckoo clocks are sold through American-inspired mail-order houses; Christmas trees, real and fake, are found in department stores far more modern than most of those in the United States. And along with the Volkswagens have come far-flung suburbs, shopping centers with acres of parking space, and motorized vacations in Greece and Spain.

Similarly, the tourist will find all the dishes he expected, but subtly different in flavor and in an incredible variety of forms. The sausages—sliced, spread, poached or fried—come in the hundreds, from delicate little *Weisswürste*, with a veal-based stuffing, to *Getrüffelte Gänseleberwurst*, a goose-

In the public market of Esslingen, farmers set up vending stalls just as they did centuries before the automobile age. On the hillside beyond the square's half-timbered gabled buildings is part of a fortress that formerly sheltered the people of Esslingen from their enemies in time of danger.

8

liver sausage fragrant with truffles. The sauerkraut will be far less coarse in texture and flavor than its American counterpart, and it may be cooked with pineapple *(page 24)*, oranges or apples (or even, in one version, with oysters); other dishes include sauerkraut cooked in beer, wine or champagne, serving as a bed for an inviting little roast partridge. *Sauerbraten* prepared in the Rhenish fashion will offer the surprise of raisins; in other versions, the meat for the dish may be marinated either in the classical wine or vinegar *(page 22)*, or marinated in buttermilk, and sauced with sweet cream and crumbs of honey cake. And the dumplings that accompany the *Sauerbraten* may be made from flour *(Recipe Booklet)*, grated potatoes or stale bread; enriched with eggs, bacon, liver or onions sautéed in butter or lard; and flavored with marjoram or parsley.

With these discoveries, an American in Germany can begin to explore a cuisine of enormous variety and scope, with unique blends of the native and the exotic, the traditional and the ultramodern. What is more, it is a cuisine that is likely to please him, for German cooking is far more suitable to the average American taste than that of other European nations. Most Americans endorse the German stress on basic "meat and potatoes," and prefer the general blandness of German food to the garlicked and spiced dishes of the Mediterranean. Even the fats used for cooking in Germany are not the relatively unfamiliar olive oil, but the butter, bacon grease or lard of home. Within this framework of pleasant familiarity, however, the American explorer of German food can find unexpected delights in every course of every meal he eats.

A glowing mural of fruits adorns the brightly lit façade of a supermodern supermarket in West Berlin. Inside, the market is just as up-to-date, offering foods premixed, freeze-dried, precooked and, of course, temptingly packaged for impulse buying, along with fresh foods from the world over.

He will begin with a selection of *Vorspeisen*, or appetizers, which may be served either hot or cold. Some of them, like the noble composite salads of lobster and crab or chicken and duck, could fill the function of a main dish. Others are less imposing but no less intricate: the *Champignon-Schnitte*, a slice of bread topped with richly sauced mushrooms and delicately browned under the broiler; or the *Königinpasteten*—puff-paste patties bursting with any number of delicate fish or meat fillings.

Germany's thick soups, made from potatoes *(page 137)*, dried peas or lentils *(page 116)*, robustly flavored with sausage and onion, and thickened with flour—these are famous throughout the world. But German cooks also produce delicious clear soups—notably, double consommés with such garnishes as tiny marrow dumplings so light you'd think they could take flight. And there are creamy asparagus, spinach, cauliflower *(page 60)* and knob-celery soups; sensuous crayfish bisque, made with veal stock and thickened with egg yolk; and soups flavored with chervil or a whole spring garden of fresh herbs.

Among the fish, the ubiquitous herring turns up in such familiar forms as rollmops *(page 39)* and filleted Bismarck herring—but herring may also be fried and then marinated, to be eaten with boiled new potatoes and a sauce of bacon and onions. Shellfish abound in the menu: rosy crayfish cooked with dill, lobsters and crabs in elaborate ragoûts and salads, mussels cooked in white wine. More simply prepared are the firm-fleshed flounder, plaice, turbot and sole of the North Sea, which are poached or sautéed and served with a simple butter or lemon sauce to keep their fla-

vor inviolate. Fresh-water salmon and trout are kings among German fish and, again, are simply cooked. But pike and carp, beloved by Germans since the Middle Ages, still appear in dishes of baroque splendor, fancifully stuffed, cooked in red or white wine and sauced with sour or whipped cream, or luxuriating in rich, dark-brown sweet-and-sour sauces redolent with raisins and spices.

Meat is the cornerstone of German cooking, and the *Braten,* or roast, is Germany's national dish. Like our American roasts, the *Braten* may be cooked in an oven; it may also be cooked with a little liquid in a tightly covered pot on top of the stove. A *Braten* may be a roast of pork (the most popular), beef or veal (the most elegant), and the last two may be larded with bacon, stuffed with *foie gras,* wrapped in puff paste, cooked with wine, vegetables or cream, basted with broth or glazed with honey. Above all, it must be *saftig*—that is, tender and juicy—and every standard German cookbook devotes pages to the problem of bringing a *Braten* to the proper stage of *Saftigkeit.*

Among the smaller meats, chops and steaks are sometimes plainly broiled, sautéed or slow-cooked; more often, they are stuffed or garnished with mushrooms, goose livers, meat dressings and the like. In their wake comes the great family of cutlets (most often of veal) called *Schnitzel,* common to the German and Austrian cuisines. There are relatively plain *Schnitzel,* such as the unbreaded *Naturschnitzel* and the sauceless *Wienerschnitzel* —and there are also such creations as the *Rahmschnitzel* (served with a cream sauce), the *Jägerschnitzel* (with mushrooms and sour cream), the *Käseschnitzel* (stuffed with ham and cheese), *Schnitzel* with cooked bacon, tongue or ragoût, and *Schnitzel* spread with fillings, wrapped in pancakes, sprinkled with cheese and baked in the oven. Most elaborate of all is the great *Schnitzel à la Holstein,* named after Baron Friedrich von Holstein, a hardworking bachelor diplomat of Imperial days who liked to eat many good things from a single plate. In its perfected form, *Schnitzel à la Holstein* is framed by tiny portions of smoked salmon, caviar, mushrooms, truffles and cooked crayfish tails; covering the meat itself is a fried egg, which is topped by anchovies, capers and a coquettish sprig of parsley.

Far more common than the *Schnitzel*—indeed, the most widely used of all meats in German cookery—is pork, fresh or cured. There are dozens of ways to cook it, all of them good. Fresh ham may be roasted to preserve a crisp crackling of skin; or marinated in wine to taste somewhat like wild boar *(page 26);* or sliced, fried in butter and sauced with sour cream. The glory of cured pork is the rosy *Kasseler Rippenspeer (page 140),* often served in a multicolored tapestry of peas, white beans, chestnuts, roast potatoes and mushrooms, or resting on a bed of sauerkraut cooked with apples.

As for ground meats, Germans are partial to veal or pork as well as beef, and often combine two of these meats or even all three in a single dish. To a German, our simple hamburger is a *Deutsches Beefsteak,* but German culinary skill is far more evident in the poached meatballs called *Königsberger Klopse (page 119),* made from ground pork and beef (or, more elegantly, pork and veal), bound with eggs and served with a piquant lemon-and-caper sauce. At the other end of the scale of complexity

Laden with blossoms, the branches of a pear tree frame a view of a small Bavarian village. The Alps in the background will still be snow-clad when the pears are ripe. They are only one of the fruits that are such a beloved part of the German diet, and orchards in bloom color the countryside everywhere in the spring.

is the famed *Beefsteak Tartar (page 26),* a dish made up of raw ground steak served with an egg yolk, chopped or sliced raw onion, anchovies, capers and pickles, which is said to be one of the most delicious and reliable of hangover cures.

The gamut of German stews ranges from the pungent *Würzfleisch* of spiced beef *(page 25)* and the robust *Pichelsteiner Fleisch* of beef, veal, lamb and pork *(page 41)* to the delicate *ragoûts fins (Recipe Booklet).* Always referred to by their French name, these *ragoûts* are sophisticated combinations of veal tongue, sweetbreads, brains and mushrooms, cooked with wine, enriched with eggs and often served in puff-paste shells. Such dishes reflect the high esteem and loving care Germans bestow upon the parts of animals that we know as "innards." Liver reaches perhaps its noblest form cooked in the Berlin way, with onions and apples, or it may be made into *Leberkäs,* a kind of Bavarian *pâté.* From several animals, but particularly from the calf, the German cook takes the tongue, kidneys, heart, sweetbreads, tripe and milt; from the cow and pig, he takes the palates, heads, shanks, hocks, tails, trotters and udders. Many an innard-hating American tourist has fallen in love with these meats in Germany without knowing exactly what he was eating.

Though the Germans have developed a number of pleasant chicken dishes, their greatest achievements in fowl cookery are based upon duck and goose. The lean, meaty ducks of Germany put our relatively fat and insipid ones to shame, and German cuisine boasts magnificent dishes of duck braised in beer or wine, or roasted with a stuffing of apples and prunes. The best of these German ducks come from Vierlande, a pretty farming district southeast of Hamburg.

It is in goose cookery, however, that Germany really triumphs, for there is a rapport between the German and his roast goose that outsiders cannot fathom. According to a saying in the Berlin dialect, which often substitutes the soft "j" for standard German's hard "g," *Eine jute jebratene Jans is eine jute Jabe Jottes*—"A good roast goose is a good gift of God"—and all Germans complain that the trouble with a goose is that there is too much for one person and not enough for two. Goose is stuffed with onions, apples and herbs; the neck is stuffed with liver and pork; the blood and giblets may be combined with dried pears, prunes and apples in the famous *Schwarzsauer,* a stew that makes strong men weep for home.

More exotic than these goose and duck dishes is the cooking of game birds and venison. All good German restaurants—and many not-so-good ones—offer a selection of saddles, haunches, loins and stews from roebuck and doe, deer and hart, hare and wild boar. Along with pheasant, partridge, woodcock and moor hen, these meats may be prepared in a variety of ways. They may be larded or barded before roasting, or larded before being marinated and braised in sour cream. Frequently, they come to the table with accompaniments of mushrooms and artichoke hearts stuffed with peas, and of stewed pear or apple halves filled with preserves or the traditional compote of *Preiselbeeren,* small, tart berries cooked into the German equivalent of cranberry sauce.

These are lordly dishes, of course, but delicious too are the dishes that have developed out of German frugality. Leftover fish or meats and leftover potatoes or vegetables or dumplings are minced, bound with a sauce or with eggs, and steamed or baked into savory puddings. Even more characteristic is the popular German way of cooking called the *Eintopf*—literally, a one-pot dish, but actually a one-dish meal—which saves the housewife both time and money. In *Eintopf* cookery, fish, bacon or other meats are combined with vegetables, potatoes, rice, barley or dumplings, and simmered long and slowly. Most of these dishes are essentially stews in which meat and vegetables are browned in hot fat, seasoned with herbs and spices, and cooked in a small amount of liquid.

The *Eintopf* represents basic German cookery. Another basic German way with foods is to combine the flavors of sweet and sour. Fish, meat, potatoes and vegetables are often cooked with vinegar and sweetened with sugar to make piquant gravies that Germans love. Still more typically, fruits are used to get the sweet-and-sour effect. I don't know of any country that uses as many dried fruits as Germany, where dried apples, pears, prunes and apricots are part and parcel of the national diet. Such fruits are combined with pork in a dish named *Schlesisches Himmelreich,* or "Silesian heaven," from the former province of Silesia, once a part of eastern Germany. In another dish, apples and potatoes are combined as *Himmel und Erde (page 164),* or "heaven and earth"; in still another, prunes, barley and bacon are simmered together in a one-dish meal.

Both dried and fresh fruits can be stewed as a compote *(page 138),* a major feature of the German and Austrian cuisines. In the main course of a meal, a compote frequently accompanies meats and dumplings in lieu of vegetables. Applesauce and freshly grated horseradish make a perfect sauce for boiled beef; *Preiselbeeren* have already been mentioned as a traditional accompaniment for game; sweet or sour cherries, brought to a quick boil and then chilled, go deliciously well with any roast meat or fowl; and prunes, an old German favorite, form the perfect foil for a rich pork roast. It may be that the Germans' taste for dried fruit stems from the days when these fruits alone broke the monotony of a winter diet of cabbage and turnip. What is certain is that the love of fruit is real and deep, and nowhere is it expressed in a more lovely way than on Germany's rural roads, planted on both sides with apples and pears, cherries and plums—trees that blossom for the traveler in the spring and shower rich gifts upon him in the fall.

Vegetables are another matter, for a German's feelings about vegetables are at once less intense and more complex than those of an American. I don't believe that any German mother would suffer as much and as visibly as an American one if a child refused to eat his vegetables—though a German child might well be scolded if he turned down a salad of fresh greens. What is more curious, each German vegetable has its own status— or lack of it. The most humble, but I think the most interestingly cooked, are winter vegetables such as cabbages and roots. At the top of the status scale are asparagus—the thick, white, unbelievably tender asparagus of Germany, eaten canned or fresh—and mushrooms, which come in six or seven standard varieties that make ours taste like foam rubber. Whenever a guest is to be honored for dinner in a German home, these two vegetables are piled on.

The meal is coming to an end, in a selection of desserts called *süsse Speisen*, or "sweet dishes." Perhaps more than any other foods, these pleasant, wholesome dishes evoke the nostalgia of a German childhood. They may be rice puddings, sometimes cooked with fruits, or puddings of farina, tapioca or fruit. Apple or other fruit pancakes *(page 65)* alternate with fruit dumplings, which come to the table with a suitable sweet sauce. Magnificently rich, yet subtle and delicate, are the egg custards, the almond or hazelnut *(page 87)* creams, and the fruit or wine jellies *(page 123)* embellished with rococo swirls of whipped cream.

Our American tourist will probably be pleased and certainly surprised by the enormous richness and variety of German food. He may be equally surprised by some of the ways in which that food is sold. He would expect the Old World flavor of town markets, set up in the open air, with stalls that feature meats and cheeses, breads and sweets, vegetables and fruit. Here, housewives roam about with wicker shopping baskets, string sacks or plastic tote bags, comparing prices. Most German food, however, is now sold in brand-new supermarkets.

German supermarkets are superstocked with thousands of different foods from every corner of the world. An American will find the cereals, coffees and canned fruits of home under their familiar brand names. He will also find mushrooms from Holland, tomatoes from Italy, lettuce from France, potatoes from Denmark, oranges from Israel, mangoes from the Caribbean and grapes from Algeria. He will see an endless number of convenience foods —jam and mustard sold in tubes; scores of excellent dehydrated soups;

hundreds of canned and bottled vegetables, meats, fruits and juices; puddings by the dozen; and a bewildering assortment of cheeses, candies, cigars and cigarettes, wines and spirits.

If these supermarkets remind the tourist of home, other food stores are very German. The butcher shops stock huge assortments of fancy meats prepared in ready-to-cook portions, such as stuffed veal birds and skewers of herbed liver. Special shops sell venison, hare, wild boar and game birds. Pork butchers, laws unto themselves, stagger a visitor with vast arrays of fresh, pickled and smoked pork—and with more sausages of more varieties than he ever thought possible. At Christmastime he may be touched and amused, as I once was, by a pork butcher's window containing a complete family of stuffed pigs and piglets—papa, mama, son and daughter. Dressed in human costumes, they sat around a table piled high with gift-wrapped presents, under a Christmas tree tastefully hung with sausages of all kinds.

But the sight that will convince our tourist that he has really left home is the *Feinkostgeschäft* (literally, "fine food shop"), a delicatessen raised to the *nth* degree of gourmandise. In Frankfurt's Kleine Bockenheimer Strasse, known locally as the *Fressgasse*, or "gorging street," he will be overwhelmed by their number, and wherever he goes he will hear someone eulogizing the merchandise, service and décor of a favorite superdelicatessen.

The greatest gastronomic temple of them all, perhaps, is Munich's Dallmayr's, where 550 employees work in a four-story establishment of vaulted arches and beer-keg-shaped marble columns. At Dallmayr's, wooden curlicues and polished brass conceal modern refrigerators, and such perishable items as Iranian caviar are displayed on beds of ice. Three bubbling streams of water gush from marble fountains supported by marble nymphs, filling pools where trout, crayfish, carp and pike swim by the hundred. Some 180 different cheeses and 130 kinds of sausages provide for all tastes. One department is devoted to Oriental delicacies, another to wild fowl and game, still another to fruit from all over the world.

If the supplies of foods in Germany do not dazzle a tourist, the places in which to try them certainly will. In any city he visits, he can enjoy all this *gutes Essen*—"good eating"—in such establishments as *Gasthöfe, Ratskeller, Weinstuben, Bierhallen* and *Restaurants,* all serving different foods at different levels of elegance. A tourist in a hurry can have a stand-up meal at a *Schnellimbiss-Stube,* or quick-lunch counter, or he can tote his own tray in an American-style cafeteria. *Austernstuben*—oyster bars—will serve him seafood in style. A vegetarian need not be deprived, for every German city has a vegetarian restaurant. If the tourist is poor, a student restaurant will fill him up for a pittance. And he can refresh himself with milk shakes in *Milchbars,* or with gaily colored ices in *Eissalons.*

The tourist need not limit himself to German foods. If he craves an international atmosphere, he will find the country studded with Italian, French, Hungarian, Serbian, Russian, Greek and Chinese restaurants. And if he is still hungry at bedtime, corner stalls will serve him sausages, meatballs and barbecued meats in the wee hours of the night. As he strolls off to bed, our well-fed tourist may reasonably feel that he has finally found the true land of *gutes Essen.*

Versatile Sauerkraut: A Food with a History

Sauerkraut plays at least a minor role in the cooking of most countries where cabbage is grown, but in the German cuisine it is a star. German cooks not only serve it, suitably cooked and seasoned *(page 24)*, as an accompaniment to meat dishes, but use it in provocative combinations with other foods. Combined with grapes *(Recipe Booklet)*, it becomes a tangy side dish; mixed with pineapple and served as shown here in the shell of the fruit *(page 24)*, it is both decorative and a surprisingly appetizing addition to a meal. From cabbage seed to finished product, the task of getting sauerkraut to German tables engages thousands of pairs of hands. Cabbage is the principal crop on many farms around Stuttgart, and is sold mainly to large sauerkraut factories, though some of it still goes to housewives who make their own kraut. The technique of making sauerkraut has hardly changed since it was recorded by the ancient Romans, who seem to have acquired it from the Orient. It consists of adding salt to shredded cabbage and then allowing the cabbage to ferment. The method was forgotten by Europeans until the conquering Tatar hordes, bringing it from China, reintroduced it to Austria in the 13th Century. The Austrians gave sauerkraut its name (literally, "sour plant") and passed it along to their neighbors, among whom none welcomed it more warmly than the Germans.

Overleaf: On its way to becoming sauerkraut, cabbage is tossed into a factory truck by a farm wife in southern Germany.

Sauerkraut for family use is made the old-fashioned way by a Swabian village woman and her grandson. She is shredding a head of *Spitzkraut* (savoy cabbage) on a board with an inset blade, while the boy presses layers of the vegetable, mixed with layers of salt, into a crock. When the container is full, the cabbage will be covered with a weighted lid slightly smaller in width than the jar—to force the brine to the top—and allowed to stand until it has fermented.

On a much bigger scale, two workers in an Esslingen sauerkraut factory alternate layers of shredded cabbage with layers of salt.

To serve 6 to 8

½ cup dry red wine
½ cup red wine vinegar
2 cups cold water
1 medium-sized onion, peeled and
    thinly sliced
5 black peppercorns and 4 whole
    juniper berries coarsely crushed
    with a mortar and pestle
2 small bay leaves
4 pounds boneless beef roast,
    preferably top or bottom round
    or rump, trimmed of fat
3 tablespoons lard
½ cup finely chopped onions
½ cup finely chopped carrots
¼ cup finely chopped celery
2 tablespoons flour
½ cup water
½ cup gingersnap crumbs, or 1 cup
    crumbled honey cake made from
    the recipe on page 181, or 1 cup
    crumbled ready-made imported
    honey cake

Sauerbraten

MARINATED POT ROAST IN SWEET-AND-SOUR SAUCE

In a 2- to 3-quart saucepan, combine the wine, vinegar, water, sliced onion, crushed peppercorns and juniper berries, and bay leaves. Bring this marinade to a boil over high heat, then remove it from the heat and let it cool to room temperature. Place the beef in a deep crock or a deep stainless-steel or enameled pot just large enough to hold it comfortably and pour the marinade over it. The marinade should come at least halfway up the sides of the meat; if necessary, add more wine. Turn the meat in the marinade to moisten it on all sides. Then cover the pan tightly with foil or plastic wrap and refrigerate for 2 to 3 days, turning the meat over at least twice a day.

Remove the meat from the marinade and pat it completely dry with paper towels. Strain the marinade through a fine sieve set over a bowl and reserve the liquid. Discard the spices and onions.

In a heavy 5-quart flameproof casserole, melt the lard over high heat until it begins to splutter. Add the meat and brown it on all sides, turning it frequently and regulating the heat so that it browns deeply and evenly without burning. This should take about 15 minutes. Transfer the meat to a platter, and pour off and discard all but about 2 tablespoons of the fat from the casserole. Add the chopped onions, carrots and celery to the fat in the casserole and cook them over moderate heat, stirring frequently, for 5 to 8 minutes, or until they are soft and light brown. Sprinkle 2 tablespoons of flour over the vegetables and cook, stirring constantly, for 2 or 3 minutes longer, or until the flour begins to color. Pour in 2 cups of the reserved marinade and ½ cup of water and bring to a boil over high heat. Return the meat to the casserole. Cover tightly and simmer over low heat for 2 hours, or until the meat shows no resistance when pierced with the tip of a sharp knife. Transfer the meat to a heated platter and cover it with aluminum foil to keep it warm while you make the sauce.

Pour the liquid left in the casserole into a large measuring cup and skim the fat from the surface. You will need 2½ cups of liquid for the sauce. If you have more, boil it briskly over high heat until it is reduced to that amount; if you have less, add some of the reserved marinade. Combine the liquid and the gingersnap or honey-cake crumbs in a small saucepan, and cook over moderate heat, stirring frequently, for 10 minutes. The crumbs will disintegrate in the sauce and thicken it slightly. Strain the sauce through a fine sieve, pressing down hard with a wooden spoon to force as much of the vegetables and crumbs through as possible. Return the sauce to the pan, taste for seasoning and let it simmer over a low heat until ready to serve.

To serve, carve the meat into ¼-inch-thick slices and arrange the slices attractively in overlapping layers on a heated platter. Moisten the slices with a few tablespoons of the sauce and pass the remaining sauce separately in a sauceboat. Traditionally, *Sauerbraten* is served with dumplings or boiled potatoes and red cabbage *(page 63)*.

NOTE: If you prefer, you may cook the *Sauerbraten* in the oven rather than on top of the stove. Bring the casserole to a boil over high heat, cover tightly and cook in a preheated 350° oven for about 2 hours.

Almost entirely covered with marinade, a cut of top-round beef begins its 2- to 3-day metamorphosis to *Sauerbraten*.

To serve 4 to 6

2 pounds fresh sauerkraut
1 tablespoon lard
½ cup finely chopped onions
1 tablespoon sugar
2 cups cold water
5 whole juniper berries, 6 whole
  black peppercorns, 2 small bay
  leaves, ¼ teaspoon caraway seeds
  (optional) and 1 whole allspice,
  wrapped together in cheesecloth
½ pound boneless smoked pork loin
  or butt, in 1 piece, or substitute
  ½ pound Canadian-style bacon in
  1 piece
1 large raw potato, peeled

Gedünstetes Sauerkraut

STEAMED SPICED SAUERKRAUT

Drain the sauerkraut, wash it thoroughly under cold running water, and let it soak in a pot of cold water for 10 to 20 minutes, depending upon its acidity. A handful at a time, squeeze the sauerkraut vigorously until it is completely dry.

In a heavy 3- to 4-quart casserole or saucepan, melt the lard over moderate heat until a light haze forms above it. Add the chopped onions and cook, stirring frequently, for 8 to 10 minutes, or until the onions are light brown. Add the sauerkraut, sugar and 2 cups of water, and mix together thoroughly, separating the strands of sauerkraut with a fork. Bury the bag of spices in the sauerkraut and place the pork or bacon on top of it. Bring to a boil over high heat, then reduce the heat to its lowest point, cover the casserole and cook, undisturbed, for 20 minutes.

Grate the raw potato directly into the casserole, and with a fork stir it into the sauerkraut mixture. Cover the casserole tightly, and cook over low heat for 1½ to 2 hours, or until the sauerkraut has absorbed most of its cooking liquid and the meat is tender when pierced with the tip of a fork. Remove and discard the spices. Taste for seasoning.

To serve, cut the meat into ¼-inch slices. Then transfer the sauerkraut to a large heated platter. Spread the sauerkraut into an even mound and arrange the slices of meat on top.

NOTE: To prepare this as an *Eintopf*, or one-dish meal, which is so popular in Germany, use a 2-pound piece of smoked pork or Canadian-style bacon and cook it as described above. To serve, cut the meat into ¼-inch slices and arrange the slices attractively around the mound of sauerkraut.

To serve 6 to 8

2 pounds fresh sauerkraut
5 cups unsweetened pineapple juice
  (2 twenty-ounce cans)
A 1½- to 2-pound ripe pineapple

Sauerkraut mit Ananas

PINEAPPLE SAUERKRAUT

Drain the sauerkraut, wash it thoroughly under cold running water, and let it soak in a pot of cold water for 10 to 20 minutes, depending upon its acidity. A handful at a time, squeeze the sauerkraut until it is completely dry.

Combine the sauerkraut and pineapple juice in a heavy 3- to 4-quart saucepan, and bring to a boil over high heat, stirring with a fork to separate the sauerkraut strands. Reduce the heat to its lowest point and cover the pan tightly. Simmer, undisturbed, for 1½ to 2 hours, or until the sauerkraut has absorbed most of its cooking liquid.

With a long, sharp knife, cut the top 1½ inches off the pineapple and set the top aside. Hollow out the pineapple carefully, leaving a ⅛- to ¼-inch layer of the fruit in the shell. Remove and discard the woody core of the hollowed-out fruit and cut the fruit into ½-inch cubes.

Stir the diced pineapple into the cooked sauerkraut, cook for a minute or two, then pour the entire mixture into a large sieve set over a bowl. When all the liquid has drained through, pile the sauerkraut into the pineapple shell. Cover with the reserved pineapple top and serve on a large plate. If you like, any remaining sauerkraut may be presented mounded on the plate around the pineapple.

Pineapple sauerkraut is traditionally served with roasted smoked pork or with roasted game birds.

oons of the flour with the salt and pep-
ned flour one at a time, then vigorously
12-inch skillet, melt 2 tablespoons of
aze forms above it. Add the beef and
heat so the meat browns quickly and
meat to a platter and add the remain-
hen drop in the onions and cook over
r 5 to 8 minutes, or until the onions
prika, peppercorns, allspice, bay leaf
it to a boil, meanwhile scraping into
ottom and sides of the skillet.
heat to low, and cover tightly. Sim-
it occasionally with its cooking liq-
with the tip of a fork, transfer it to
keep it warm.
e sieve into a small bowl, pressing
...s with the back of a spoon before discarding them.
There should be 1½ to 2 cups of liquid in the bowl. If there is less than that
amount add canned or fresh beef stock; if more, boil the liquid briskly over
high heat until it is reduced to 2 cups. Return the liquid to the skillet, bring
to a simmer over high heat, then reduce the heat to low. With a whisk, beat
the remaining tablespoon of flour into the sour cream. A few tablespoons at
a time, beat the sour cream into the simmering liquid and cook, whisking constantly, until the sauce is hot and slightly thickened. Do not let it boil. Return the beef to the skillet, baste it well with the sauce, and cook just long
enough to heat it through. Stir in the Madeira and taste for seasoning. To
serve, arrange the meat on a heated platter. Moisten the slices with a few tablespoons of sauce and serve the rest separately in a sauceboat. Traditionally,
Würzfleisch is accompanied by dumplings or boiled or mashed potatoes.

4 tablespoons flour
1 teaspoon salt
½ teaspoon freshly ground black
   pepper
2 pounds top round steak, sliced ½
   inch thick and cut into 4 pieces
3 tablespoons lard
½ cup finely chopped onions
1 teaspoon paprika
6 whole black peppercorns
3 whole allspice
½ small bay leaf
1 whole clove
2 cups water
1 cup sour cream
1 tablespoon Madeira

Pilze mit Tomaten und Speck
MUSHROOMS WITH TOMATOES AND BACON

Cut away any tough ends of the mushroom stems. Wipe the mushrooms
with a damp paper towel, and cut them, stems and all, into ⅛-inch slices.

In a heavy 10- to 12-inch skillet, melt the butter over moderate heat.
When the foam subsides, add the bacon and cook, stirring frequently, until
the bacon is crisp and light brown. Add the onions and cook, stirring frequently, for 5 minutes, or until the onions are soft and transparent but not
brown. Then drop in the mushrooms and season with salt and a few grindings of pepper. Cook over high heat, turning the mushrooms frequently, for
3 or 4 minutes.

When the mushrooms are lightly colored, stir in the chopped tomatoes
and simmer over low heat for about 10 minutes.

If there are more than 2 or 3 tablespoons of liquid left in the pan, increase
the heat and boil briskly for a minute or so to reduce the excess. Then add
the parsley and taste for seasoning. Serve at once from a heated bowl as an accompaniment to meat.

To serve 4

1 pound fresh mushrooms
2 tablespoons butter
½ cup finely diced lean bacon
½ cup finely chopped onions
½ teaspoon salt
Freshly ground black pepper
3 medium-sized tomatoes, peeled,
   seeded and coarsely chopped
2 tablespoons finely chopped fresh
   parsley

To serve 2

½ pound lean boneless beef,
   preferably beef tenderloin, or top
   or eye round, ground 2 or 3 times
2 egg yolks
2 tablespoons salt
2 tablespoons freshly ground black
   pepper
2 tablespoons capers, thoroughly
   drained
2 tablespoons finely chopped onions
2 tablespoons finely chopped fresh
   parsley
8 flat anchovy fillets, thoroughly
   drained
Dark bread
Butter

To serve 6 to 8

2 cups dry red wine
½ cup red wine vinegar
1 cup finely grated onions
15 whole juniper berries, crushed
   with a mortar and pestle or
   wrapped in a towel and crushed
   with a rolling pin
2 tablespoons grated fresh lemon
   peel
6 small bay leaves, coarsely crushed
2 teaspoons dried tarragon
1 teaspoon ground cloves
1 teaspoon ground allspice
1 teaspoon ground ginger
1 teaspoon freshly ground black
   pepper
A 5- to 6-pound fresh ham, rind
   removed and the ham trimmed of
   fat
1 tablespoon salt
2 tablespoons lard
2 cups water
3 tablespoons flour
3 tablespoons cold water

Beefsteak Tartar
BEEFSTEAK TARTAR

Traditionally the beef for beefsteak Tartar is ground very fine and served as soon as possible thereafter. Shape the beef into two mounds and place them in the center of separate serving plates. Make a well in the middle of the mounds and carefully drop an egg yolk in each.

Serve the salt, black pepper, capers, chopped onions, parsley and anchovy fillets in small separate saucers. The beef and other ingredients are then combined at the table to individual taste. Serve beefsteak Tartar with dark bread and butter.

Falscher Wildschweinbraten
FRESH HAM, MOCK-BOAR STYLE

For the marinade pour the wine and vinegar into a mixing bowl and stir in the grated onions, juniper berries, grated lemon peel, bay leaves, tarragon, cloves, allspice, ginger and black pepper. Place the ham in a deep dish just large enough to hold it comfortably and pour the marinade over it. Cover with foil and marinate in the refrigerator for two days, turning it over once or twice a day.

Preheat the oven to 325°. Remove the ham from the marinade, and dry it thoroughly with paper towels, brushing off any bits of onion or herbs clinging to it. Rub the salt evenly into its surface. Strain the marinade into a bowl or saucepan, pressing down hard with a spoon on the solid ingredients to extract all their liquid before throwing them away.

In a heavy casserole or Dutch oven just large enough to hold the ham comfortably, melt the lard over high heat until a light haze forms above it. Add the ham and brown it well on all sides, turning the ham frequently and regulating the heat so the meat colors quickly and evenly without burning. Transfer the ham to a plate. Combine the strained marinade with 2 cups of water and pour the mixture into the casserole. Bring the liquid to a boil over high heat, meanwhile scraping in any brown bits clinging to the bottom and sides of the casserole.

Return the ham to the casserole, cover tightly, and bake in the middle of the oven for about 2 hours, basting it every 30 minutes or so with the cooking liquid. The ham is done when it can easily be pierced with the tip of a sharp knife. (You may use a meat thermometer, if you like, for more predictable results. After the ham is browned, insert the thermometer into the thickest part without letting the tip touch any bone. Roast until the thermometer reads 170° to 175°.) Transfer the ham to a heated platter and set it aside to rest for 10 to 15 minutes for easier carving.

Meanwhile, strain the cooking liquid into a small saucepan and skim off as much fat as possible from the surface. Measure the liquid, then boil it briskly to reduce it to 2 cups. Reduce the heat to low. Make a smooth paste of the flour and 3 tablespoons of cold water and, with a whisk or spoon, stir it gradually into the simmering liquid. Cook, stirring frequently, for about 10 minutes, or until the sauce thickens slightly. Taste for seasoning.

To serve, carve the ham into ¼-inch slices and arrange the slices attractively in overlapping layers on a large heated platter. Serve the sauce separately in a sauceboat.

Beefsteak Tartar is a mound of raw ground beef with an egg yolk in the center; to this the diner adds other ingredients to taste. Suggested here *(clockwise from the tray handle):* salt, pepper, capers, chopped onions, anchovies, chopped parsley.

27

II

How to Eat Five Meals a Day

Aleke Brinkama slips a morsel of food to the family dachshund as she and her husband Eduard, a well-to-do Hamburg antique dealer, dine informally at home. Their meal, a fillet of veal with rice and a green salad, reflects the trend to a relatively light and simple cuisine in upper-class German homes today.

The Germans never followed the American tradition of three square meals a day. Their tradition is *five* meals. They start, as we do, with breakfast, *Frühstück,* and only a few hours later follow it with a second breakfast, *Zweites Frühstück,* that would make a lunch for many an American. At midday comes dinner, *Mittagessen,* the main hot meal of the day. *Kaffee*—a sociable snack that often includes much more than a cup of coffee—is served in late afternoon. And finally the day of hearty, frequent eating is closed with a comparatively light supper called *Abendbrot.*

This traditional pattern persists, although radical changes in German society have weakened it. Some meals are lighter now, and not all are eaten at home. And yet, even though most German men work in offices or factories, half the women hold jobs and all children attend school full time, the old custom of five meals a day is still part of the German way of life, particularly among members of the older generation.

Breakfast is much more a sit-down meal in Germany than in most American homes, with freshly prepared food on a properly set table. Crisp little rolls and rye and dark breads are served with butter and jam. The rolls are invariably just out of the oven; if the bakery does not deliver them, the lady of the house or her children will fetch them before breakfast. Eggs turn up often, especially in northern Germany, and are generally boiled rather than fried or scrambled.

These boiled eggs, like the coffeepot, sit warmly under their own little cozies. In days gone by, richly embroidered cozies, like fretwork picture frames and handpainted teacups, embodied the artistic inclinations of the lady of

Continued on page 32   29

A boned breast of veal called a *Kalbsrolle,* or veal roll, is combined with freshly cooked vegetables to create the kind of opulent and elegant dish that German women take pride in serving. In this main course for a midday meal, the veal roll is accompanied by peas, cauliflower, carrots, green beans and braised leeks. It contains a stuffing of ground beef and sausage meat flavored with onion, parsley and nutmeg. The recipe is on page 40.

the house. Nowadays, mercifully, the cozies are less "artistic," but they are still the best and most painless way of keeping eggs and beverages hot. The eggs are eaten, opened but unpeeled, from egg cups. In more genteel homes, the top is snipped off with a pair of egg scissors and the egg is eaten with a little ivory spoon. I still have my scissors, the delight of my childhood, and I can still taste the opaque, bland, solid egg white from the tip of the egg, which the scissors cut off into a precise half dome.

In the colder climate of northern Germany, cheese is often served at breakfast and slices of ham and cold cuts often appear on the breakfast table.

Between 9 and 10 o'clock, most Germans stop whatever they are doing to refuel with their second breakfast, the *Zweites Frühstück*. At school, children have a sandwich—called a *belegtes Brot* (literally, "covered bread"), or simply a *Brot*—with a banana or an apple. Men and women take a bag of meat or cheese sandwiches to work, and eat them with a bottle of beer or a cup of coffee made on the job.

But the *Zweites Frühstück* need not be that simple. In more settled days, it was a splendid meal, taken at about 11 o'clock—a meal for which gentlemen repaired to elegant restaurants, staffed by very distinguished waiters, to keep up their strength with the best smoked salmon, goose liver pâté, oysters and caviar, all washed down by glasses of good Bordeaux or Burgundy. Some of these temples of gastronomy still function—Schlichter, in Berlin; Dallmayr, in Munich; and the famous oyster parlor of Johann Coelln, in Hamburg, founded in 1833. At Johann Coelln's, even today, Hamburg shipowners tuck away their lobster and their Malassol caviar under Bismarck's photograph, signed in his own angular, unforgettable hand, and bearing the inscription: "Wenn sich der Deutsche seiner Kraft recht bewusst werden soll, dann muss er erst eine halbe Flasche Wein im Leibe haben, oder besser noch, eine ganze. Stammkunde Bismarck." ("If a German wants to be properly conscious of his strength, he must first have a half bottle of wine inside him—or better yet, a whole bottle. Regular customer Bismarck.")

A lovable morning institution—for those who can afford it—is the *Sektfrühstück*, the champagne breakfast. Lobster, caviar, salmon and *foie gras* are the classic four dishes that grace these affairs, preceded perhaps by a noble consommé to strengthen those who have danced or played all night. Another soothing morning meal—for those who need it—it is the *Katerfrühstück*, the hangover breakfast, which in Germany is far removed from black coffee. Herring under various piquant guises, such as sour cream and dill, with fresh horseradish; sausages and country ham with pumpernickel; goulash soup (a watered-down, or rather, a bouilloned-down version of goulash)—all these help the sufferer regain his poise. The correct beverage at a *Katerfrühstück*, incidentally, is neither coffee nor tea, but a hair of whatever dog it was that bit you.

Mittagessen, the midday dinner, is the meal that has changed most radically in recent decades, and it is still changing. The employment of women in offices and industry, the urbanization of the country, and the modern demand for a more varied, lighter diet—all these have tended to reduce the importance of Germany's traditional main meal. Most husbands cannot go home for their *Mittagessen*, many wives do not have the time to prepare it prop-

erly, and even the propriety of eating heavily in the middle of the day is often questioned.

Yet the *Mittagessen* survives. The vast majority of German factories and offices maintain employee cafeterias, where substantial midday meals are sold below cost. The firms that underwrite the losses on the food say that without this amenity they could not recruit their workers, who cling to their hot midday meal and consider sandwiches, however substantial, as mere snacks. At home, a housewife still prepares a midday dinner for her children, who are seldom able to eat in school. If she is a working woman, she will prepare a one-dish meal the night before or early in the morning and hurry home to heat it up. Or she will whip up one of the dishes that go under the name of *Schnellküche*, or quick cookery. Such a meal might consist of deep-frozen fish sticks, frozen spinach and stewed fruit.

But it is the *Eintopf*, the one-dish meal, that is at the heart of this kind of family eating. A friend of mine, the owner of a vineyard in the Mosel Valley, cooks massive casseroles late at night to feed her harvest help the following day. She herself must be among the grape vines, supervising the temporary employees, who are frequently young office and factory girls spending their vacations at hard work and play in the vineyards. Incidentally, for those who think that grape harvesting is romantic, with maidens in dirndls wearing Bacchic wreaths in their hair, I have news. Grape pickers wear jeans, sweaters and high rubber boots. The pretty dresses and stupendous beehive hairdos come later, at the *Winzerfeste*, or local vintners' fêtes, where the merriment is astonishing indeed.

At the top and the bottom of the social scale, the traditional *Mittagessen* is

On many labor-short German farms grandmother presides in the kitchen while both parents help gather the crops. This woman in Westphalia is shredding home-grown potatoes to make crisp pan-fried cakes. The standard accompaniment is apple butter, but her grandson prefers blueberry preserves; he wolfs down a dozen pancakes at a sitting.

An example of the popular timesaver, an *Eintopf*, or one-pot dish, is this traditional German stew, known as *Pichelsteiner Fleisch* (*page 41*).

more enduring than it is among the middle-class majority. Many well-to-do men still go home for their midday dinner, sometimes zipping along in their fast Mercedes, more often fuming at traffic jams. As in more leisurely days, entertaining may be done over the *Mittagessen* table. (In the '20s, my own father, then a diplomat who frequently entertained official guests, preferred midday parties because people could not stay until all hours, as they do in the evening.) But workers and farmers, too, continue to eat their main meal in the middle of the day, after a long morning's work. The difference in social status is reflected not only in what is eaten at this substantial dinner but in the hour when it is eaten. A farmer will eat his *Mittagessen* around noon and his supper at 6. High-ranking civil servants or businessmen never dine before 1 and often have *Mittagessen* as late as 2 or 2:30; such men eat their evening meal, at the earliest, at 7:30.

Such class distinctions in eating habits are fading today, as prosperity and industrialization spread over the country. But before the First World War, a man's social standing could accurately be gauged by his *Mittagessen* menu, and such menus can be resurrected from the cookbooks of the time. Germans have always thought highly of cookbooks; a newly married couple frequently receives one from the civil authorities along with the marriage certificate. One particularly revealing cookbook is Henriette Davidis-Holle's *Praktisches Kochbuch,* a constantly revised bestseller since its appearance in 1844, and a mainstay of the upper-middle class. In its menus and recipes can be seen the variety—and length—of dinners among the well-to-do.

According to one pre-World War I edition of the *Praktisches Kochbuch,* a proper *Mittagessen* began with soup, which might be a clear bouillon with marrow dumplings, a clear oxtail, a shrimp bisque or a cream of carrot or cauliflower. A fish course followed, perhaps a combination of carp and eel, turbot with butter sauce or a *vol-au-vent* of flounder. Then came one or two meat dishes, such as a haunch of venison with red cabbage *(page 63),* a loin of pork with applesauce, roast veal with fresh peas and asparagus, mutton chops with knob-celery salad, roast chicken, duck or goose with artichokes or a green salad; with the meat was almost always a compote of stewed fruits *(page 138).* The dessert might include an apple pudding, quince ice cream, wine jelly *(page 123),* or a tricolor cream of almonds or vanilla. But this was not the end. There was still cheese, served with butter (the bread that came to the table with the other courses was served without butter). And then a final *Nachtisch,* a sort of second dessert favored especially by the ladies, might be homemade bonbons, elaborate cookies or candied fruits.

Going down the social scale to the house of one of the Kaiser's middle-rung-of-the-ladder civil servants, we might find a simple and shorter but still substantial *Mittagessen* consisting of cream soup with dumplings, cutlets with cauliflower, and stewed fruit; barley soup and hare ragoût with rice and applesauce; lentil soup *(page 116),* pike with dumplings, and chocolate pudding; or cauliflower soup *(page 60)* and *Deutsches Beefsteak* (that is, hamburger) with home-fried potatoes and cucumber salad. On Sundays, the meal was considerably more elegant. A typical Sunday *Mittagessen* might include clear bouillon served in cups, shirred eggs, roast partridge with sauerkraut, and grapes in gelatin, or perhaps creamy wine soup, roast beef with cauliflower and potatoes, and gooseberry tarts with whipped cream.

Still further down the social scale a family meal might consist of herring, boiled potatoes and salad; of broad beans and bacon and stewed fruit; of a one-dish meal of beans, potatoes with bacon and sausage; or of a thick lentil or pea soup with sausage or smoked pork and stewed fruit. Fresh meat was Sunday and holiday fare, and so were such relatively elaborate desserts as sweet rice or an almond or fruit cream or tart.

In those days, the very poor ate very poorly indeed: kraut and potatoes, potatoes and kraut, or a watery soup. But even in somewhat better-off families, Saturday and Monday meals were especially simple. On Saturday, when the house was turned upside down for its weekly cleaning, dinner might be rice pudding and stewed fruit, beans and sour gravy, or cabbage and sausage. I own a crumbling, handwritten old cookbook in which the Saturday menu reads: "Potato ragoût. For the *Hausherrn* [the master of the house], a squab." Monday was washday, with much boiling in copper kettles in the steamy *Waschküche,* or laundry room; on that day, the master of the house was often asked to eat at a restaurant while the family had a severely simple *Mittagessen* of noodles with leftover ham and salad, cabbage rolls, or rice pudding with a fruit juice as a sauce.

Saturday and Monday dinners are no longer so Spartan, now that vacuum cleaners and automatic washers have lightened the load on German housewives. On the other hand, neither are the regular *Mittagessen* as elaborate as they were. Even among the rich, only very formal and socially important occasions warrant a fish dish before the entrée. The *Mittagessen* of the middle class is much simpler, too. For one thing, soup is often dropped, for Germans are convinced that soup is the most fattening of all foods. A family dinner might consist of a goulash, dumplings and a cottage-cheese dessert; sausage with kale and roast potatoes and oranges; or paprika fish, rice and salad with a wine jelly. Even the Sunday middle-class dinner, while richer than the daily meal, has shed some of its heavy elegance. Typical menus include mushroom soup, fillet of beef with various vegetables and boiled potatoes, and vanilla cream; bouillon with pancake strips, roast pork with red cabbage *(page 63)* and boiled potatoes, and nougat ice cream; or a tomato cocktail, venison cutlets with cream sauce, *Spätzle (page 164),* applesauce and cranberry preserves followed by éclairs.

The radical changes in German society have led some people to eat light lunches at midday and make the evening meal the heavy dinner. But the traditional *Abendbrot* (literally, "bread of the evening") was and is just that: white, rye or dark bread, spread with butter, and an assortment of cold cuts, sausages and cheeses. Each diner makes up his own open-face sandwich at the table, and eats it with a fork and knife.

This is where the Lucullan delicatessen foods sold in the *Feinkostgeschäfte* come in. Those who can afford them eat them every day; others, whenever they are able to, as a change from simpler sausages and cheeses. Another alternative is a salad made with meat, fish or vegetables, or a platter of raw vegetables. Small hot dishes (often leftovers) or an egg dish might also be served. Desserts are not served for the *Abendbrot.*

I have saved the most *gemütlich* of all the five meals for last. *Kaffee,* or afternoon coffee, is unquestionably one of the true delights of German life. It may be simple, with merely a cup of coffee and a cookie, or expansive, with lots of little sandwiches and cakes. In either case, its pleasure derives partly from the fact that it is eaten at the hour of the afternoon when friends meet and let their hair down.

Going out for *Kaffee* is one of the most charming of German treats. In every German town there are *Konditoreien*, or pastry shops, that are part of their patrons' hearts, and there are such famed establishments as Berlin's Kranzler, Hamburg's Alsterpavillon and Munich's Café Glockenspiel. More than coffee and cake is served in these temples of friendship and flirtation; even at *Kaffee*, a patron can order small steaks on toast with mushrooms, turtle soup, three-egg omelets, and cheese and cold-cut sandwiches. But it is cake that makes a *Konditorei*. The number and diversity of cakes that are offered on the Kranzler cake buffet, for example, are awesome: five different fruit *Torten*, eight whipped-cream *Torten*, 15 cream *Torten*, 21 coffeecakes and 21 miscellaneous pastries.

But at home, too, *Kaffee* is a special event, and here particularly the social differences that weave in and out of German life turn up. In modest households on Saturdays and Sundays, when the family is together, coffee and cake will be served at the dining table; in upper-class homes, a table will be set in the living room. Even the size of the pieces of cake varies: it is considered far more elegant to keep the pieces small, or even to omit cake in favor of a dish of cookies. Whatever the social setting, however, the quality of the coffee is immensely important. A thoughtful guest will praise the coffee even more than the cakes, for coffee, good and strong, is an emotion in Germany, as tea is in England.

German coffee comes in a dozen qualities and corresponding prices, and it is a matter of pride for the hostess to treat her guests to the best. More often than not, she will grind her own just before making it. What I have never understood, however, is how the Germans tolerate canned cream in their good coffee. Pure cream is the rare exception in cafés and homes. It is not a matter of cost, but one of taste—a taste that I deplore.

An invitation for afternoon coffee is among the choicest and most welcome forms of hospitality. I remember with fondness an afternoon at the coffee table in Ulla Groth's Munich living room, a low round table set with an embroidered cloth and flowers in a low vase. Before me was a plate with a napkin, a fork and knife, and a plate of tiny thin open-face sandwiches garnished with tomato and parsley, eggs and anchovies. A dish held a variety of cookies, and a small tray the sugar bowl and cream pitcher. On a side table, a candlewarmer kept the coffeepots warm, and there was tea and a jug of hot water. The mood was one of intimacy and relaxation.

A handsome coffee table is the pride of every German woman; flowers, embroidered cloths and special dishes are as much part of *Kaffee* as the food and drink. Indeed, an attractive table at any meal is an essential element in German culinary life. Flowers will grace even a table set in the kitchen; a tablecloth and china, flowered in the traditional manner or decorated with modern linear designs, will bring an extra dimension to a meal that, by American standards, is a very simple one. *Schön decken* (to set a table beautifully) is one of the things by which a German woman is judged. A career woman entertaining you for coffee, a company president's wife officiating at a business lunch, or your old aunt who has you over for a simple supper—all will take the same loving care with their tables.

Schinken in Burgunder
HAM BRAISED IN BURGUNDY

To serve 6 to 8

Half a precooked smoked ham, butt
   or shank end, about 5 to 6 pounds
2 cups water
2 cups red Burgundy or other dry
   red wine
1 medium-sized onion, peeled and
   thinly sliced
1 medium-sized tomato, peeled,
   seeded and coarsely chopped
1 whole clove, crushed with a mortar
   and pestle
1 small bay leaf
1 tablespoon butter, softened
1 tablespoon flour

Preheat the oven to 350°. With a small, sharp knife, separate the rind from the ham and place the rind in a 1- to 2-quart saucepan. Trim the ham of all but a ¼-inch layer of fat. Pour 2 cups of water over the rind, bring to a boil over high heat, then reduce the heat to low and simmer uncovered for 20 minutes. Strain the liquid through a sieve into a bowl and discard the rind.

Pour 1 cup of the rind stock into a shallow roasting pan just large enough to hold the ham comfortably. Add 1 cup of the wine, and the onion, tomato, clove and bay leaf. Place the ham, fat side up, in the pan and bake uncovered in the middle of the oven for about 1 hour. Baste the ham thoroughly every 20 minutes with the pan liquid. The ham is done when it can easily be pierced with a fork. Transfer the ham to a heated platter and let it rest for easier carving while you prepare the sauce.

Skim and discard all the fat from the pan liquid and stir in the remaining 1 cup of wine. Bring to a boil over high heat, meanwhile scraping in any brown bits clinging to the bottom or sides of the pan, and boil briskly for a minute or two. In a small bowl, make a paste of the butter and flour, and stir it bit by bit into the pan. Cook over low heat, stirring constantly, for 5 minutes, or until the sauce is smooth and slightly thickened. Strain it through a fine sieve into a small saucepan and taste for seasoning.

To serve, carve the ham into ¼-inch slices and arrange the slices attractively, in overlapping layers, on a large heated platter. Moisten the slices with a few spoonfuls of the Burgundy sauce, and serve the remaining sauce separately in a sauceboat.

Rollmops—herring rolls filled with onion and pickle—are popular in all parts of Germany as everyone's snack. They go well with beer or *Schnaps;* garnished with parsley and onion slices *(right),* they become an attractive dish for the traditional light supper. On a morning after, they are prized as a pick-me-up.

Rollmöpse
ROLLMOPS

Place the herring fillets in a bowl and pour in enough water to cover them by about 1 inch. Soak them for at least 12 hours in the refrigerator, changing the water once or twice. Drain them well, rinse under cold running water and pat them dry with paper towels. Remove and discard any bones.

For the marinade, combine the vinegar, water, juniper berries, allspice, cloves, peppercorns and bay leaf in a 2- to 3-quart saucepan and bring them to a boil over high heat. Reduce the heat to low and simmer uncovered for 5 minutes. Then cool to room temperature.

Lay the herring fillets, skin side down, on a board or table. Spread 1 teaspoon of mustard evenly on each fillet and scatter ½ teaspoon of capers and several onion rings over the mustard. Cut the dill pickles lengthwise into quarters; if they are much longer than the width of the herring fillets, cut them crosswise into halves. Place a wedge of pickle at one narrow end of each of the fillets, and then roll the fillets jelly-roll fashion around the pickle into small, thick cylinders. Skewer the rolls with 2 or 3 toothpicks to secure them. Pack the rolls flat on their sides in a 2-quart glass loaf dish in two layers with the remaining onion rings scattered between the layers and over the top. (Do not use a metal pan, for the fish may pick up a metallic flavor.) Pour the marinade over the herring, then cover the dish with foil or plastic wrap and refrigerate it for 5 or 6 days before serving.

Serve the rollmops as an hors d'oeuvre on individual plates or arrange them attractively on a large platter. In either case, you may garnish the herring with the marinated onion rings and parsley.

NOTE: If salt herring fillets are not available, substitute 12 bottled Bismarck herring fillets. Drain them well, wash them thoroughly under cold running water and pat dry with paper towels. Then proceed with the recipe.

To serve 6 to 8

12 salt herring fillets, preferably *Matjes* herring
2 cups cider vinegar
2 cups cold water
3 juniper berries, 3 whole allspice, 3 whole cloves and 6 whole black peppercorns, bruised with a mortar and pestle or wrapped in a towel and bruised with a rolling pin
1 small bay leaf
¼ cup Düsseldorf-style prepared mustard, or substitute other hot prepared mustard
2 tablespoons capers, drained
3 medium-sized onions, peeled, thinly sliced and separated into rings
3 large dill pickles
Parsley sprigs

To serve 6 to 8

POACHING STOCK

The bones from a leg or breast of
    veal, sawed into 2-inch lengths
4 cups water
½ cup coarsely chopped onions
½ cup coarsely chopped celery,
    including the leaves
6 whole black peppercorns
1 small bay leaf

STUFFING

2 slices homemade type fresh white
    bread
⅓ cup milk
1 tablespoon butter
½ cup finely chopped onions
½ pound ground beef chuck
½ pound fresh sausage meat
1 egg, lightly beaten
3 tablespoons finely chopped parsley
⅛ teaspoon ground nutmeg
Salt
Freshly ground black pepper

A 4- to 4½-pound breast of veal,
    boned and trimmed
3 tablespoons lard

Kalbsrolle

BRAISED STUFFED VEAL ROLL

In a heavy 3- to 4-quart saucepan, bring the veal bones and water to a boil
over high heat, skimming off any foam and scum that rise to the surface.
Add the ½ cup of coarsely chopped onions, the celery, peppercorns and bay
leaf, reduce the heat to low and partially cover the pan. Simmer, undisturbed,
for 1 hour. Strain the stock through a fine sieve set over a bowl, discarding
the bones, vegetables and spices. Set the stock aside.

Tear the slices of bread into small pieces and soak them in the milk for 5
minutes, then gently squeeze them and set them aside in a large mixing
bowl. In a small skillet, melt the butter over moderate heat. When the foam
subsides add ½ cup of finely chopped onions and cook, stirring frequently,
for 5 minutes, or until they are soft and transparent but not brown. With a rubber spatula, scrape the contents of the skillet into the bowl with the bread,
and add the beef, sausage meat, egg, parsley, nutmeg, ¼ teaspoon of salt
and a few grindings of pepper. Knead the mixture with your hands or beat
with a large spoon until all the ingredients are well blended.

Preheat the oven to 325°. Place the boned veal flat side down on a board
or table, sprinkle it with salt and a few grindings of pepper and, with a knife
or spatula, spread the ground-meat stuffing mixture evenly over the veal. Beginning with a wide side, roll up the veal jelly-roll fashion into a thick cylinder. Tie the roll at both ends and in the center with 8-inch lengths of
white kitchen cord.

In a heavy flameproof casserole just large enough to hold the roll comfortably, melt the lard over high heat until a light haze forms above it. Add
the veal roll and brown it on all sides, regulating the heat so that it browns
quickly and evenly without burning. Pour in the reserved stock and bring it
to a boil over high heat.

Cover the casserole and transfer it to the middle of the oven. Cook for
1¾ hours, turning the roll over after the first hour. Then remove the cover
and cook, basting occasionally with the pan juices, for 30 minutes longer,
or until the veal is tender and shows no resistance when pierced with the tip
of a small, sharp knife.

To serve hot, carve the veal into ¼-inch slices and arrange them attractively in overlapping layers on a heated platter. Skim and discard the fat
from the juices in the casserole, taste for seasoning, and either pour over the
veal or serve separately in a sauceboat. (If you would like to make a sauce,
measure the skimmed juices. If there is more than 2 cups, boil briskly to reduce it; if there is less, add water. Melt 2 tablespoons of butter over moderate
heat and, when the foam subsides, stir in 3 tablespoons of flour. Cook, stirring, over low heat until the flour browns lightly. Gradually add the pan
juices, beating vigorously with a whisk until the sauce is smooth and thick.
Taste for seasoning.)

To serve cold, transfer the veal roll to a loaf pan and pour the degreased
cooking juices over it. Cool to room temperature, then refrigerate overnight.
When cold, the juices should jell into a light aspic. Serve the veal cut into
thin slices.

Traditionally, Kalbsrolle is accompanied by plain boiled potatoes and a selection of boiled or braised vegetables such as peas, leeks, cauliflower, green
beans and carrots.

Pichelsteiner Fleisch

MIXED MEAT AND VEGETABLE CASSEROLE

In a heavy 10- to 12-inch skillet heat 2 tablespoons of the lard over high heat until a light haze forms above it. Add the cubed lamb, beef, veal and pork (in any order you like) a few pieces at a time, and brown them well on all sides, regulating the heat so the cubes brown quickly and evenly without burning. Replenish the lard in the pan as needed, and transfer the browned meats to a bowl as you proceed.

When all the meat is browned, pour the 2 cups of water into the skillet and bring to a boil, meanwhile scraping in any brown particles clinging to the bottom and sides of the pan. Boil briskly for a few seconds, then set the skillet aside off the heat.

In a large mixing bowl combine the carrots, cabbage, green beans, celery root, parsnips, leeks, kohlrabi, peas, onions, ½ teaspoon of salt and a few grindings of black pepper. Toss the vegetables about with a spoon to mix them thoroughly.

Spread the marrow in the bottom of a heavy 6-quart casserole, and arrange about a third of the meat cubes over it. Sprinkle the meat with a little salt and freshly ground pepper and spread it with a third of the mixed vegetables. Repeat the layers in thirds similarly. Scatter the diced potatoes over the final layer of vegetables, sprinkle lightly with salt and pepper, and pour in the reserved liquid.

Bring to a boil over high heat, then reduce the heat to its lowest point and cover the casserole tightly. Simmer, without stirring at any point, for 1½ hours. Serve directly from the casserole.

NOTE: Traditionally, this dish is made from whatever vegetables are in season, but in modern Germany frozen vegetables are often substituted for the fresh ones. Celery may replace celery root, and additional onions may replace the leeks. Be sure to use 8 or 9 cups of vegetables, whichever they are.

Bratwurst mit saurer Sahnensosse

STEAMED BRATWURST IN SOUR-CREAM SAUCE

Drop the bratwurst into 2 quarts of boiling water, remove from the heat, and let the sausages soak for 5 minutes. Drain and pat the bratwurst dry with paper towels.

Melt the butter over moderate heat in a heavy 10- to 12-inch skillet, add the bratwurst and cook, turning them frequently with tongs until they are a golden brown on all sides. Add the ¼ cup of water to the skillet, reduce the heat, and simmer, uncovered, for 15 to 20 minutes, turning the bratwurst over after 10 minutes. Replenish the water with a few tablespoons of boiling water if the cooking water boils away. Transfer the sausages to a plate, and cover them with foil.

With a whisk, beat the flour and salt into the sour cream. Then, a few tablespoons at a time, stir the sour-cream mixture into the liquid remaining in the skillet. Cook over low heat, stirring constantly, for 5 to 8 minutes, until the sauce is smooth and slightly thickened. Do not let it boil. Slice the sausages into ¼-inch rounds, drop them into the skillet, baste with the sauce and simmer only long enough to heat the bratwurst through. Transfer the entire contents of the skillet to a large, deep platter and serve immediately.

To serve 6

2 to 4 tablespoons lard
½ pound boneless shoulder of lamb, cut into 1-inch cubes
½ pound boneless beef chuck, cut into 1-inch cubes
½ pound boneless veal, cut into 1-inch cubes
½ pound boneless pork, cut into 1-inch cubes
2 cups cold water
2 cups scraped carrots, cut into 1-inch lengths
1½ cups cored savoy or green cabbage, cut into 1½-by-1-inch pieces
1 cup fresh green beans, cut into 1½-inch lengths
1 cup peeled celery root (celeriac), cut into ½-inch dice
1 cup scraped parsnips, cut into 1-inch lengths
1 cup leeks, sliced into 1-inch lengths (including 1 inch of the green part)
½ cup kohlrabi, if available, cut into ¼-inch slices
½ cup freshly shelled green peas, or substitute ½ cup thoroughly defrosted frozen green peas
½ cup coarsely chopped onions
Salt
Freshly ground black pepper
¼ pound beef marrow, coarsely diced
3 medium-sized boiling potatoes (about 1 pound), peeled and cut into ½-inch cubes

To serve 4

8 bratwurst sausages, separated
2 tablespoons butter
¼ cup cold water
1 tablespoon flour
½ teaspoon salt
1 cup sour cream

41

To serve 6 to 8

9 medium boiling potatoes (about
   3 pounds), scrubbed but not
   peeled
½ pound bacon, finely diced (about
   1½ cups)
½ cup finely chopped onions
¼ cup white wine or cider vinegar
¼ cup water
½ teaspoon salt
¼ teaspoon freshly
   ground black pepper
2 tablespoons finely chopped parsley

Warmer Kartoffelsalat mit Speck

HOT POTATO SALAD WITH BACON

Drop the unpeeled potatoes into enough boiling water to cover them completely. Boil them briskly until they show only the slightest resistance when pierced with the point of a sharp knife. Be careful not to let them overcook or they will fall apart when sliced. Drain the potatoes in a colander, then peel and cut them into ¼-inch slices. Set the potatoes aside in a bowl tightly covered with aluminum foil.

In a heavy 8- to 10-inch skillet, cook the bacon over moderate heat until brown and crisp. Spread it out on paper towels to drain. Add the onions to the fat remaining in the skillet and cook, stirring frequently, for 5 minutes, or until they are soft and transparent but not brown. Stir in the vinegar, water, salt and pepper, and cook, stirring constantly, for a minute or so. Pour the hot sauce over the potatoes, turning the slices about gently with a large spoon or spatula to coat them evenly with the onion-and-vinegar mixture. Gently stir the reserved bacon pieces into the salad. Taste for seasoning.

Serve at once or cover and set the salad aside at room temperature until you are ready to serve it. Just before serving, stir the salad gently and sprinkle the top with parsley.

To serve 4

2 pounds fresh firm beets
2 teaspoons salt
½ cup dry red wine
½ cup cider vinegar
1 onion, peeled and thinly sliced
4 whole cloves
½ teaspoon ground coriander seeds
6 whole black peppercorns
3 tablespoons olive oil
1 teaspoon freshly grated
   horseradish, or substitute 1
   tablespoon bottled grated
   horseradish, thoroughly drained
   and squeezed dry in a towel

Rote Rübensalat

PICKLED-BEET SALAD

With a small, sharp knife cut the tops from the beets, leaving about 1 inch of stem on each. Scrub the beets under cold running water, then combine them in a 4- to 5-quart saucepan with enough cold water to cover them by 2 inches. Add 1 teaspoon of the salt and bring the water to a boil over high heat. Reduce the heat to low, cover the pan, and simmer until the beets show no resistance when pierced with the tip of a small, sharp knife. This may take anywhere from 30 minutes for young beets or as long as 2 hours for older ones. The beets should be kept constantly covered with water; add boiling water if necessary.

Drain the beets in a colander and, when they are cool enough to handle, slip off the skins. Cut the beets crosswise into ⅛-inch slices and place them in a deep glass or ceramic bowl.

In a 1½- to 2-quart enameled or stainless-steel saucepan, bring the red wine, vinegar, onion, cloves, coriander, peppercorns and the remaining 1 teaspoon of salt to a boil over high heat. Immediately pour the mixture over the beets. It should cover them completely; if it doesn't, add more wine. Cool to room temperature, cover the bowl tightly with aluminum foil or plastic wrap, and refrigerate for at least 24 hours.

Just before serving, discard the whole cloves and the peppercorns. Beat the olive oil and horseradish together in a small bowl and add it to the beets, turning the slices about with a spoon to coat them thoroughly with the dressing.

NOTE: If you prefer a somewhat thinner dressing, add up to ½ cup of cold water to the oil and horseradish. (Whole canned beets may be substituted for the cooked fresh beets. Slice them ⅛ inch thick and pour the hot marinade over them as described above. Use the canned beet juice in place of water if you wish to dilute the marinade.)

Bohnensalat

GREEN BEAN SALAD

To serve 4

In a small bowl combine the vinegar, oil, chicken stock, 1 teaspoon of the salt and a few grindings of pepper, and beat them vigorously with a whisk to blend thoroughly. Stir in the dill and parsley, and taste for seasoning. Cover the bowl and set the dressing aside.

With a small, sharp knife, trim the ends off the beans, and cut them into 2-inch lengths. In a 3- to 4-quart saucepan bring 2 quarts of water, the remaining 1 teaspoon of salt and the summer savory to a bubbling boil over high heat. Drop the beans in by the handful. Return the water to a boil, reduce the heat to moderate, and boil the beans, uncovered, for 10 to 15 minutes, or until they are tender but still slightly firm. Do not overcook them. Immediately drain the beans in a colander and run cold water over them for a few seconds to set their color and keep them from cooking further. Spread them out on paper toweling and pat them dry.

Transfer the beans to a large mixing bowl and pour the dressing over them. Stir thoroughly to coat them well, taste for seasoning, and chill for at least 1 hour before serving.

3 tablespoons red or white wine vinegar
3 tablespoons olive oil
½ cup chicken stock, fresh or canned
2 teaspoons salt
Freshly ground black pepper
1 teaspoon finely chopped fresh dill
1 teaspoon finely chopped parsley
1 pound fresh green beans
1 sprig fresh summer savory, or ¼ teaspoon dried summer savory

Zitronencreme

LEMON-CREAM DESSERT

To serve 6

In a heatproof measuring cup or small bowl, sprinkle the gelatin over ¼ cup of cold water. When the gelatin has softened for 2 or 3 minutes, set the cup in a small skillet of simmering water and stir until the gelatin dissolves completely. Remove the skillet from the heat, but leave the cup of gelatin in the skillet.

With a wire whisk or a rotary or electric beater, beat the egg yolks with ½ cup of the sugar until the yolks are pale yellow and thick enough to fall back in a ribbon when the beater is lifted from the bowl. Stir in the dissolved gelatin, the lemon juice and the lemon peel. With the same whisk or beater whip the cream in a large chilled bowl until it is firm enough to hold its shape softly. Then, with a rubber spatula, gently but thoroughly fold the cream into the egg and lemon mixture, using an over-under cutting motion rather than a stirring motion.

Wash and dry the whisk or beater; then, in a separate bowl, use it to beat the egg whites until they are frothy. Sprinkle in the remaining 3 tablespoons of sugar and continue beating until the egg whites are stiff enough to stand in unwavering peaks when the whisk is lifted from the bowl. Gently fold the egg whites into the lemon mixture and continue to fold until no trace of white can be seen in the mixture.

Spoon the lemon cream into six individual dessert dishes or into a large serving bowl. Cover it tightly and refrigerate it for at least 3 hours before serving.

If you like, you may garnish the dessert with lemon slices and whipped cream. Whip the cream with a wire whisk or a rotary or electric beater until it holds its shape softly, sprinkle it with confectioners' sugar, and beat until the cream is stiff enough to form firm, unwavering peaks. With a pastry bag fitted with a decorative tip, pipe rosettes or decorative swirls of whipped cream on top of the dessert.

1 envelope unflavored gelatin
¼ cup cold water
3 egg yolks
½ cup plus 3 tablespoons sugar
¼ cup fresh lemon juice
2 teaspoons finely grated lemon peel
1 cup heavy cream
3 egg whites
1 lemon, cut lengthwise into halves and cut crosswise into paper-thin slices (optional)
½ cup heavy cream (optional)
1 teaspoon confectioners' sugar (optional)

III

The Pleasures
of Dining Out

In the United States, the national sport is dieting; in Germany, it is *gut essen gehen* (dining out well). In a vast number of establishments where one can dine away from home, the German national sport is practiced on every level of cuisine, service and cost.

Naturally, Germans differentiate between the meals they eat away from home. After an evening at the theater in Berlin, one may go to Hardtke in the Meinekestrasse to enjoy a *Berliner Riesenbratwurst mit Kartoffelsalat,* an irresistible, crispy giant fried sausage accompanied by a savory potato salad that has never been desecrated by chilling. More ambitiously, the theatergoer might order a *delikate Kleinigkeit,* a "delicate little something," as only a Berliner would call a tender veal steak sautéed to a golden blush, prettied up with a béarnaise sauce and served with snowy, buttery asparagus on toast. Afterward, the diner could reasonably say that he had eaten well—but this aftertheater snack, for all its generosity, is not at all the same as a deliberate restaurant expedition.

When a Bonn government official takes his wife and friends to Sunday dinner at the Haus Maternus in nearby Bad Godesberg, it is indeed *gut essen gehen.* Like many of the best German restaurants, the Haus Maternus is part of a real house, with small paneled rooms, wall lanterns, candles, very good food and a proprietress of genius. Frau Ria has made her Haus Maternus a gathering place for diplomats and politicians: it is said that more government business is transacted at her tables than in most offices.

The menu at the Haus Maternus is, I think, typical of top German restaurants. Though more than adequate, it is selective rather than all-embracing,

In Castle-Hotel Kronberg near Frankfurt, guests dine in royal splendor. This 19th Century castle-turned-hotel-restaurant is one of many in Germany offering romance-seeking tourists a package of Old World pomp, gastronomic pleasure and modern plumbing.

as the menu of a more popular establishment is likely to be. The soups include a clear *consommé double,* a clear oxtail and a clear turtle soup. Shrimp are served with an imaginative creamy dill sauce; a sole is poached in vermouth and garnished with mussels. The beef Stroganoff and its complement of mushrooms come with an inspired garnish of crisp cucumbers; the *Kalbsfilet Diplomaten Art,* or fillet of veal *à la diplomate,* is charmingly surrounded by a ragoût of chicken, scrambled eggs, a veal kidney, asparagus, and a sauce Choron (a tomato-flavored sauce béarnaise), all gratinéed with Parmesan cheese and served with potato balls browned in butter. Lovers of more exotic dishes can indulge in the Indonesian *nasi goreng,* the Spanish *paella valenciana,* the Italian *piccata napolitana* and an Indian dish consisting of skewered beef fillet served with a curried sauce, chutney, almonds, pineapple and a banana-and-rice combination.

The glory of the Haus Maternus is the way they prepare game. I think game cooking is about the best of all of Germany's cooking; I have eaten venison as good only in Austria, and never in France or Sweden. German venison comes from either *Hirsch,* a big stag, or *Reh,* a smaller deer. This meat is all venison, of course, but each type is treated differently. First-class cooks never marinate the tender *Reh,* while *Hirsch* is invariably marinated, without trimming or larding beforehand, to tenderize the meat of this enormous, muscular animal. Vinegar, especially a sharp vinegar, is not desirable as a marinade, for it kills the venison's flavor. The ideal short-term marinade, for periods up to two days, is sour cream; red wine is suitable for longer marinating times. The difference in the tenderness of the two meats is reflected in their relative roasting times. *Hirsch* requires 20 to 30 minutes per pound; *Reh,* only 10 to 15 minutes.

At the Haus Maternus, I enjoyed sautéed medallions of *Reh* gently bathed in a cream sauce and distinctively flavored with juniper berries, the best of all spices for venison. With it came *Pfifferlinge,* the wild mushrooms that the French call chanterelles, whose flavor embodies all the sweet wildness of a summer forest, and *Preiselbeeren,* Germany's small, tart cousins to our cranberries and the perfect counterfoil for the sweetish taste of venison. Crisp little potato croquettes provided a contrast of texture. For dessert, I had *Sahnegervais in Pfirsich,* a cream cheese served in a peach (in November, alas, a canned peach) and flamed with kirsch.

Gut essen gehen! How I wish I could describe the scores of great meals I have eaten in Germany's restaurants, served by attentive and dignified waiters and their acolytes—apple-cheeked youths who are learning the trade, and who hover behind their instructors in much the way that interns hover behind a great surgeon on his hospital rounds. How can I convey the infinite joy of perfect service, beginning with an immaculate table with flowers, fine crystal and good silver? Or the delight of fish brought on a silver platter for your inspection before being faultlessly boned, drizzled with just a drop of butter and served with nut-sweet dilled potatoes? How to describe the clean, swift strokes of the knife cutting a partridge golden under its mantle of bacon, and the deft arrangement of the sliced bird on the hot plate with green grapes, sauerkraut and potato purée? Or how to thank the German wine waiters who conferred with a single woman with the same gravity as if she were the Grand Panjandrum himself, exploring her tastes before advising a dry rather than a fruity Moselle for a dish of fresh asparagus with hollandaise, a not-too-sweet Rhenish *Beerenauslese* for a sautéed scallop of veal, or the right Château Haut-Brion to go with a saddle of young boar larded with truffles and served with grilled mushrooms and fresh sweet corn in cream? (This last dish, in all its glory, was served to me at the Walterspiel Restaurant in Munich, the restaurant I most enjoyed in all of Germany, of which more later.)

Gut essen gehen often means sheer opulence, the more baroque the better. This opulence shows in menus that grow longer as an establishment gets more popular. The menu of Munich's famous Franziskanerbräu lists 164 standard dishes, from hors d'oeuvre to dessert and cheese, plus 66 daily specialties; that of the Funkturm Restaurant, atop Stuttgart's lofty TV tower, offers some 115 dishes. Typical of such menus are the massive meat dishes so esteemed by the Germans. The Franziskanerbräu, essentially a vast beer palace, caters to the robust taste of the Bavarians with any number of pork specialties—boiled pork, trotters, livers and kidneys, roast pork, pork chops and roast pig—all served in immense quantities. Veal steaks, richly garnished with peas and french-fried potatoes or with pineapple, bananas and curried rice, are the pride of the Funkturm. But I have also had an extremely good *Forelle blau* (a trout *au bleu*) there, fished alive from the trout and carp tank that is part and parcel of any good German restaurant. (It comes as a surprise to all Germans that our most astronomically priced restaurants do not normally stock live fish.)

I rather doubt that the dishes and garnishes listed on Germany's monster menus are really as different from each other as they are represented: many of them may come out of the same kettle or the same pan. But it is the feeling of choice, of wide, wide choice, that many Germans revel in. This feeling is part of what almost amounts to a national ideal—the ideal of *sich verwöhnen lassen* (let yourself be pampered), a phrase that occurs again and again in conversation and is used as the final clincher in advertisements for perfume, liquor or travel.

Not all German restaurants sport such a plethora of edibles, but those that do are among the most popular. I myself don't care for them. Not too much, but perfect, is what I crave; and this I found at the Walterspiel Restaurant, in Munich's palatial, exquisitely furnished Vier Jahreszeiten Hotel, the Hotel of the Four Seasons, where James Bond was wont to stay and where one of the public rooms is the graceful Damensalon, in which ladies can entertain in privacy. Alfred Walterspiel, who founded the restaurant now run by his sons, was an internationally famous hotelkeeper and, above all, a great and passionate cook. Walterspiel did the seemingly impossible: He refined German dishes to the point of creating a German *grande cuisine*. His cookbook *Meine Kunst (My Art)* is an invaluable text for anybody who wants to learn to cook exquisitely.

The classical beauty of Walterspiel's cookery is reflected in the restraint and elegance of his restaurant. Among its rooms, the Nymphenburg Room is my favorite, a white chamber decorated with nacreous china of museum quality in the rococo shapes and patterns that recall the glorious Nymphenburg Castle where it is still made. The menu offered in the Nymphenburg Room is not an extensive one, containing fewer than 50 dishes. The first

Continued on page 54

The Signs of Dining Out Well

Gut essen gehen, "dining out well," has long been a traditional part of family and social life in Germany. In following this popular custom, the Germans have a tremendous choice of eating places, which vary widely in cuisine, atmosphere and local lore. Among these are inns and taverns that in a few German towns still exhibit time-honored signs like these flamboyant wrought-iron devices in Rothenburg, in northern Bavaria. Such signs were originated by medieval craftsmen's guilds to indicate their trades. The signs on these pages are used today by eating and drinking houses to denote their names or symbols—Golden Stag, Griffin, Swan—sometimes with the names of their owners underneath.

Gasthof

Gasthof Greifen

Family Outings beneath the Trees

Whenever the weather is pleasant enough, whole
families spend sunny hours in the Gutsschänke
Neuhof, a garden restaurant near Frankfurt. This
establishment, which is also a working farm,
caters to motorists from the city with rustic
dining rooms and bars, a leafy terrace and garden,
a children's playground and a spacious parking
lot. But the main attraction is solid country fare,
which often includes fresh game such as venison
and wild boar, and plenty of rich desserts like
the whipped-cream-smothered parfait the little
girl above is shoveling into her mouth. The
Gutsschänke Neuhof makes its own bread and *Wurst*
on the premises and even provides its own wine
from a vineyard owned by the estate.

Gemütlichkeit for Townsfolk and Students

Germans intent on "dining out well" seek not only good food and drink but *Gemütlichkeit,* an atmosphere of warmth and fellowship. For centuries they have enjoyed this ambiance in student taverns like the one shown at right, and in *Ratskeller* restaurants, which are traditionally situated in the vaulted cellars of city halls. One of the more famous of the latter type is Bremen's *Ratskeller (above).* Reputedly the oldest of its kind, it is rich in anecdotes about celebrated poets and artists who dined there—and richer still in vintage German wines; nearly a half million bottles, of 925 types, are ensconced in its cellars.

University students in Münster, clad in the uniform of their student association, gather at Pinkus Müller's tavern for a *Dämmerschoppen* (a drink at twilight), singing and drinking beer from a traditional glass boot. The beer is Müller's famous *Altbier,* from the tavern's own 150-year-old brewery.

course includes a choice of Dutch oysters, Malassol caviar, game pâté with Cumberland sauce, smoked breast of goose, and smoked salmon with a sauce made from fresh thick cream and freshly grated horseradish. It also includes a delicate, almost bland chicken salad with slices of Persian melon, which I used to order by room service late at night, after the theater, with a cup of clear hot bouillon of pheasant and a half bottle of the 1966 Bernkasteler Doktor *Auslese,* one of the most glorious Moselles of its decade.

Among the fish, the eel *aux fines herbes* and the carp boiled blue, with butter and creamy horseradish—both of them fish that I usually don't care for—evoke tender memories. So do the other courses. I once reveled in a plate of thick, fresh white asparagus flown from South Africa to a November-gray Munich, and in a superlative breast of partridge served on croûtons spread with the bird's liver, sautéed in butter. This dish was accompanied by sautéed tart apples, wild mushrooms, and mashed potatoes as fluffy as a cumulus of summer clouds.

Yet the most distinctive quality of the Walterspiel cuisine, I think, lies not in its gourmet creations but in the perfection of certain simpler dishes, such as grilled pork chops with peas and potatoes, or tips of tenderloin steak cooked with mushrooms and served with *risotto*—dishes that depend upon the very freshest of ingredients and upon a cook's light hand and intellect. This is true of desserts as well. The sweet that made the deepest impression on me was *Reis Trautmannsdorf,* basically a rice pudding with fruit, custard, cream and liqueur. After a childhood spent in British boarding schools, where tasteless rice pudding ended every dinner, I have generally been willing to leave the stuff alone, but the Walterspiel version of rice pudding was so light and so balanced in its relation of ingredients that I felt I was eating the very idea, the spirit of the dish rather than its earthly components.

Another German restaurant I like immensely is the Frankfurter Stubb, local dialect for the Frankfurt Room, of the famed Hotel Frankfurter Hof in Frankfurt. The Frankfurter Hof is one of the great luxury hotels of Europe and its restaurant features many local dishes, superbly done. Here, too, refinement of cooking has relieved the native heaviness of some of the dishes without altering their regional quality, as in the famed green sauce of Frankfurt *(Recipe Booklet),* made from herbs and served as an accompaniment for hard-cooked eggs or boiled beef, or added to a modest dish of lentils and sausage. Once again, the menu is not an especially extensive one, but it is enormously sophisticated, as is the generous wine list. Apart from its contents, this menu is as beautifully produced as an art book, with colored illustrations, recipes and amusing dialect mottoes and adages. It is sold to visitors—and cheerfully bought by them—as a souvenir at a price of almost three dollars.

Needless to say, not all German restaurant food is either exuberant or exquisite; I have merely described these qualities as the ideals of *gut essen gehen.* But by and large, the choice and presentation of food in a German town that corresponds in size to, say, Wiscasset, Maine, will be surprisingly large and varied. Even the humbler guest houses and beer halls will offer you a choice of *Schnitzel,* pork dishes, sausages and similar hearty fare that you will not find in the United States. But the food in the small, nondescript eating places of Germany will not approach that of similar establishments in France or Italy, where you will almost certainly find a well-prepared sole or a mouth-watering display of *hors d'oeuvre variés*.

Germany is not the country for bistro exploring, as I found out when I toured the length and breadth of the country, eating where I could whenever it was time to eat. Sometimes I made my explorations with guidebook in hand, using the invaluable Varat series, which gives information not only on the quality and price of various restaurants, but also on their coziness, tranquillity and proximity to points of interest. More often, to gain a realistic view of how the local people ate, I simply went into whatever likely *Lokal,* or place, presented itself at mealtimes. I had few, if any, delicious surprises; for the most part, the food was indifferent and much too heavy. The exceptions were invariably the *Schnitzel,* made from the excellent German veal, and the equally excellent sausages. These vary from locality to locality, and they are worth exploring, as are the local beers and the local open wines, called *Schoppenweine.*

I soon grew proficient in matters of *Wurst,* which is divided into four basic types, with their own subdivisions, local variations and local names. *Rohwurst* is cured and smoked by the butcher, then eaten as it is without further cooking. *Brühwurst* is both smoked and scalded by the butcher; it may be eaten as it is or heated by simmering. *Kochwurst,* which corresponds to what we in America generally call cold cuts, may be smoked and is always well cooked by the butcher. And *Bratwurst* is sold raw by the butcher and must be pan-fried before eating.

By restricting himself to this kind of food, the traveler can avoid the flour-thickened sauces that are manna to the less sophisticated eaters of Germany. It will also help him avoid the fantastic lavishness of many of Germany's most popular restaurants.

This lavishness is one of the more deplorable aspects of *gut essen gehen,* but there is a simple historical explanation for it. According to a popular rhyme, "Wer Geld hat, mag Austern essen; wer keines hat, muss Kartoffeln fressen" —"He who has money may eat oysters; he who has none must feed on potatoes"—and the words reflect not only the Germans' taste for opulent foods, but also the bitter periods of food rationing during two world wars and the periods of near starvation that followed them.

In those days, potatoes were a luxury; coffee was made from acorns and tea from apple peelings; six-foot men weighed less than a hundred pounds and children combed the fields for rotting cabbages and turnips. In some ways, the period of near starvation after World War II was worse than the war itself, and it probably provided the unconscious motive behind the food crazes that have swept Germany since the war.

First came the *Fresswelle* (devouring wave) during which people indiscriminately devoured everything and anything they could swallow. This wave produced the image of the fat Germans of the *Wirtschaftswunder* (economic miracle), who transformed the war-devastated German people into one of the world's most prosperous populations.

More recently, Germany has been passing through an *Edelfresswelle* (exotic-food devouring wave), as a glance at almost any German restaurant menu will show. Even relatively simple establishments offer turtle, shark's fin and

Continued on page 58

55

THE TWO MAIN TYPES OF GERMAN BEER: *DUNKLES,* OR DARK, AND *HELLES,* OR LIGHT

The Many Faces of German Beer

As an accompaniment to dining out, and as a pastime in itself, beer-drinking is one of Germany's oldest and best-known customs, involving a consumption of some two billion gallons a year. Generally distinguished as dark or light *(opposite page)*, German beers also come in sweet and bitter, weak and strong, top- and bottom-fermented varieties (depending on the type of yeast, which floats or sinks during the brewing). Among the bottom-fermented beers is *Lager* (meaning "to store"), which is aged about six weeks to clear and mellow it. *Export* is a stronger beer, stored two to three months so it will not cloud up during shipment. Another is the bitterish *Pilsener*, originally brewed in Pilsen, Czechoslovakia. *Pilsener* and other light beers are often served with *Schnaps (left)*. The dark, strong and seductive *Bock* is brewed in winter and consumed in spring. *Märzenbier*, with a color between light and dark, is served at the Oktoberfest in Munich.

Top-fermented beers are cloudy as a result of after-fermentation in the bottle. Among them is the weak, frothy *Weissbier* or "white beer," which in Munich is served with a lemon slice *(bottom left)*. The delicate, champagne-like *Berliner Weisse*, lovingly nicknamed "cool blonde" by Berliners, is brewed entirely from wheat and customarily is served *mit Schuss* ("with a shot of syrup," *bottom right*). Other top-fermented beers include the light *Altbier* ("old beer"), derived from a Rhenish favorite called *Kölsch*, and the sweet, dark, malty *Malzbier*, favored by women and children because it is nutritious but very low in alcohol.

PILSENER, ACCOMPANIED BY *SCHNAPS*

WEISSBIER, SERVED WITH LEMON

BERLINER WEISSE, WITH AND WITHOUT A SHOT OF RASPBERRY SYRUP

sea-cucumber soup—all canned, but exotic in concept if not in taste. At one time the magic apparently lay in an indiscriminate use of pineapple, bananas, mangoes, papayas or whatever other tropical fruit could be obtained, served with such unlikely mates as veal steaks, and preferably flamed to a fare-thee-well. Such dishes are now rather old hat, the tide having turned to the lure of the romantic Balkans. Dishes abound with names like *Serbisches Reisfleisch* ("Serbian meat and rice," which is just that, and highly seasoned), *Pusztafeuer* ("fire of the Puszta," or pork chops on a mixture of rice and peppers, garnished with a pepper stuffed with the delicate mixture of meats and vegetables called *ragoût fin*), and *Ungarische Rhapsodie* ("Hungarian rhapsody" consisting of a veal steak on toast with a ragoût of ham, mushrooms and paprika). The romance of the flaming Balkans is also expressed in an enormous number of skewered shashliks, brilliantly flamed whenever possible.

But *gut essen gehen* outside the home is more than a current craze. There is in Germany a tradition of fine inns at least five centuries old, dating back to the days when pilgrims crossed the European continent on their way to Canterbury or Loreto. German literature celebrates many of these inns, and so does German song; innumerable German *Lieder* tell of Herr Wirt, the innkeeper, his wife Frau Wirtin and their *schönes Töchterlein* (beautiful young daughter). In the course of time the innkeeper turned into the kind of hotel or restaurant owner who is far more than a purveyor of food and drink, and the tradition has never gone out of fashion.

It is a tradition alien to America, where "innkeepers," for want of a better name, seldom get to know their guests in any intimate way, however much the guests may like the bed and board. Not so in Germany. The most famous German restaurateurs and hotelkeepers of our time, Lorenz and Louis Adlon, were personal friends of the Kaiser, of Frederick Ebert, first president of the German Weimar Republic, of Hugo Stinnes, the famous industrialist, and of other personages too numerous to mention. Their hotel, the Adlon, is now a burnt-out shell in East Berlin, but in its day it was the one place in Germany where you were sure to meet both foreign potentates and impoverished, brilliant intellectuals, and the Adlons were the friends, confidants and supporters of all of them.

To this day, the relation between a German restaurateur and his clients is infinitely closer than it is in the United States. When a German has a favorite restaurant, he will know the owner intimately and consult with him closely on such important matters as the best menu for a confirmation or an engagement dinner party. Perhaps the intimate relation between a German and his inn is best seen in the *Stammtisch*, a table reserved at all times for a group of men who meet daily, after work and before supper, for a drink of wine or beer and for simple conviviality. An old and honored institution, the *Stammtisch* plays the role of a club for its "members." Even today, in small German towns, you will see the *Stammtisch* of the *Honorationen*, or leading citizens, such as the doctor, the mayor, the tax collector, the apothecary, the school principal and the most important merchants. In this group, the innkeeper is both peer and friend. There is nothing that the host of a *Stammtischlokal* does not know about his town and its people (which may be all to the good or the bad, depending on how you look at it), and he himself is invariably one of the best known and most respected of the townsmen.

Hanover *Hausfrauen*, shopping in a *Konditorei*, confront an abundant choice of cream pastries, *Torten* and fruit tarts.

Rehschnitzel mit Pilzen
VENISON CUTLETS WITH MUSHROOMS

To serve 6

10 whole juniper berries
5 whole black peppercorns
1 small bay leaf, crumbled
½ teaspoon salt
6 six-ounce venison cutlets,
 preferably from the leg, cut ½
 inch thick and pounded slightly
½ cup plus 1 tablespoon flour
4 tablespoons butter
1 cup thinly sliced fresh mushrooms
¾ cup light cream

With a mortar and pestle, pulverize the juniper berries, peppercorns, crumbled bay leaf and salt together. Then firmly press the mixture with your fingertips into both sides of the venison cutlets. Dip the cutlets in ½ cup of the flour and shake off any excess. In a heavy 12-inch skillet, melt the butter over moderate heat. When the foam subsides, add the cutlets (in two batches if they crowd the pan), and cook them for 2 or 3 minutes on each side, regulating the heat so that they color evenly without burning. Don't overcook; when done, the cutlets should be slightly pink inside. Place the cutlets side by side on a heated platter and cover with foil to keep them warm while you prepare the sauce.

Add the sliced mushrooms to the fat remaining in the skillet and cook them over moderate heat, stirring frequently, for 3 or 4 minutes. Then stir in 1 tablespoon of flour and cook, stirring constantly, for a minute or two. Add the cream and cook, stirring until the sauce thickens slightly. Taste for seasoning. Pour the sauce over the cutlets and serve.

NOTE: In Germany, the venison cutlets are sautéed in butter alone. To avoid the danger of burning the butter, you may prefer to use 3 tablespoons of butter combined with 1 tablespoon of vegetable oil.

Blumenkohlsuppe
CREAM OF CAULIFLOWER SOUP

To serve 4

1 large cauliflower (about 1½
 pounds)
2 cups chicken stock, fresh or canned
2 cups cold water
4 tablespoons butter
⅓ cup flour
1 cup milk
1 teaspoon salt
¼ teaspoon white pepper
⅛ teaspoon ground nutmeg
1 egg yolk
¼ teaspoon fresh lemon juice

Cut away the thick stem at the base of the cauliflower and tear off the green leaves. Separate the flowerets and wash them under cold running water. Reserve 10 small flowerets, and chop the rest coarsely. Combine the stock and water in a 2- to 3-quart saucepan, and bring to a boil over high heat. Drop in the whole flowerets, and boil briskly, uncovered, for 10 minutes, or until they are tender but still somewhat resistant to the point of a small, sharp knife. Remove the flowerets and set them aside in a bowl. Reserve the stock.

Melt the butter over moderate heat in a 4-quart stainless-steel or enameled saucepan. Stir in the flour and cook over low heat, stirring constantly, for 1 or 2 minutes. Do not let the flour brown. Pour in the stock and the milk, beating constantly with a whisk. Cook, stirring, until the mixture comes to a boil and is smooth and somewhat thick. Reduce the heat to low, and simmer for 2 or 3 minutes. Then add the chopped cauliflower, salt, pepper and nutmeg. Simmer, half covered, for 15 minutes, or until the cauliflower is soft enough to be easily mashed against the side of the pan. Pour the cauliflower and all of its cooking liquid into a sieve set over a bowl. With a wooden spoon, force the cauliflower through the sieve. (If you prefer, purée the cauliflower in a food mill. Don't use a blender; it will make the mixture too smooth.) Return the purée to the pan. Beat the egg yolk with a fork or whisk to break it up, then beat in ½ cup of hot purée, 2 tablespoons at a time. Now whisk the mixture back into the saucepan. Add the reserved flowerets and cook over moderate heat for 2 or 3 minutes, stirring occasionally. Do not let it boil. Add the lemon juice, taste for seasoning, and serve.

Wildgeflügel mit Burgunder
GAME BIRDS IN BURGUNDY

Wash the birds quickly under running water and dry them inside and out with paper towels. Season the birds generously with salt and pepper, roll them in flour, then vigorously shake off the excess. In a heavy 10- to 12-inch skillet, melt 3 tablespoons of the butter over moderate heat. When the foam subsides, brown the birds, turning them frequently, until they are a light golden color on all sides. Remove the birds from the skillet and set aside. Melt 2 more tablespoons of butter in the skillet. Add 3 tablespoons of shallots and cook them over moderate heat, stirring frequently, for 4 or 5 minutes, then drop in the mushroom slices and chopped ham. Cook, stirring occasionally, for 3 to 4 minutes, until the mushrooms are lightly browned. With a rubber spatula, transfer the mixture to a bowl and set aside.

Melt the remaining 2 tablespoons of butter in the skillet and in it cook the remaining 1 tablespoon of shallots for 2 or 3 minutes, until they are soft and lightly colored. Add the wine and brandy, and bring to a boil over high heat, meanwhile scraping in any brown bits clinging to the bottom and sides of the pan. Add the thyme, tarragon, bay leaf, nutmeg, ½ teaspoon of salt and a few grindings of black pepper, stir, and then return the birds to the skillet. Baste the birds thoroughly, reduce the heat to low, cover the skillet and simmer for 20 to 30 minutes, or until the birds are tender. Test by pressing a drumstick with your finger; it should show no resistance when the bird is fully cooked. Transfer the birds to a heated platter and cover them with foil; let them rest while you prepare the sauce.

Bring the juices remaining in the skillet to a boil, and boil briskly until the liquid is reduced to about 1 cup. Remove the bay leaf, stir in the mushroom-ham mixture and simmer for a minute or two. Taste for seasoning, and stir in the parsley. Pour the sauce into a sauceboat and serve with the birds.

To serve 4

4 one-pound, oven-ready young partridge, baby pheasant, quail, woodcock or grouse
Salt
Freshly ground black pepper
1 cup flour
7 tablespoons butter
¼ cup finely chopped shallots
2 cups thinly sliced mushrooms (about ½ pound)
2 tablespoons finely chopped cooked ham
2 cups red Burgundy or other dry red wine
2 tablespoons brandy
⅛ teaspoon dried thyme
⅛ teaspoon dried tarragon
½ small bay leaf
Pinch of ground nutmeg
2 tablespoons finely chopped fresh parsley

Lauchsalat
LEEK SALAD

With a sharp knife, cut off the roots of the leeks and strip away any withered leaves. Line up the leeks in a row and cut off enough of their green tops to make each leek 6 or 7 inches long. Then slit the green parts in half lengthwise, stopping where they shade into white. Carefully spread the leaves apart and wash the leeks under cold running water to rid them of all sand.

Lay the leeks in 1 or 2 layers in a heavy stainless-steel or enameled skillet or a flameproof casserole just large enough to hold them flat. Pour in enough cold water to cover them and bring to a boil over high heat. Reduce the heat to low, and simmer gently for 10 minutes, or until the leeks show only the slightest resistance when pierced with a fork. Do not overcook.

With tongs or a slotted spoon, transfer the leeks to a double layer of paper towels and let them drain for a minute or two. Then arrange the leeks in a serving dish or deep platter just large enough to hold them. In a small bowl, combine ¼ cup of the leek cooking liquid with the sour cream, vinegar, mustard, horseradish, salt and a few grindings of black pepper. Beat the mixture with a whisk or spoon until it is well blended, and taste for seasoning. Pour the dressing over the leeks. Cool to room temperature, then refrigerate the leeks for about an hour, or until chilled.

To serve 4

8 firm fresh leeks, 1 to 1½ inches in diameter
¼ cup sour cream
¼ cup cider vinegar
½ teaspoon Düsseldorf-style prepared mustard, or substitute other hot prepared mustard
½ teaspoon freshly grated horseradish, or 1 teaspoon bottled grated horseradish, drained and squeezed dry in a towel
½ teaspoon salt
Freshly ground black pepper

A rich, brown roulade of beef, accompanied by red cabbage, dumplings and beer, makes a satisfying German midday meal.

Rouladen

BRAISED STUFFED BEEF ROLLS

To serve 6

Cut the steak into 6 rectangular pieces about 4 inches wide and 8 inches long. Spread each rectangle with a teaspoon of mustard, sprinkle it with 2 teaspoons of onions, and place a slice of bacon down the center. Lay a strip of pickle across the narrow end of each piece and roll the meat around it, jelly-roll fashion, into a cylinder. Tie the rolls at each end with kitchen cord.

In a heavy 10- to 12-inch skillet melt the lard over moderate heat until it begins to splutter. Add the beef rolls, and brown them on all sides, regulating the heat so they color quickly and evenly without burning. Transfer the rolls to a plate, pour the water into the skillet and bring it to a boil, meanwhile scraping in any brown particles clinging to the bottom and sides of the pan. Add the celery, leeks, parsnip, parsley and salt, and return the beef rolls to the skillet. Cover, reduce the heat to low, and simmer for 1 hour, or until the meat shows no resistance when pierced with a fork. Turn the rolls once or twice during the cooking period. Transfer the rolls to a heated platter, and cover with foil to keep them warm while you make the sauce.

Strain the cooking liquid left in the skillet through a fine sieve, pressing down hard on the vegetables before discarding them. Measure the liquid, return it to the skillet, and boil briskly until it is reduced to 2 cups. Remove from the heat. Melt the butter in a small saucepan over moderate heat and, when the foam subsides, sprinkle in the flour. Lower the heat and cook, stirring constantly, until the flour turns a golden brown. Be careful not to let it burn. Gradually add the reduced cooking liquid, beating vigorously with a whisk until the sauce is smooth and thick. Taste for seasoning and return the sauce and the *Rouladen* to the skillet. Simmer over low heat only long enough to heat the rolls through. Serve the rolls on a heated platter and pour the sauce over them. *Rouladen* are often accompanied by red cabbage (*below*) and dumplings or boiled potatoes.

3 pounds top round steak, sliced ½ inch thick, trimmed of all fat, and pounded ¼ inch thick
6 teaspoons Düsseldorf-style prepared mustard, or substitute 6 teaspoons other hot prepared mustard
¼ cup finely chopped onions
6 slices lean bacon, each about 8 inches long
3 dill pickles, rinsed in cold water and cut lengthwise into halves
3 tablespoons lard
2 cups water
1 cup coarsely chopped celery
¼ cup thinly sliced leeks, white part only
1 tablespoon finely chopped scraped parsnip
3 parsley sprigs
1 teaspoon salt
1 tablespoon butter
2 tablespoons flour

Rotkohl mit Äpfeln

RED CABBAGE WITH APPLES

To serve 4 to 6

Wash the head of cabbage under cold running water, remove the tough outer leaves, and cut the cabbage into quarters. To shred the cabbage, cut out the core and slice the quarters crosswise into ⅛-inch-wide strips.

Drop the cabbage into a large mixing bowl, sprinkle it with the vinegar, sugar and salt, then toss the shreds about with a spoon to coat them evenly with the mixture. In a heavy 4- to 5-quart casserole, melt the lard or bacon fat over moderate heat. Add the apples and chopped onions and cook, stirring frequently, for 5 minutes, or until the apples are lightly browned. Add the cabbage, the whole onion with cloves, and the bay leaf; stir thoroughly and pour in the boiling water. Bring to a boil over high heat, stirring occasionally, and reduce the heat to its lowest possible point. Cover and simmer for 1½ to 2 hours, or until the cabbage is tender. Check from time to time to make sure that the cabbage is moist. If it seems dry, add a tablespoon of boiling water. When the cabbage is done, there should be almost no liquid left in the casserole. Just before serving remove the onion and bay leaf, and stir in the wine and the currant jelly. Taste for seasoning, then transfer the entire contents of the casserole to a heated platter or bowl and serve.

A 2- to 2½-pound red cabbage
⅔ cup red wine vinegar
2 tablespoons sugar
2 teaspoons salt
2 tablespoons lard or bacon fat
2 medium-sized cooking apples, peeled, cored and cut into ⅛-inch-thick wedges
½ cup finely chopped onions
1 whole onion, peeled and pierced with 2 whole cloves
1 small bay leaf
5 cups boiling water
3 tablespoons dry red wine
3 tablespoons red currant jelly (optional)

To serve 6 to 8

FILLING

¼ cup dried currants

¼ cup rum

½ cup fresh, white bread crumbs

2 tablespoons melted butter

6 medium-sized tart cooking apples
(about 2 pounds), peeled, cored
and cut into slices about ¼ inch
thick

PASTRY

2 cups all-purpose flour

¼ pound plus 4 tablespoons
unsalted butter, softened

4 egg yolks

2 tablespoons sugar

2 tablespoons finely grated lemon
peel

CUSTARD

2 whole eggs

2 egg yolks

⅓ cup sugar

1¾ cups heavy cream

2 tablespoons sugar combined with
2 tablespoons melted butter

To make about 6 pancakes

FILLING

6 tablespoons butter

3 pounds tart cooking apples, peeled,
cored and sliced into ¼-inch-thick
wedges

2 tablespoons sugar mixed with 1
teaspoon ground cinnamon

PANCAKES

8 eggs

2½ cups milk

1 cup flour

4 teaspoons sugar

½ teaspoon salt

6 tablespoons butter

Confectioners' sugar

Apfelkuchen
APPLE AND RUM CUSTARD CAKE

Place the currants in a small bowl, pour the rum over them, and let them soak for at least 20 minutes. Preheat the oven to 350°.

Meanwhile make the pastry. Combine the flour and ¼ pound plus 4 tablespoons of butter in a large bowl and, working quickly, use your fingertips to rub the flour and fat together until they look like flakes of coarse meal. With a large spoon, beat in 4 egg yolks, one at a time, then beat in 2 tablespoons of sugar and the lemon peel. With your fingers pat and press the pastry evenly into the bottom and sides of an 8-inch springform cake pan 2 inches high.

Now begin to fill the pastry shell in the following fashion: Stir the bread crumbs and 2 tablespoons of melted butter together in a small bowl, sprinkle the mixture evenly over the dough and spread the apples over it. Drain the currants and set the rum aside. Then scatter the currants over the apples. Bake in the middle of the oven for 10 minutes.

During this first stage of baking, beat the 2 eggs, the 2 egg yolks and ⅓ cup of sugar with a wire whisk or a rotary or electric beater until they are thick and lemon colored. Beat in the reserved rum and the cream and pour half of it evenly over the apples in the partly baked cake. Bake the tart for 20 more minutes, or until the custard is set, then pour in the remaining liquid custard and bake for 30 minutes longer. Sprinkle the top of the tart with the 2 tablespoons of sugar mixed with the melted butter. Bake in the top third of the oven for 15 or 20 minutes, or until the top of the tart browns lightly. Remove the pan from the oven and let the tart cool completely before removing the springform. With a wide spatula, slide the tart onto a cake plate and serve.

Apfelpfannkuchen
APPLE-FILLED PANCAKES

In a heavy 12-inch skillet, melt 6 tablespoons of butter over moderate heat. When the foam subsides, drop in the apple slices and sprinkle them with the mixed sugar and cinnamon. Cook, stirring gently from time to time, until the apples soften slightly and begin to color. Don't overcook. Set the skillet aside, off the heat.

Preheat the broiler to its highest point. To make the pancake batter, combine the eggs and milk in a large mixing bowl and beat them with a whisk or fork only long enough to blend them. Do not overbeat. Mix the flour with 4 teaspoons of sugar and ½ teaspoon of salt and add it to the eggs and milk a few tablespoonfuls at a time, stirring constantly all the while.

In a heavy 10-inch skillet, melt 1 tablespoon of butter over moderate heat. When the foam subsides, pour in ½ cup of the batter and tip the pan from side to side so that the batter quickly covers the bottom. Strew ¾ cup of apples evenly over the batter and let the pancake cook for 3 minutes. Watch carefully for any sign of burning and regulate the heat accordingly. Pour a second ½ cup of batter over the apples and slide the skillet under the broiler 6 or 7 inches from the heat. Cook the pancake for 2 or 3 more minutes, or until the top is golden brown and firm to the touch. Watch carefully for any sign of burning.

Loosen the sides and bottom of the pancake with a metal spatula and slide the pancake onto a heated individual serving plate. The pancakes are best served at once but they may be covered with foil to keep them warm until they are all ready to be served. Add 1 tablespoon of additional butter to the skillet for each successive pancake. Just before serving, sprinkle the pancakes lightly with confectioners' sugar.

NOTE: Traditionally *Apfelpfannkuchen* are cooked entirely on top of the stove—a delicate process that involves turning the filled pancake without dislodging the apple filling. Finishing the pancake under the broiler is easier and safer for most cooks—and produces almost the same result.

Schokoladenpudding
STEAMED CHOCOLATE PUDDING

To serve 8

With a pastry brush and 2 tablespoons of softened butter, coat the bottom and sides of a 2-quart steamed pudding mold, that is, a mold with a snugly fitting cover. Pour in 3 tablespoons of sugar, and tip the mold from side to side to spread the sugar evenly. Then turn the mold over and knock out the excess sugar. Set aside.

Preheat the oven to 350°. Spread the almonds out evenly in a shallow roasting pan. Toast them in the middle of the oven for about 10 minutes, stirring them occasionally until they are light brown. Be careful not to let them burn. Set them aside in a bowl.

Melt the chocolate with the coffee, stirring constantly, in a heavy 1-quart saucepan over low heat or in a double boiler placed over simmering water. Then cool to lukewarm.

In a large mixing bowl, beat the ½ pound of butter and 1⅓ cups of sugar together, with a large spoon, mashing and beating against the side of the bowl until the mixture is light and fluffy. Beat in the egg yolks, one at a time, then little by little add the melted chocolate and coffee, and continue to beat until the batter is smooth. Stir in the almonds.

In a separate bowl, with a wire whisk or a rotary or electric beater, beat the egg whites until they form soft peaks on the beater when it is lifted out of the bowl. Stir about one quarter of the whites into the chocolate mixture to lighten it, then pour it over the remaining egg whites and gently but thoroughly fold them together. Spoon the pudding into the prepared mold, smooth the top with a spatula and cover the mold tightly.

Place the mold in a large pot and add enough water to come two thirds of the way up the side of the mold. Bring the water to a boil over high heat, reduce the heat to its lowest point, cover the pot and simmer undisturbed for 1 hour. Then remove the mold from the water and wipe it dry. Remove the cover and unmold the pudding in the following fashion: Run a long, sharp knife around the inside edges of the mold, then place a heated serving plate over the mold. Grasping mold and plate together turn them over. Rap the plate on a table and the pudding should slide out easily.

With a wire whisk or a rotary or electric beater, whip the chilled cream in a large chilled bowl until it thickens slightly. Sprinkle the cream with the confectioners' sugar and vanilla and continue to beat until the cream is stiff.

Serve the pudding while it is still hot, accompanied by the whipped cream presented separately in a bowl.

2 tablespoons butter, softened
1⅓ cups plus 3 tablespoons sugar
2½ cups blanched almonds, coarsely chopped
½ pound semisweet chocolate, cut into small chunks
3 tablespoons strong coffee, made from 1 teaspoon instant coffee and 3 tablespoons boiling water
½ pound unsalted butter, softened
10 egg yolks
10 egg whites
2 cups heavy cream, chilled
3 tablespoons confectioners' sugar
⅛ teaspoon vanilla extract

IV

Old and New Ways of Party Giving

Ursula von Kardorff's *Feste Feiern Wie Sie Fallen* (which can be loosely translated as "make hay with parties while the sun shines") is a witty, literate book that clearly illustrates the drastic changes of recent years in the way the Germans entertain. The author, one of Germany's best-known writers and one of Munich's most famous hostesses, belongs to Germany's old aristocracy, a class known in the past more for its formality than for any free-and-easy view of social obligations. Yet her book is a model of unpretentious common sense, and its chapters are full of practical advice on giving parties that are at once amusing, unstuffy and feasible in a servantless world. Above all, the book attains its basic objective: to alleviate the insecurity of the traditional German hostess.

To understand that insecurity, one must look back to the days of Imperial Germany and to the formality of German life before World War I. There was lavish entertaining on a grand scale among the rich aristocracy. On the huge country estates of East Prussia, platoons of guests came for a weekend and stayed for months. But in the cities, the lesser gentility restricted their entertaining and regulated it according to rules that now seem ludicrously rigid. Even today, in respect to entertaining at home, Germany has not completely shaken off the dead hand of that past.

In those days, the home of every self-respecting middle-class citizen had a front parlor, *die gute Stube*, reserved for visitors. In the center of the room lay the best carpet, and in the center of the carpet was the best table. The table bore a knitted or embroidered doily, topped by the best flower vase. Chairs upholstered in plush ringed the table, and the best silver, china and crystal re-

The easier mood of German parties has not eliminated tradition, and Ursula von Kardorff welcomes a bouquet and a formal *Handkuss* from one of her guests, Professor Rolf Trauzettel. The setting is her small Munich apartment, where limited space relegates the buffet table to the kitchen. Three guests enjoying the food there are foreign correspondent Werner Holzer and his wife, and Frau Detre von Varczy. In addition to Frau von Kardorff's goose-fat spread, the buffet consists of meatballs, Westphalian ham, liver sausage, smoked meat, cheeses, salads, cauliflower with dips, baked eggs mixed with dill and parsley, and assorted breads.

posed in the best sideboard, next to a windowsill bearing the best plants. Using *die gute Stube* and its contents for everyday affairs would have been a desecration as sacrilegious as dipping into capital. Nevertheless, the room was cleaned from top to bottom once a week.

Visitors did not come to such a home uninvited except on mandatory formal calls, which entailed a ritual as fixed as that of any primitive society fearful of offending its gods. Such calls were made only by one's social inferiors; socially superior acquaintances were called *upon*. The call was brief and totally impersonal: One rang the doorbell, was admitted to the hallway by a maid, left with her an engraved calling card, and departed. It is no wonder that, under such circumstances, easy and spontaneous hospitality did not flourish, and that both host and hostess contemplated an entertainment as elaborate as a formal dinner with trepidation.

For such a dinner, it was customary to hire the services of a *Kochfrau*, a freelance cook who went from house to house as the need for her services arose. These women cooked as well as any chef, with specialties that were famous throughout the town. Apple-cheeked, sturdy-armed *Minna* (the generic name for a family's cook and general maid) was relegated into the background for these splendid occasions. Not all *Minnas* took kindly to this second-class role; my aunts told me of battles whose savage infighting might have served as models for modern guerrilla warfare.

But times have changed. *Minna*, miniskirted and beehived of hair, has taken herself to an office or a factory bench; the wandering cook has been sup-

planted by the caterer. And for older German women, who are not as self-assured as American ones, the almost total lack of servants for their entertaining has been a heavy blow. Americans have learned to accept the fact that a hostess must often be her own cook and waitress, and that a less-than-perfect meal is not a final catastrophe. In contrast, German women worry—perhaps too much—about their food and service, and about matters of appearance. (Can the curtains stand critical glances? Do the glasses match?) Consequently, they entertain dinner guests less than we do, and with much greater formality. Many Germans, to the surprise of American visitors, entertain in restaurants—not out of any lack of hospitality, but out of a wish to offer their guests the best that can be had and a doubt that this can properly be done at home. Others prefer to invite guests into their homes for a relatively informal afternoon *Kaffee*, or for a glass of wine or beer in the evening after supper. These unpretentious gatherings are often the most enjoyable of all, for they give a visitor an intimate glimpse of the kind of cozy geniality that Germans call *Gemütlichkeit*.

I remember with affection some of the *Kaffeevisiten* to which I have been asked spontaneously, without great ado. "Kommen Sie zu mir Kaffee trinken," said Sigrid Lanzrath, who works for the German government in Bonn. Her home was charming: two rooms in a modern apartment building, furnished with Biedermeier antiques from a former, more spacious home. She set the coffee table with an embroidered cloth and, on old Meissen plates, she served me little sandwiches and cakes bought on the way home from

Most of the 30-odd guests at Frau von Kardorff's party are members of Munich's upper-class intelligentsia who devote more time to intent conversation than to food or drink. In this corner are Frau Anna Schröder, an editor's wife *(left)*, the actress Marianne Hoppe and sociologist Herbert Thiele-Fredersdorf. By the time the last guests depart at 2:30 a.m. (the first having arrived at 5:30), Frau von Kardorff has dispensed 42 bottles of wine, 15 bottles of beer—and a single bottle of gin.

"Kaffee" with great aunt at the "Stift."

work. As in almost all German homes, a profusion of house plants filled the room. When we had finished our coffee, Sigrid brought out liqueurs and cognac, as German tradition demands.

Another *Kaffee* I remember with pleasure was in a suburb of Berlin, miles from the center of town, where I went to see a house in which I had often played as a child. Now small, old and shabby, but miraculously surviving after the last war, the house was an anachronism among the tall concrete buildings that surrounded it. But the garden was as I remembered it, and in the garden a workman's family was preparing afternoon *Kaffee* at a table set under the old apple tree that I had climbed so long ago. I was invited to join them, and the youngest child was quickly dispatched to a bakery to fetch some *Pflaumenkuchen* (plum tarts) and *Windbeutel* (cream puffs) to supplement the *Streuselkuchen* (yeast cake with sugar-crumb topping, *page 141*) that were already waiting under a throw of bead-fringed insect netting.

Yet another *Kaffeevisite* touched me deeply. In East Berlin, a sick, old, old woman showed me the traditional courtesy of baking me a cake, a delicious *Apfelkuchen (page 64)*, for *Kaffee*. And when I kept an appointment with Hellmut Jaesrich, editor of *Der Monat*, probably the best of all German magazines, he set a coffee table for me in his office, serving freshly made coffee in charming china cups, cookies and the convivial bottle of after-coffee brandy.

In the past, *Kaffee* parties could be more ceremonious, even formidable. I remember my mother's, with dozens of pretty little sandwiches; the *Obsttorten*, fruit tarts made with seasonal fruit *(page 178);* the *Sandtorte*, dry of texture and redolent of lemon peel and brandy; the bowls of whipped cream; the tea cart on which all the paraphernalia was wheeled in; and the lemon for tea, squeezed in an unforgettable gadget—a spouted two-piece Meissen squeezer that I still own today.

I also remember being taken to the still more formidable coffee parties of a great aunt who lived in a *Stift*, a foundation for old ladies established by a long defunct member of the minor royalty. My great aunt presided, encased in her long-jacketed tailored suit with a high, boned net collar reaching from décolletage to chin, and wearing a brooch with the initials of the *Stift*'s founder outlined in diamond splinters under her Adam's apple. In the middle of her living room sat a round table with a lace cloth and a bunch of roses. An old woman servant, who had followed my great aunt to the *Stift*, poured coffee from a silver pot; then she spooned great dabs of whipped cream into it and gave me lumps of sugar, two delights that were forbidden at home. To accompany the coffee, my great aunt passed around two serving plates, one with slices of cherry tart and one with chocolate cake, and fed us delicious vanilla-flavored pretzels from a silver tray. After that I was given a copy of Doré's illustrated Bible to amuse me while the grownups talked.

As the afternoon went on, the maid appeared again with a large crystal bowl of *Vanillecreme* decorated with rosettes of whipped cream and candied violets. And a short while before the end of the visit, a veritable Persian tapestry of tiny open-face sandwiches was brought in, along with a decanter of Madeira. I was not allowed any sandwiches with capers, anchovies or olives, for my great aunt said that they were bad for children, but a liqueur glass of Madeira was poured for me.

Nothing could be more different from such entertainment than a modern after-supper gathering. *Kommen Sie doch auf ein Glas Wein oder Bier nach dem Abendessen* (come for a glass of wine or beer after supper) is an invitation that always results in a relaxed, congenial evening, when one gets to know one's hosts far better than over most meals. It is a time, too, to get to know German wine at its best. I think that if I were a poet I would not sing of young love under the June moon, but praise the elegance, the sheer delight of Germany's great Moselles and Rhine wines. Ah, those *Spätlesen* and *Trockenbeerenauslesen*, made from almost resinous grapes specially picked during the early-morning frosts of the late autumn, delicate in flavor and light in body but with such a flowery bouquet that they will scent the room when the bottle is uncorked.

These are wines of supreme elegance, wine for wine's sake. Food, however refined, sometimes gets in their way, for many of them are not essentially table wines. This is particularly true of the best Moselles and Rhine wines, which in my opinion are infinitely better on their own. That is how the Germans drink them (at all times of the day, incidentally, for these wines are not very strong). And that is how a host will serve his prize wine to his after-supper guests, with perhaps an almond or a nibble of salty biscuit, the *Salzgebäck* the Germans make so well.

Instead of offering evening guests wine straight from the bottle, a *Bowle* may be "constructed," as the Germans say. Though its name derives from the English word "bowl" and it is indeed made in a punch bowl, a *Bowle* is the most German of drinks. It is not a punch, for it does not contain as many ingredients, nor is it ever made with hard liquor. In a classic *Bowle* there is wine—good or very good wine—sometimes champagne, and almost always a flavoring of strawberries, peaches or other fruits. But fruit is not an essential ingredient of a *Bowle*. The most famous of all *Bowlen*, in fact, is not made with fruit, but with *Waldmeister*, the sweet-scented herb we call woodruff, which blooms in May, deep in the woods, and has a distinctive, haunting flavor all its own.

Whether the evening's drink is a festive *Bowle*, fine wine or some of the justly renowned German beer, the snack accompaniment is always simple; cheese or salt crackers are most common. As the evening draws on, the hostess may ask her guests if they would like some sandwiches, or she may bring out a modest plate of them. But at a spontaneous party she must not come out with a tea wagon piled with fancy sandwiches or an opulent composite salad. A German manual for hostesses explains the delicate question of protocol that such an act would raise: "The evening would then have a note of obligation. The guests would want to reciprocate the invitation, and to serve more than was served to them." The rule of simplicity may be relaxed a bit around midnight, when guests are weary but ought to take on ballast for the journey home; then a glass of beer and a plate of the little sausages called *Würstchen* will give them the strength they need.

The wine and beer parties I have been describing are evening or late-evening affairs. Cocktail parties, in Germany, figure only in the lives of the rich, the American-minded or people out to impress their friends. To be sure, all the hostess manuals and magazines give suggestions for cocktail parties, but more often than not the drinks are wild and woolly. Something called a domino cocktail consists of equal parts of Jamaica rum, orange juice and brandy, with dashes of vermouth and sugar syrup. The *Einsiedler* (hermit) cocktail, apparently designed for unsociable guests, may well assuage their loneliness with its combination of vermouth, peach brandy, brandy, bitters and lemon juice. I've never known anybody who went in for such concoctions, but someone must. The German sophisticates I know drink Scotch or, if they are *very* rich, bourbon. Others down native *Schnaps—einen Klaren, Steinhäger* or *Korn*—when they want something strong, or they stick to brandy.

The entertainment at which an American might most expect to be served a drink—the full-scale dinner party—is the very occasion on which he is least likely to get one. When you receive a dinner invitation in Germany you must be punctual almost to the minute, for there is little or no before-dinner drinking there. This generalization is not one I would wish to lay my life down for, because the possibility of drinks before dinner depends partly on the kind of circle you move in. At dinner in an elegant circle—at the house of a Hamburg shipowner, say, or that of a high government official— a variety of drinks might be served, even if it is a midday dinner. In the house of a school principal in a small Bavarian town you will sit down to eat very soon after you arrive. Elsewhere, you may get sherry, vermouth or the ubiquitous Italian apéritif Campari. Perhaps the matter is best summed up by saying that drinking before meals is considered chic by some Germans— but very few Germans are chic in this way.

Other aspects of a German dinner party may be equally surprising to an American guest. It is customary, for example, to bring flowers when you visit somebody's house the first time, and it is quite correct to do so every time you go. If the occasion is a formal one you should send the flowers beforehand, so that your hostess will not have to cope with a dozen bunches of roses at one time. When you do bring flowers in person, be sure to take off the wrapping in the outer hall, before you meet your hostess and present your gift. In Germany's rigid etiquette it is considered rude not to do so, because the hostess is expected to express gratitude for specific flowers rather than an amorphous paper bundle.

I think these gifts of flowers one of the nicest of all German customs; though I have lived in America for many years, I have never grown used to the fact that guests seldom send or bring flowers. But at a dinner party, even flowers take second place to the cardinal rule of punctuality. If you are ever forced to choose between being on time and stopping to pick up flowers, choose punctuality and send the flowers later.

These rules of punctuality and gifts reflect some of the formality that has survived in German entertaining. It is typical of Germans, too, that they like to have a formal reason for entertaining guests. Thus, the *Konfirmation* ceremony of the Lutheran Church, an important event in the life of a boy or girl because it marks his or her entry into the adult world, will be celebrated in a restaurant or at home with a festive *Mittagessen*. Such a meal might consist of a lobster or crab-meat cocktail (both almost inevitably canned), a clear bouillon with marrow, roast beef with mixed vegetables and potatoes, and a lemon cream *(page 43)* with cookies. Sherry or a glass of *Sekt* (German champagne) would precede this ceremonious meal, and wine rather than beer would accompany it.

A *Verlobung,* or engagement—a relationship that in Germany is almost as binding as matrimony—is often announced in a local newspaper or by a card. Friends will pay a festive visit to congratulate the families, or they may be invited to a more formal reception (traditionally, in the late morning), where sherry, port or champagne will be offered with suitable crackers or even a cold buffet. A proper engagement party, however, takes place at a festive meal in the house of the bride's parents. The excitement of the event knows no bounds, especially if it is the first time that the respective families meet. Usually there are speeches, initiated by greetings from the girl's father and followed by a response from the future bridegroom. Then the field is wide open; it is significant, however, that all the German books on etiquette make a point of warning a prospective guest at a *Verlobungsfeier* to avoid endless speechifying.

Weddings in Germany are celebrated much as they are in America, but Germans also enjoy a wedding-eve party called *Polterabend* that is unknown to us. The institution dates back for centuries. In earlier days, friends and acquaintances attended a *Polterabend* bearing armloads of old crockery, which they smashed against walls and doors in accordance with the proverb *Scherben bringen Glück,* "Broken dishes bring good luck." At the same time, the couple was teased, often unmercifully, in songs and humorous sketches. Today, a *Polterabend* is no longer the all-out bash it used to be, perhaps because the current generation does not have the stomach for this kind of robust celebration. But it is still a customary entertainment, socially valuable in providing an opportunity for receiving friends who are not asked to the wedding proper.

Another very German form of entertaining is *der Herrenabend,* an evening for gentlemen alone. A *Herrenabend* may be an evening dinner, or it may follow the evening meal. No ladies may be present for a moment, not even to greet the guests. For a dinner, there must be male servants to pass the courses; for an evening party, the mistress of the house may arrange sandwiches, cheeses or a buffet beforehand, the wines being the concern of the host. Though such an evening often sinks deep into drink, it does not have the connotations of an all-out American stag party, for it takes place among men who have business or politics to discuss. Thus, a German diplomat or politician might give a relatively formal *Herrenabend,* and many of these entertainments, such as those of Bismarck and the Kaiser, and more recently, those of Munich's Prince Constantin of Bavaria, have become famous.

I remember *Herrenabende* of my father's which, like all *Herrenabende,* waxed loud with song as the hours grew smaller, while my mother sat in her bedroom growing more and more furious at the middle-of-the night bedlam. The high point of my father's *Herrenabend* was a punch called *der Warschauer Tod,* "The Warsaw Death," a potent concoction of Russian or Polish cavalry origin that had been popular in the East Prussia of his youth. It was made by heating almost to the boiling point two bottles of excellent Burgundy, a little lemon peel, one or two whole cloves and an inch or so of stick cinnamon.

In the original version of *der Warschauer Tod* two sabers were laid crosswise over the punch bowl and topped by a large piece of rum-soaked sugar cone. (Sugar cones wrapped in the traditional blue paper can be bought to this day in the grocery stores of East Germany. I brought one home to America with me, to the delight of a very old Vermont lady who had known these cones in the general store of her distant youth.) The lights were then put out and the sugar cone flamed while the cavalry officers sang their favorite songs. In our own antimilitaristic household there were no sabers, and we were beyond sugar cones. Instead, two long-handled ladles were filled with rum-soaked lump sugar and ignited, amidst songs that were exhilarating in other than a military way.

Along with "The Warsaw Death" I remember two other powerful drinks that came from the Baltic of my father's youth. One was designed for the early hours of the morning; the other was a hangover cure. *Der Göttertrunk,* or "The Drink of the Gods," consisted of equal parts of port, brandy and very strong black coffee, the whole well shaken and served at the end of an all-night party with open-face cheese sandwiches on pumpernickel. The hangover cure, called *der Nikolaschka* after some Russian czar, was made by filling a liqueur glass with brandy and topping it with a slice of lemon that had been trimmed of its rind and sugared. Half a teaspoon of ground coffee was placed on the lemon. To consume this restoring potion, one removed the lemon slice and ground coffee, downed the brandy in one gulp, and then ate the coffee-covered lemon.

These potables from eastern Germany bring back to my mind the unparalleled prewar hospitality of those ancient provinces. In Silesia, Pomerania and East Prussia, then still German, the landed gentry practiced hospitality with the abandon of Arab potentates. Visitors came for a few days and stayed for months on the big estates, which resembled the antebellum plantations of our own South in their self-sufficiency. As a child and young girl, I was lucky enough to have snatched glimpses of this life on occasional visits to friends and to distant branches of my father's family.

I remember especially one long, low, ocher-painted manor house in East Prussia, the heart of an estate that had been in the same family for 600 years, and the home of magnificent hunt parties. A flight of steps led up from a circular graveled drive that was raked twice a day. In the entrance hall, stuffed stags' heads and antlers lined every inch of the wall, and a chandelier made of antlers hung from the ceiling, waiting to be lit with dozens of candles on festive occasions.

The original "Warsaw Death."

Off the hall, the sun streamed against the silk-lined walls of the yellow and green salons with their huge ornate Meissen-tiled stoves, their elegant Louis XV furniture, all gilt and satin, and the ancestral portraits and silhouettes, framed in fading brown velvet, of warriors, divines and bewigged ladies. The bedrooms, all named for the colors of their wallpapers, had curtains of the same ball-fringed dimity that I was to see again, decades later, in Jefferson's Monticello. The beds were covered with enormous white hand-crocheted spreads, which were made by past generations of ladies of the house during the long winter months and were as lacy as the snow blanketing the pine and birch forests of the region.

Our first act, after a creaky old Mercedes brought us some 40 miles from the little local railroad station, was to drink coffee on the garden terrace.

The "Mamsell," as the housekeeper was called, had had her kitchenmaids bake small, round, buttery caraway cakes, round cheese tarts, triangular red currant tarts, and mountains of waffles, heart-shaped and flower-patterned by the old long-handled waffle irons. Great bowls of newly picked, incredibly sweet gooseberries and raspberries sat on the table, to be eaten with clouds of whipped cream; I can still see the rococo shapes and crimson flowers of the old Nymphenburg bowls.

During coffee, plans were made for the hunting, for which people had come from as far as Berlin. The men went out well before dawn, with sandwiches and batteries of thermos bottles filled with scalding coffee or tea laced with rum. At noon the lady of the house sent a hot meal out into the woods—usually a *Bigos,* a Polish hunter's stew containing venison, game birds and sauerkraut.

To a young guest, one of the most exciting events of a visit was the ritual of early summer preserving. It became a kind of *fête champêtre* to which old and young from neighboring estates were bidden. All the estates of the region had extensive berry gardens and orchards, where the children and young people picked raspberries and currants, gooseberries and cherries. The older ladies trimmed and stoned the fruit, and the young matrons cooked it. This was done in large, wide copper pans over stacks of firewood that had been piled up in one corner of the large *Gutshof,* or central yard, a square surrounded by low stables, barns and the buildings that housed the farm machinery. The preserves were brought to a boil, then cooled and allowed to boil up once again. After their second cooling the housekeeper and her maids immediately sealed the cooked fruit in jars for the long winter ahead, preserved like bottled memories of the short, sweet, hay-scented summer of those northern latitudes.

These domestic activities were like games to us youngsters, but there were also croquet, horseshoes and dancing. Sometimes we sang to the accompaniment of a guitar in the evening, after one of the hearty dinners for which East Prussia was renowned. Such a dinner might have included *Beetensuppe* (the beet soup called borscht in the U.S.); *Krebse in dill,* crayfish from the local brooks, cooked in dill; and *Schmandschinken,* sliced fresh ham cooked in the oven with onions and cream. The dessert I remember best, called *Tulaer Kirschkuchen,* was a cherry tart baked with a custard of egg yolks, sugar, sour cream and beaten egg whites.

The food in those distant parts of Germany had much in common with that of Russia, Poland and the tiny Baltic republics that now are parts of the Soviet Union, but in those days were independent. The ties with the countries of the Baltic region were close, for many East Prussian families had branches there from the days when the Teutonic Order of knights settled those parts, and many boys were sent to the university at Dorpat, in Estonia, rather than to one in Germany.

It was a spacious life, and one that is indeed gone with the wind. But I will always have the memory of the *Tantenbesuche,* when for days or weeks we went visiting all the real and honorary aunts up and down the country; the harvest festivals with their pagan rituals; the balls called *Lämmerhüpfen* (literally, "lamb jumps") for the young people; and the immense hospitality, as vast and comforting as the clear summer sky over a landscape of gently rolling country, deep forests and still lakes.

Hunters and their spaniel rest for a moment in a beech grove, while a short-haired pointer sniffs the air for scents.

Tradition Rules Hunters and Hunted

At least since the Middle Ages in Germany, the pleasures of the hunt have banded men together in the quest for wild game as a sport, often on the private preserve of a baronial host. Today, although the number of large estates has dwindled, private hunting parties—and their well-ordered customs—still survive. The pictures here and on the next pages show such a hunt, held on the estate of G. C. Frantzen, president of the Hamburg Hunting Association. On the opposite page, a morning's take of pheasant and hare hangs from the rack of a field wagon as a lunch of pea soup and *Schnaps* is served by a uniformed *Fräulein*.

Overleaf: The day's hunt comes to a dramatic climax in a semipagan, torchlit ceremony. The spoils are laid out on the ground and, as the leader of the hunt announces the kinds and quantities of animals taken, each game is honored with its own special salute from hunting horns.

Racing hares in a hunting print form a background for the spicy rabbit stew called *Hasenpfeffer*, served here with potatoes and red cabbage.

Heisse Biersuppe

HOT BEER SOUP

Pour beer and sugar into a heavy 4- to 5-quart saucepan. Bring to a boil over high heat, stirring constantly until the sugar is dissolved, then remove the pan from the heat. In a small bowl, beat the egg yolks with a wire whisk or fork to break them up, and beat in the sour cream a little at a time. Stir about ¼ cup of the hot beer into the mixture, and then whisk it into the beer. Add the cinnamon, salt and a few grindings of pepper. Return the pan to low heat and cook, stirring constantly, until the soup thickens slightly. Do not let it boil or it may curdle.

Taste for seasoning and serve at once from a heated tureen or in individual soup bowls.

To serve 4

3 twelve-ounce bottles or cans of
  light beer
½ cup sugar
4 egg yolks
⅓ cup sour cream
½ teaspoon ground cinnamon
¼ teaspoon salt
Freshly ground black pepper

Hasenpfeffer

BRAISED RABBIT IN SPICED RED WINE SAUCE

In a heavy 5-quart flameproof casserole, cook the bacon over moderate heat, stirring and turning it frequently, until it is crisp. Spread the bacon out on a double thickness of paper towels to drain and set the casserole with the bacon fat aside.

Wash the rabbit quickly under cold running water and pat it thoroughly dry with paper towels. Sprinkle the pieces with salt and pepper, then dip them in flour and shake off any excess. Heat the bacon fat in the casserole over high heat until it splutters. Add the rabbit, a few pieces at a time, and brown them on all sides, regulating the heat so that they color quickly and evenly without burning. As they are done, transfer the rabbit pieces to a plate. Pour off all but 2 tablespoons of fat from the casserole and in it cook the shallots and garlic, stirring frequently, for 4 or 5 minutes, or until the shallots are soft and transparent but not brown. Pour in the wine and stock, and bring to a boil over high heat, meanwhile scraping in any brown bits clinging to the bottom and sides of the pan. Stir in the brandy, currant jelly, bay leaf, rosemary and thyme, and return the rabbit and any juices collected around it to the casserole. Add the drained bacon, cover the casserole tightly, and simmer over low heat for 1½ hours, or until the rabbit is tender but not falling apart. (If you are substituting small rabbits, they may cook much faster. Test them for doneness after about 1 hour of cooking.) Pick out the bay leaf, stir in the lemon juice and taste for seasoning. The sauce should be quite peppery; add more pepper, if necessary, to taste.

Serve the rabbit directly from the casserole, or arrange the pieces attractively on a deep heated platter and pour the sauce over them.

NOTE: Traditionally, the sauce in which the rabbit is simmered is thickened, just before serving, with the rabbit's blood. If you hunt and dress your own rabbit, save its blood. Stir into it 1 or 2 tablespoons of vinegar to prevent it from clotting and refrigerate until ready to use. Stir the blood into the sauce after the rabbit is cooked, then simmer gently, stirring all the while, for 4 or 5 minutes, or until the sauce thickens slightly. Be careful not to let the sauce boil. Add the lemon juice, taste for seasoning and serve.

To serve 6

½ pound lean bacon, finely chopped
A 5- to 6-pound fresh rabbit or
  defrosted frozen mature rabbit, cut
  in serving pieces, or substitute two
  2½- to 3-pound fresh or defrosted
  frozen rabbits, cut in serving
  pieces
½ teaspoon salt
½ teaspoon freshly ground black
  pepper
½ cup flour
½ cup finely chopped shallots, or
  substitute ½ cup finely chopped
  onions
½ teaspoon finely chopped garlic
1 cup dry red wine
1 cup chicken stock, fresh or canned
2 tablespoons brandy
1 teaspoon currant jelly
1 small bay leaf
⅛ teaspoon dried rosemary
⅛ teaspoon dried thyme
2 teaspoons fresh lemon juice

Selleriesalat mit Äpfeln
CELERY ROOT AND APPLE SALAD

In a large mixing bowl, beat together the mayonnaise, sour cream, dill, parsley, salt and a few grindings of pepper. Gently stir in the apple slices, cover the bowl and set aside. With a small, sharp knife, peel the celery root and cut it crosswise into ⅛-inch slices. Drop the slices into enough lightly salted boiling water to cover them completely and cook, uncovered, over moderate heat, for 20 to 25 minutes, or until the root shows only the slightest resistance when pierced with the tip of a small, sharp knife. Drain thoroughly and pat the slices completely dry with paper towels. Add the celery root to the dressing and stir gently to coat the slices thoroughly. Taste for seasoning and serve at once, or refrigerate and serve chilled.

To serve 4

½ cup freshly made mayonnaise, or a good, unsweetened commercial variety
¼ cup sour cream
1 tablespoon finely chopped fresh dill
1 tablespoon finely chopped fresh parsley
½ teaspoon salt
Freshly ground black pepper
1 large tart cooking apple, peeled, cored and cut into ¼-inch slices
A 1¼- to 1½-pound celery root (celeriac)

Gefüllter Fasan
PHEASANT WITH GIBLET AND CROUTON STUFFING

Preheat the oven to 350°. To make the stuffing, trim off the crusts and cut the bread into ¼-inch cubes. Spread the cubes on a baking sheet and toast in the middle of the oven for 10 minutes, turning them over once or twice. When golden brown, transfer the cubes to a mixing bowl and set aside.

In a heavy 8- to 10-inch skillet, melt 2 tablespoons of butter over moderate heat. When the foam subsides, add the pheasant giblets and the chicken livers, and cook for 2 or 3 minutes, stirring occasionally, until the giblets and liver are lightly browned. Then remove them to a board, chop them very fine and add them to the toasted bread. With a rubber spatula, scrape any fat remaining in the skillet into the bread and stir in the parsley, pulverized juniper berries and pepper, allspice, thyme and marjoram.

Wash the pheasant quickly under cold running water and pat it thoroughly dry inside and out with paper towels. Beat the 3 tablespoons of butter, lemon juice and salt together with a spoon and rub it into the pheasant inside and out. Fill the cavity loosely with the stuffing, and close the opening by lacing it with skewers or sewing it with heavy white thread. Fasten the neck skin to the back of the pheasant with a skewer. Lay the bacon slices side by side across the bird and wrap them around it, pressing the slices snugly against the body to keep them in place.

Place the pheasant, breast side up, on a rack set in a shallow baking pan just large enough to hold the bird comfortably. Roast undisturbed in the middle of the oven for 30 minutes. Then increase the oven heat to 400°, remove the bacon slices and set them aside. Baste the pheasant with ¼ cup of chicken stock and roast for about 30 minutes longer, basting every 10 minutes or so with another ¼ cup of stock. To test for doneness, pierce the thigh of the bird with the tip of a small, sharp knife. The juice should spurt out a clear yellow; if it is slightly pink, roast for another 5 to 10 minutes.

Transfer the pheasant to a heated platter, drape the bacon slices over it, and let the bird rest covered with aluminum foil for 10 minutes before carving. Meanwhile, make the sauce by pouring any remaining stock into the pan, bringing it to a boil over high heat, and scraping in the brown bits clinging to the bottom and sides of the pan. Stir in the sour cream a few tablespoons at a time, and simmer long enough to heat it through. Taste for seasoning. Pour the sauce into a heated sauceboat and serve it with the pheasant.

To serve 4 to 6

STUFFING
3 slices fresh white homemade-type bread
2 tablespoons butter
The heart, liver and gizzard of the pheasant
4 large chicken livers, about ¼ pound
1 tablespoon finely chopped parsley
4 whole juniper berries and 3 whole black peppercorns, finely pulverized with a mortar and pestle or wrapped in a towel and crushed with a rolling pin
Pinch of ground allspice
Pinch of dried thyme
Pinch of dried marjoram

PHEASANT
A 3½-to 4-pound oven-ready pheasant
3 tablespoons butter, softened
1 tablespoon fresh lemon juice
1 teaspoon salt
4 slices lean bacon
1 cup chicken stock, fresh or canned
½ cup sour cream

A saddle of venison is accompanied by jelly-filled pears, vegetables and beer.

3 cups dry red wine

3 cups cold water

5 whole juniper berries, 2 whole
cloves and 8 whole black
peppercorns, bruised with a mortar
and pestle or wrapped in a towel
and bruised with a rolling pin

1 large bay leaf

1 tablespoon salt

A 5-pound saddle of venison

4 ounces slab bacon, sliced ⅛ inch
thick and cut into lardons ⅛ inch
wide and about 8 to 10 inches
long

4 tablespoons lard

1 cup thinly sliced scraped carrots

½ cup finely chopped onions

¼ cup thinly sliced leeks, white
part only

1½ cups thinly sliced celery,
including some of the leaves

3 tablespoons flour

½ cup heavy cream

1 teaspoon fresh lemon juice

4 poached fresh pears or 8 canned
pear halves, thoroughly drained
(optional)

½ cup lingonberry *(Preiselbeeren)*
preserves (optional)

Rehrücken mit Rotweinsosse

ROAST SADDLE OF VENISON WITH RED WINE SAUCE

In a heavy 3- to 4-quart stainless-steel or enameled saucepan, bring the wine, water, juniper berries, cloves, peppercorns, bay leaf and the salt to a boil over high heat. Remove the pan from the heat and let the marinade cool to room temperature.

Place the venison in an enameled or stainless-steel roasting pan just large enough to hold it comfortably and pour in the marinade. Turn the meat to moisten it thoroughly on all sides. Marinate at room temperature for at least 6 hours, turning the venison once or twice. Or cover it tightly with foil or plastic wrap and marinate in the refrigerator for as long as 3 days, turning the venison over at least once each day. Because marinades are tenderizers, the older the animal, the longer it should marinate.

Remove the venison from the marinade and set the marinade aside in a bowl. Pat the meat completely dry with paper towels and lard it in the following fashion: Insert the tip of a bacon lardon into the clip of a larding needle. Force it through the roast by pushing the point of the needle into the surface of the meat at an angle toward the backbone. Pull the needle through and trim the ends of the lardon so that ¼ inch protrudes from each end of the stitch. Space the lardons about an inch apart in 2 horizontal rows along both sides of the saddle.

If you do not have a larding needle, cut the lardons into short strips about 2½ inches long. Make small stitchlike holes through the surface of the meat with a skewer, ice pick or small knife, and use its tip to push the short lardons through the holes.

Preheat the oven to 350°. Dry the roasting pan and in it melt the lard over high heat until it splutters. Add the saddle and brown it on all sides, regulating the heat so that the meat colors evenly without burning.

Transfer the saddle to a platter, and add the carrots, onions, leeks and celery to the fat remaining in the pan. Cook over moderate heat, stirring frequently, for 4 or 5 minutes, or until the vegetables are soft and lightly colored. Sprinkle 3 tablespoons of flour over the vegetables and cook over low heat, stirring constantly, for 2 or 3 minutes to brown the flour slightly. Watch carefully for any sign of burning.

Now place the venison on top of the vegetables and pour in enough of the marinade to come about 2 inches up the side of the saddle. (Reserve the re-

Larding a saddle of venison takes only minutes—and makes the roast moist. If you have a larding needle with a clip, insert one lardon into it at a time and, as shown at right, make 1-inch larding stitches through the surface of the meat. Space the stitches as evenly as you can about an inch apart in two rows across both sides of the saddle. Snip off the ends of the lardons as you go. If you don't have a needle, cut the lardons into 2½-inch lengths, make holes for them with the tip of a skewer, an ice pick or even a small, sharp knife, and poke them into place.

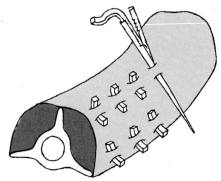

A saddle of venison is best carved in the kitchen on a cutting board. Stand the saddle on its rib side, as shown at right. Then cut each loin entirely away from the backbone and rib bones. Carve the loins crosswise into ¼-inch slices, cutting at a slight diagonal so that the first slice from each loin has a tapered wedge shape. Reassemble the saddle on a platter and it is ready to serve.

maining marinade.) Roast the venison uncovered in the middle of the oven for 1½ hours, or until the meat is tender (ideally it should be slightly pink), basting it occasionally with the pan juices, and adding more marinade to the pan if the liquid cooks away.

Transfer the venison to a large heated platter and let it rest for 10 minutes or so for easier carving.

Strain the liquid in the roasting pan through a fine sieve into an 8-inch skillet, pressing down hard on the vegetables with the back of a spoon before discarding them. Skim thoroughly of all surface fat. There should be about 2 cups of liquid. If more, boil it rapidly over high heat until reduced to the required amount; if less, add as much of the reserved marinade as necessary. Bring to a boil over high heat and pour in the cream, whisking constantly. Reduce the heat to low and simmer the sauce for 5 minutes, whisking occasionally, then stir in the lemon juice. Taste for seasoning.

To carve the saddle, separate each loin from the bones by holding the carving knife against the ridge on either side of the backbone and cutting down through the meat along the contours of the bones. Cut the loins crosswise into ¼-inch slices as shown in the diagrams below, carving at a slight angle so that the first slice from each loin is tapered. Reassemble the saddle on the platter and garnish it, if you like, with pear halves filled with lingonberry (*Preiselbeeren*) preserves.

Traditionally, the roast saddle of venison is also accompanied by a variety of such vegetables as green beans, carrots, cucumbers, mushrooms and red cabbage *(page 63)*.

NOTE: To poach fresh pears, peel them, cut them in half lengthwise and scoop out the cores with a teaspoon. In a 10- to 12-inch enameled or stainless-steel skillet, combine 4 cups of water, 2 tablespoons of sugar and 1 teaspoon of fresh lemon juice. Bring to a boil, add the pears, reduce the heat to low and simmer uncovered for 5 to 15 minutes, or until the pears show almost no resistance when pierced with a fork. Baste the pears occasionally if they are not completely covered by the liquid. Drain, cool to room temperature and refrigerate until ready to serve.

If a saddle of venison is not available, a 4- to 5-pound boned and rolled venison leg or shoulder roast may be substituted. In that case leave the lardons in long strips and insert them completely through the meat from one side of the roast to the other.

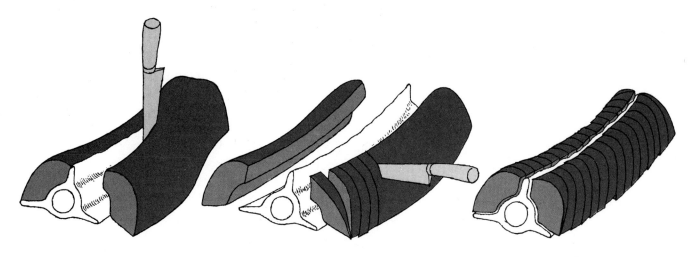

Golden-roasted partridges are stuffed and garnished with plump grapes; the wine is a chilled Rheingau *Cabinet* from Eltville.

To serve 4

10 slices lean bacon

4 partridge hearts, gizzards and livers

4 one-pound oven-ready young partridges

Salt

Freshly ground black pepper

8 whole juniper berries, coarsely crushed with a mortar and pestle

2 cups seeded green or red grapes, or 2 cups green seedless grapes

8 canned grape leaves, or 8 washed fresh grape leaves

½ cup dry white or red wine

¾ cup chicken stock, fresh or canned

½ cup sour cream

3 or 4 small bunches of green or red grapes (optional)

Rebhühner mit Weintrauben
ROAST PARTRIDGES WITH GRAPES

Preheat the oven to 400°. Cook 2 of the bacon slices over low heat in a small skillet only until they are somewhat translucent and soft but not brown. Drain them on a double thickness of paper towels and then cut each strip into 6 equal pieces. Wash the hearts, gizzards and livers of the birds and pat them dry with paper towels. Then wrap them individually in small pieces of the cooked bacon, keeping the giblets for each bird aside separately.

Wash the partridges quickly under running water and dry them thoroughly inside and out with paper towels. Sprinkle the cavities of the birds with salt and a few grindings of pepper, then stuff each bird with its wrapped giblets together with 2 of the juniper berries and ½ cup of the grapes. Neatly truss the partridges with white kitchen string. Drape 2 uncooked slices of bacon across the breast and thighs of each bird, pressing the bacon snugly against the bird to keep it in place. Drape 2 grape leaves over each partridge.

Place the birds on their backs on a rack in a large, shallow roasting pan

86

and roast them in the middle of the oven for 20 minutes, basting them every 10 minutes with 2 tablespoons of the wine. Reduce the heat to 350°, and carefully remove and discard the grape leaves and bacon from the birds. Continue roasting for 15 to 20 minutes, basting every 5 minutes or so with the remaining wine and then with the juices as they collect in the pan. The birds are done when they are a golden brown and the drumsticks feel tender to the touch. Remove the string, transfer the partridges to a heated platter and cover loosely with foil to keep them warm while you make the sauce.

Pour the pan juices through a fine sieve set over a mixing bowl. Measure the strained liquid, add enough chicken stock to make 1¼ cups and pour it into a small saucepan. Bring to a boil over high heat, reduce the heat to low and beat in the sour cream, a few tablespoonfuls at a time. Cook for a moment or two to heat the cream through. Do not let it boil. Taste and season with as much salt and pepper as you think it needs. Then spoon the sauce over the partridges and serve at once. Traditionally, the birds are accompanied by *Weinkraut (Recipe Booklet)* and mashed potatoes. If you like, you may garnish the partridges with bunches of grapes or line the platter with additional grape leaves, arrange the birds on the leaves and garnish them with grapes. Then serve the sauce separately in a sauceboat.

Haselnusscreme
HAZELNUT CREAM PUDDING

To serve 4

2 teaspoons unflavored gelatin
2 tablespoons cold water
1 cup shelled and blanched hazelnuts, pulverized in a blender or with a nut grinder or mortar and pestle
1¼ cups milk
3 egg yolks
½ cup sugar
1 teaspoon vanilla extract
1 cup heavy cream

In a heatproof measuring cup, sprinkle the gelatin over the cold water. When the gelatin has softened for 2 or 3 minutes, set the cup in a small skillet of simmering water and cook over low heat, stirring constantly, until the gelatin dissolves completely. Remove the skillet from the heat, but leave the cup of gelatin in the water to keep warm.

Combine the nuts and milk in a heavy 2- to 3-quart saucepan and heat, stirring constantly, until bubbles form around the edge of the pan. Remove from the heat. With a whisk or a rotary or electric beater, beat the egg yolks and sugar together in a mixing bowl for 3 or 4 minutes, or until the yolks are pale yellow and thick. Beating constantly, pour the hot milk in a thin stream over the yolks, then pour this custard mixture into the saucepan. Cook over low heat, stirring constantly, until it thickens enough to coat a spoon heavily. Do not let the custard come to a boil or it may curdle.

Remove the pan from the heat and stir in the dissolved gelatin and the vanilla extract. Transfer the custard to a mixing bowl, preferably stainless steel, and set it aside and let it cool to room temperature. With a whisk or a rotary or electric beater, beat the cream in a large chilled bowl until it holds soft peaks. Set the bowl of custard into a pot or another larger bowl filled with crushed ice, and stir the custard with a metal spoon until it is cold but not set. Beat thoroughly with a wire whisk if any lumps form. Immediately pour the whipped cream over the custard and with a rubber spatula fold them together gently but thoroughly. Spoon the mixture into a 1-quart serving bowl or four individual 8-ounce dessert dishes, cover tightly with foil or plastic wrap, and refrigerate for at least 3 hours, or until firm.

NOTE: If you cannot buy blanched hazelnuts, drop shelled nuts into a pan of water and boil them briskly for 2 minutes. Drain the hazelnuts in a sieve, and with a small, sharp knife peel them while they are still hot.

V

A Cooking History 2,000 Years Old

The history of German cooking and the history of Germany itself match each other in colorfulness and complexity. On the one hand, German food habits vary enormously, depending upon geographical location and social status. On the other, the German "nation," for most of its history, has been a loose conglomeration of tribes, fiefdoms, townships, dukedoms, principalities and petty kingdoms, each with its own rigid social structure and individual ways of living. Like Italy, but unlike such nations as England and France, Germany was never united until very recent times—not in fact until 1871, when Otto von Bismarck persuaded or compelled the various German states to accept the King of Prussia as the Emperor of all Germany. This interplay of political individualism, social stratification and human diversity is mirrored in the story of German cooking.

The earliest reliable records are found in the writings of the Roman historian Tacitus, who lived in the latter part of the First Century A.D. In his *Germania*, Tacitus remarks that German food was "of a simple kind," and by the sophisticated Roman standards of the time he was probably right. Hunters, nomads and primitive farmers, the ancient Germans lived on gruels; on breads made from oats, barley and millet; on milk and cheeses; on wild fruits and berries; and on game and fowl taken in their hunts.

But the first 10 centuries of the Christian era brought enormous changes to the peoples of the lands we now call Germany. First, they came into close contact with Rome—and eventually conquered it. Inevitably, some of Rome's civilization rubbed off on the Germans; for example, their rulers developed luxurious tastes for gold and silver plate and drinking vessels. What was more important, these were the centuries when Christianity conquered Europe, and its influence went far beyond religion, into art, manners and daily life. In the monasteries that preserved and transmitted civilization through the Dark Ages, there were orchards and gardens in which the monks maintained high standards of food production. Charlemagne, the ruler who united most of the people of Europe into a single Christian community around 800, gave his empire not only peace and good government, but also advice on how to plant herb gardens and vineyards, and directions on the amounts of food to be used at every meal.

By the time of the Middle Ages, Europe was a world united in customs and religion. Thus, the food of Germany differed little from that of other regions with the same natural resources. Large pieces of beef or even whole oxen, roasted on a spit over an open fire, were the great culinary feature of the period. It sometimes took three men to carry these great roasts to the lord's table. But smaller meat dishes were also known; we read, for example, of a dish of kidneys, onions and raisins in a sharp wine sauce. Game such as hart and wild boar was highly prized in Germany, but eating it was the privilege of king and nobles, who alone were allowed to hunt. Salt pork, sausages and black puddings were liked then as they are today.

Among fowl, the goose was as popular with Germans in the Middle Ages as it is now, and stuffings of apples were known even then. But the methods of cooking fowl were cruel. Geese and chickens were plucked live, a procedure that was believed to improve their flavor. The greatest pride of the medieval table was the peacock. The bird was cooked in an elaborate manner. First skinned, with the skin and plumage kept intact, it was rubbed with caraway and other spices, doused with egg yolk, roasted and then sewed again into its own skin. Pheasants were another prize of the courtly table; Charlemagne himself particularly liked them.

The people of the Middle Ages ate enormous amounts of fish, far more than we do now. Carp, pike and flatfish were readily available, and a great number of fast days in the Church calendar called for a fish diet. (Salt cod from northern Norway was, in fact, known as *Fastenfleisch*, or fast-day meat.) Medieval cookery included many ways of preparing fish, from stewing it with raisins, ambergris, pepper, honey and brine to roasting it on a spit.

All of this food was prepared with a spiciness we can hardly imagine today. In those times, spices were at once a necessity and a luxury more precious than gold. They helped to preserve food, and they also covered the taste of tainted or spoiled food in a day when refrigeration and canning were unknown. At the same time, spices, which had to be imported at great cost from the Orient, were used to display one's riches. In turn, spices made the fortune and greatness of many a family, and of such cities as Nürnberg, and rich merchants were called *Pfeffersacke* (pepper bags).

The usual drinks of the people were beer, cider and milk; only the rich drank wine, and they often drank it hot and spiced. Because the wines of Germany were then relatively sour, sweet wines from Spain, Italy and Hungary were highly esteemed, as were the sweet liqueurs that began to flow from convents and monasteries toward the end of the period.

Sweets were highly prized. Honey rather than sugar, which was rare and expensive, was used in heavily spiced and scented pastries and confections that were extravagantly formed into the shapes of castles, warriors and animals, and sometimes covered with silver or gold leaf. Recipes dating back to about 1350 tell how to make sour-cherry or apple fritters and how to crystallize rose leaves.

In earlier days, the rulers of the German tribes ate with their vassals, but the court of Charlemagne, which deeply influenced medieval Europe, fostered new customs. A contemporary writer tells us that Charlemagne ate alone, served by his subject kings and dukes. These noble attendants ate only after the Emperor was finished, and they in turn were served by their counts and chief vassals; then these dignitaries were served by *their* inferiors. This series of meals went on down the line until, around midnight, the most menial servants had their turn. Such ritualized formality became the rule among medieval royalty, and kings and emperors continued to eat alone, seated on platforms higher than those of their nobles, into the 17th Century.

At lesser banquets, men and women ate together as couples, sometimes sharing plates and drinking vessels. The ladies usually withdrew at the end of the meal, leaving the men to their heavy drinking. The drinking was often rowdy, but during a meal table manners were rigid, as we know from manuscripts dating back to the 12th Century. People ate with their fingers, but it was considered inelegant not to wash one's hands before a meal or to get them inordinately greasy during one. In an early etiquette book, cast in the form of a conversation between father and son, the son is admonished not to stuff his mouth, or to drink before he has swallowed his food.

The formal banquets of the Middle Ages, with their great number of courses and dishes and their appeal to all the senses, were part of the exuberant festivities of the times. Among the most spectacular features of the great banquets of medieval Germany were the *Schauessen,* or "foods for show," splendid dishes that were designed to appeal more to the eye than to the palate. Whole lambs, calves and deer were brought to the table covered with gold or silver; pheasants, swans and peacocks appeared in the full glory of their plumage, with gilded beaks and feet. The luxury of such banquets was extraordinary. Archbishop Albrecht of Bremen, for example, once entertained 500 people in Hamburg at a dinner served on plates of gold and silver. The chronicler of that banquet reports that the service also included golden houses, golden towers and golden mountains from which flew live birds. Fanciful table fountains were much in fashion; Philip the Good of Burgundy had one in the shape of a naked woman whose breasts spouted wine.

Such banquets, frequently held out of doors under tents, lasted as long as five hours. Entertainment—pantomimes, declamations and music—was offered between the courses. Tableaux of performing animals or of dancers masked as asses, bears and monkeys were also much admired. These extravaganzas, which literally made a meal into a work of art, are almost impossible to grasp for people of our matter-of-fact century. Their height was reached at such occasions as the banquet given in Paris in 1378 by Charles V of France for his uncle, the German Emperor Charles IV. Before more than 800 guests, the conquest of Jerusalem by the Crusader Godfrey of Bouillon was re-enacted, with scenes showing the ships carrying the Crusaders, the city of Jerusalem held by the Saracens, and the ensuing battle.

Despite all the formality and ceremony of these banquets, the food was served in a curiously helter-skelter sequence. In one banquet, given in 1303, three "courses" were served. The first consisted of "egg-soup with saffron, peppercorns and honey, millet, vegetables, mutton with onions, roast chicken with prunes." The second course consisted of "salt cod with oil and raisins, *Brassen* [a fish] fried in oil, boiled eel with pepper, roast herring with mustard." The third course included "a sour stew of fish, fried fish, small birds fried in lard with horseradish, leg of pork with cucumbers."

Amidst all the feasting, the common people were not forgotten in that age of pious charity. Some of the great events were truly *Volksfeste,* or feasts of the people. When Maximilian I was crowned King of Germany at Aix-la-Chapelle in 1486, whole oxen were roasted for all comers in the marketplace, and whole roasted lambs, fish and hares were thrown to the populace from the windows of the palace in which the Emperor was dining.

As the Middle Ages drew to a close and the Renaissance began, German life changed. Cities became more powerful, and with them, a new urban middle class. An age of trade began, bringing new goods and great wealth to Germany. The greatest commercial association of the times was the mercantile and trading confederation of some 70 cities known collectively as the Hanseatic League, which was organized in the 13th Century and survived until

Der halz im pfeffer

A cook in a puffed-sleeve doublet, shown in a 16th Century woodcut, skins a hare in preparation for the traditional *Hasenpfeffer (Hasz im Pfeffer* in old German), or "hare in pepper" *(picture, page 80; recipe, page 81).* On the stove a bubbling pot awaits the making of the stew, a dish almost as old as German cooking itself and still popular.

the 17th. The League consisted mainly of cities on the northern coasts of Germany, but also included Bergen in Norway and Bruges and Antwerp in Belgium. A sort of early European Common Market, the Hanseatic League traded in fruits from the Mediterranean, salt cod and herring from Norway, oil from Provence, wines from Spain and Italy, leather, skins and fats from Russia, grain from the Baltic region, copper and iron from Sweden, and textiles from Flanders, Germany and England. In terms of food, the results of the trading reached down to the actual consumer; at the end of the 15th Century, Bozen and other markets of the inland Tyrol sold such imported delicacies as capers, rice, almonds, figs, pepper, ginger, nutmeg, currants from Smyrna, Polish mustard, cinnamon and precious sugar.

Though the Renaissance brought the triumphant expansion of the cities of Germany, these cities had been developing for some time. Over the centuries, their organization had become rigidly structured in a way that we may now find hard to comprehend. Most citizens were members of monopolistic craft guilds, fraternal societies for artisans that regulated every aspect of their members' work. There were guilds for each trade and profession, and they controlled all everyday activity, including the production and distribution of food. In the overcrowded German cities, many of the poor did not have their own kitchens, but cooked food was sold in the *Garküchen*, where a customer could buy boiled or roasted meats. A contemporary report on the town of Wismar mentions the sale of cooked lamb and young pigs; in Munich, boiled sausage was one of the attractions. So strict was the guild organization that the cooks who ran these establishments were not allowed to slaughter the animals they prepared, and bakers were not allowed to grind their own flour. Even the kitchens were sharply divided. In some, food could only be boiled; others were set aside for roasting, frying or baking by cooks of those particular guilds.

As the Renaissance progressed, the art of fine cooking sifted down from the nobles to the rising middle classes, who quickly adopted an extravagant style of eating and drinking. In Germany, the age of Humanism and the Reformation brought a new freedom of behavior and a new luxury of living. Now the rich new bourgeoisie could keep up with princes and nobles when it came to feasting.

Seven hundred guests were invited to the wedding of a Berlin maiden at the end of the 16th Century. The meal started with a beer soup heavily spiced with pepper and ginger, served on a table set with enormous cheeses. The first full course included a gruel of millet tinted with saffron and enriched with sausages, mutton with kale, veal tinted with saffron, roast venison with garlic and onions, and roast boar and spice cakes. The second course brought ham and bread, a second gruel of millet, bread with caraway and fennel, boiled fish, a selection of venison baked in a crust, and a cream of almonds. The beverages included spiced wine and four kinds of beer.

Elsewhere, the tables of the Renaissance groaned under such delicacies as turtle soup, preserved beaver legs, lark pies, stews of lampreys, and the famous marzipan—the exquisite confection of sugar and almonds drenched with rose water. For weddings, always the most festive occasions, whole towns were often treated to a sequence of free meals and to free drink from barrels set outside the celebrants' houses. In 1627, the daughter of a Berlin pa-

Cum Priv. Maj.

Mart. Engelbrecht exaud. A.V.

trician brought her groom a dowry of 12,000 thalers, butter, bacon, eggs and four barrels of Bernau beer.

The new preoccupation with food resulted in a number of cookbooks. One of the bestsellers of the 15th Century was the *Küchenmaysterey (Mastery of the Kitchen)*, which was originally written for a nobleman's kitchen. First published in Nürnberg in 1485, the book remained in print for 200 years, no mean testimony to its excellence. It contains five parts, dealing respectively with fast-day foods, meats, baked and fried foods, sauces and vinegar and wine. Some of its advice is curiously modern. The anonymous author recommends that fish and crayfish be cooked in wine rather than beer or vinegar, and gives recipes for such vegetables as turnips, spinach, peas and sauerkraut.

Another famous cookbook of the time, written by a certain Max Rumpolt, appeared in Nürnberg in 1531. It lists 83 recipes for beef dishes, 59 for veal, 45 for mutton, 55 for salads and 225 for vegetables and miscellaneous dishes. Still another, *Welsch Kochpuech verteutscht von Bartlme Scrappi*, was translated from the Italian, indicating the importance then given to the food of Italy. During the early 16th Century, Italian cuisine was the *grande cuisine* of Europe; it became the inspiration for French cooking after Catherine de' Medici, daughter of Lorenzo de' Medici, brought her cooks to the French court at the time of her marriage to Henry II of France in 1533.

As part of Renaissance luxury and elegance, even carving became a sort of fine art. At a banquet, a good carver was expected to be able to hold a goose above the table on a fork and carve it with 20 strokes of his knife without laying the bird down. Carving is a major concern of a wide-ranging culinary manual published by Paul Fürst of Nürnberg in 1652. The first part of Fürst's book contains instructions on how to set a table, with hints on ways of folding napkins into bizarre shapes. The second deals with the carving of pheasant, goose, duck, hare, rabbit, boar, pig, lamb and fish; even desserts such as marzipan, *Torten*, candies, melons, oranges and other fruit called for special carving instructions. The third part of the book is a kitchen calendar of seasonal foods, the fourth provides guidance for the preparation of formal banquets and "show foods," and the fifth goes into table manners and questions of table etiquette. It is clear from the last section that drinking was heavy in Fürst's time, for he says: "Whosoever does not follow the laws and rules on how to fill oneself with drink should drink water instead of wine."

The luxury of the Renaissance was nowhere better expressed than in table furnishings, particularly in drinking vessels, which were made from such exotic materials as whalebone, ivory, coconut and ostrich eggs, and carved into the shapes of birds, snails, ships, grapes and strawberries. At an exhibition of historic tableware held in Innsbruck, Austria, I once saw a lidded octagonal jug of gilded silver, embossed with the signs of the zodiac. A silver wedding cup, made in Augsburg, was supported by a carved silver lady in a wide silver skirt, chased and embossed with incredible richness. And there was an engraved silver carving set consisting of eight perfectly wrought pieces, including saws, picks and a pointed hammer.

The might and splendor of the great German trading cities were ended by the Thirty Years' War of 1618 to 1648. Prompted by religious antagonisms between Catholics and Protestants and by the territorial ambitions of various Bohemian, Austrian and German princes, this savage conflict left the coun-

Opposite: Portrayed as a walking kitchen, a German cook in a humorous 18th Century engraving is festooned with equipment and supplies as he plies his trade. Numbers indicate: *(1)* suckling pig; *(2)* frying pan; *(3)* kettle; *(4)* pot cover; *(5)* sausages; *(6)* ham; *(7)* pot; *(8)* salt container; *(9)* grill; *(10)* spit; *(11)* pitcher; *(12)* kettle; *(13)* scoop; *(14)* knives; *(15)* tray of fruits. In the background the cook deals with tradesmen *(left)* and later serves the completed meal.

try in the hands of the autocratic princes and laid the foundations of a courtly society that ended only with the First World War. The birth pangs of this new society were terrible. Plundering mercenaries of six nationalities—German, Danish, Bohemian, Swedish, Spanish and French—brought devastation immense even by our modern, hardened standards. The Swedes alone were accused of destroying nearly 2,000 castles, 18,000 villages and over 1,500 towns; such was their remembered ferocity that in the time of my father's childhood, during the latter part of the last century, nursemaids still threatened naughty charges with the warning: "The Swedes will come and get you." More than a generation after the end of the war a third of the farmland in northern Germany still lay untilled. The people ate dogs, cats, rats, acorns and grass; an English observer of the time records: "So difficult are conditions here [on the right bank of the Rhine] that poor people are found dead with grass in their mouths." It has been estimated that in 1618 the population of Germany was 21 million. By 1648, it was less than 13½ million.

As the country recuperated, a new quality of delicacy and refinement of life made its appearance. The numerous courts of Germany, large and small, came under the spell of the absolute kings of France, especially that of Louis XIV, *le Roi Soleil,* who built Versailles and influenced the forms of European court society for centuries to come. Food became sophisticated and was eaten with comparative moderation; the enormous metal drinking vessels of earlier times were displaced by smaller ones made of glass. Even the kinds of drinks changed in the direction of temperance, for around 1700, coffee, tea and chocolate became popular in Germany.

This was an age of handwritten cookbooks that circulated from family to family and from court to court. All of them reveal the influence of the great chef La Varenne, who reformed French cookery in the 17th Century. These German books included such subtle dishes as a pie of hare, squabs served with a salad of chervil and cucumber, and a venison stew sauced with capers. Their most interesting innovations, however, were new, refined desserts —yeast pastries, delicate egg-and-almond cakes, and *Torten,* all of which came to be preferred over the sharply spiced honey cakes of an earlier day.

Opposite: A menu for a sumptuous banquet reflects the culinary tastes of German high society at the turn of the century. The gala feast was given in Berlin by Prince Albrecht of Prussia on January 23, 1897. The first course, consommé, was followed by oysters, baked pike-perch, fillet of beef, stuffed chicken with lobster, goose liver in aspic, saddle of venison with tossed salad and compote of fruit, green asparagus, Savarin cake with pineapple, butter, cheese and a final sweet dessert. The menu's border is embellished with the Prince's crest and vignettes of various royal estates, garlanded by the bounty of the land.

The Baroque style was lending a new richness to art and architecture, and its achievements are embodied not only in churches and palaces, but also in table furnishings. The earliest German faïence and porcelain factories were established in Meissen and other cities, sponsored by local princes who were tired of paying enormous prices for fine tableware imported from China.

These colorful, exquisitely painted services were matched by a table silver less massive than that of the Renaissance but no less beautiful. Around 1680, silver sets consisting of matching spoons, knives and forks first came into their own. Packed in rich velvet cases or silver chests, and augmented with silver bowls, basins, ewers and toothpick cases, they became prized gifts of the time, and their elaborate decoration is a revelation of the silversmith's craft. About the same time, the shape of table silver began to take on the forms we know today. The two-tined fork of the past became three-tined; in spoons, oval bowls replaced the round ones of earlier days; and the tip of a table knife became rounded rather than pointed. By the end of the Baroque era, not only silverware but all the appurtenances of the table had crystallized in the shapes and functions they have today. There were to be further re-

Berlin, den 23. Januar 1897.

Consommé.

Austern.

Zander au four.

Rinderfilet.

Farcirte Poularden mit Hummer.

Gänseleber in Aspic.

Rehrücken
Salat, Compot.

Grüner Spargel.

Savarin mit Ananas.

Butter, Käse.

Nachtisch.

finements, but no radical innovations. By that time too, class differences in living habits of the aristocrats, bourgeoisie, workers and peasants became rigid, even in such matters as choices of foods and ways of cooking and eating.

The aristocratic food and drink that became increasingly popular later in the 18th Century exhibit something of the playfulness of the exuberant gold, white and pastel Rococo architecture of the times. We find recipes for rose or violet sugar, for capons stuffed with oysters or cooked with almonds, and for an extraordinary variety of cakes and sweetmeats. The taste for coffee, chocolate and tea, introduced earlier, became a passion and led to the establishment of coffeerooms and pastry shops in such nations as Germany and Austria. The vast consumption of these beverages can be judged from the amount of appropriate services imported from China at a time when fine domestic porcelain was available from the German factories in Meissen, Fürstenberg, Höchst, Berlin, Frankenthal, Ludwigsburg and Nymphenburg. In 1780, for example, the Dutch East India Company imported 450,000 tea sets, 40,000 chocolate sets and 24,000 coffee sets from China.

This was the most Frenchified period in German history, a time when all Germans who could afford it tried to model their lives upon French ideals. The greatest ruler of the age, Frederick the Great of Prussia, vastly preferred speaking French to German. He imported French cooks and a master chef by the name of Noël, to whom he once wrote a grateful ode. Though Frederick's own tastes were on the frugal side, and he enjoyed such simple foods as herring, green peas, eel pie, and ham with cabbage, he was fussy. He made numerous suggestions before his food was cooked, and at the table he wrote notes on the various dishes set before him, using his menu card as a sort of notebook. Then, at the end of the meal, he discussed with his chef the dishes he liked or disliked. Chronicles of the time report that the King repeatedly called for more and different spices, for he preferred his simple food hot and piquant.

As the Rococo age died out at the end of the 18th Century, to be followed by the bourgeois cultures of the Empire and Biedermeier periods, attitudes toward food changed once again. Cookbooks of all kinds proliferated, but they were no longer written exclusively by professional cooks, but also by educated people with an interest in gastronomy. The literate upper-class gourmet, exemplified in France by Brillat-Savarin, made his appearance. In Germany, Eugen Baron von Vaerst, born in 1792, emerged as one of the wittiest gastronomical writers of all times. Squabs and pigeons, much admired as table birds in his time, were to him "amiable" birds, beautiful in the air but ugly in the dish. But the nearest German equivalent to Brillat-Savarin was probably Karl-Friedrich von Rumohr, born in 1785, whose *Geist der Kochkunst (The Essence of the Art of Cookery),* is one of the soundest cookbooks I have ever read. Rumohr had a delicate constitution, and took a strong stand against gluttony. His culinary suggestions are models of good taste, and he especially favored well-prepared home food. A typical Rumohr menu might run as follows: bouillon with bread or vegetables; a few slices of smoked ham or sausage, or a meat in aspic; boiled meat with or without vegetables, or a roast with salad; and a dessert of cheese and fruit. All in all, it is a meal that would be acceptable to people of our own day.

Not all German food, to be sure, had this sort of elegance. Peasants, workers and the poor ate traditional dishes of kraut and bacon, lentils and peas, and dumplings, and they lived simply at best. As the 19th Century progressed, German food generally became simpler and more as we know it today. At the tables of the upper classes, however, French influence remained strong. Emperor Wilhelm I employed two French chefs named Bernard and Dubois, and French chefs ruled the kitchens of other German courts and the big aristrocratic houses.

Reprints of a fascinating and unique collection of court and royal menus have appeared in—of all places—a magazine published by a German pharmaceutical firm, the Byk-Gulden Company of Konstanz. The collection was assembled by a former court chef, Rudolf Boj, a gentleman with a lifetime of experience in cooking for royalty. As the chef of Kaiser Wilhelm II in his Dutch exile, Boj probably cooked for all of Europe's royalty when they visited their German relatives.

The elegantly decorated historic menus collected by Rudolf Boj exhibit a steady progression toward simplicity. One of the oldest of these menus, composed for a dinner at the royal court of Hanover on February 19, 1854, lists no less than 12 courses. There were two soups, a pheasant and a *suprême,* followed by oysters on a bowl of crushed ice, fillets of perch cooked in white wine and served with lobster dumplings, mushrooms and truffles, and roast beef with *pommes frites* and mixed pickles. Another course included breaded fried boneless breasts of baby chicken served with new peas, asparagus with hollandaise sauce, and slices of smoked salmon and Westphalian sausage, and a cold dish of *foie gras* with aspic. Then came the main course, venison with red currants, mashed potatoes and salad. For dessert, baked apples were filled with sour cherries and sprinkled with kirsch, Bavarian cheeses were shaped into round patties, and ice cream was flavored with orange and vanilla. The menu was written in French.

Kaiser Wilhelm II, who reigned from 1888 to 1918, started the practice of having menus written in German. A dinner planned for him on January 18, 1901, included consommé, turbot with hollandaise; a pot roast with gravy, cauliflower, green beans and tiny carrots; a soufflé of venison; cold lobster with dill mayonnaise; boned roast capon served so that the breast rested on the boned legs; stewed fruit; and a salad. An ice cream *bombe* of mandarin oranges with cookies, followed by fresh fruit, nuts and raisins, ended the meal. The meal was cooked for about 1,000 guests, and it was served in the imperial palace at Berlin.

The industrialization of Germany during the late 19th Century improved the living standards of the broad middle classes. As they rose in status, they imitated the food and food habits of the aristocracy, and many of the newly rich industrialists outdid their models with food in the grand manner. Yet at the same time a streak of affection for the simple, robust dishes of traditional German cooking could be found then as now even among the highly born or highly placed. Pea soup with bacon, sauerkraut with pork, eel, carp and the rest—the upper classes never rejected such dishes in the way that the English upper classes rejected the food of their common people.

And in any case, the First World War and the birth of a German republic meant the end of aristocratic ways. Though the nobility was by no means always impoverished, the courtly style had disappeared forever. When the age of abundance eventually returned, it was an age of abundance for all.

Health and Pleasure
at Scenic Spas

Whenever the body wearies or the diet proves too robust, many Germans retreat to the time-tested cure of the spas, those elaborate health-and-pleasure domes designed to purify the system while uplifting the soul. In the 19th Century scene above, genteel visitors gather to sip restorative mineral water from the fountain at Bad Reinherz, then a highly fashionable spa in Silesia.

Modern spa-goers drink at the shrinelike spring of Bad Ems, while others promenade along the picturesque River Lahn. Since the Romans discovered the waters' powers in the First Century B.C., German spas have blossomed into full-scale vacation towns, where one can enjoy everything from thermal and mud baths, diets and massages, to riding, hiking, dancing and concerts.

A Tale Told by Boundaries: The Political and the Culinary

The map on the opposite page shows Germany as it was in 1914, a grand empire that overreached itself and no longer exists—except as a culinary heritage. German cooking still recalls the cooking of Imperial Germany, and an acquaintance with the regions of the old Germany makes it far easier to understand the richness and complexity of the three schools of German cuisine that are the subject matter of the next three chapters in this book.

Until 1871 there was no unified German nation, but only a scattering of principalities and duchies, and the separate German-speaking kingdoms of Prussia in the north and east, Saxony in the center, and Württemberg and Bavaria in the south. Their unification was achieved by Prince Otto von Bismarck at the time of the Franco-Prussian War. In the conglomerate country that he put together and then managed as Chancellor, the styles of cooking that climate, geography and ancient custom had created in the various regions gained national recognition and acceptance.

Bismarck's empire, which is bounded on the map by a dotted line, remained stable for more than four decades, long enough for the people of the northern coastal plains (*shaded in purple*), the central rolling hills (*shaded in green*) and the mountainous south (*shaded in orange*) to become familiar with, and even proud of, each other's cuisines.

Then in two world wars—the one waged by the Empire, the other by the Third Reich—the nation sought to expand by conquest. Twice it was defeated, and a look at the dotted and solid lines on the map shows the consequent drastic shrinkage of German territory in modern times. In the west, France and Belgium gained or regained lands such as Alsace-Lorraine. In the north, Denmark recovered portions of its territory. And in the east, vast reaches of the old Empire—more than 50,000 square miles—became independent or the property of Poland or Russia. In all these areas the ousted Germans left behind some traces of their ways with food, and from all of them they brought back in turn certain food habits absorbed from their temporarily conquered neighbors.

But for all this intermingling within and outside the country, the three main schools of German cuisine have never died. In a sense they have flowered: traditional north German dishes that are no longer much eaten east of the Oder River have become favorites along the Rhine in West Germany, as well as along the Elbe in East Germany. Königsberg in East Prussia is now Kaliningrad in the U.S.S.R., but *Königsberger Klopse* will always be German. Today in the restaurants of Berlin, Hamburg and other cities on both sides of the hard line that divides West Germany from East, you can eat regional specialties from all over the no-longer-united nation. But really to understand the basic structure of this panoply of German food, you have to go back to the places where it all began. Accordingly Chapter 6 will tour the old northern culinary region, Chapter 7 the central food belt and Chapter 8 the cooking of the southern lands that rise into the Alps.

The political map of Europe has undergone many kaleidoscopic rearrangements in the 20th Century, and many place names significant today—the U.S.S.R., Czecho-slovakia, East Germany, West Germany—were unheard of at the outbreak of World War I in 1914. But the three German culinary regions shown in color were established long before there was a German empire—and have survived, both in the regions of their origin and in the rest of the nation, despite all the political changes since 1871.

The Northern Belt

A lowland plain that extends from the Neth-erlands to the U.S.S.R. comprises the north German culinary belt. The plain is cut from north to south by the Weser, Elbe, Oder and Vistula Rivers. In the coastal area, largely rimmed by sand-dune beaches, food preferences and customs reflect the proximity to Scandi-navia and to the sea. Inland, most of the soil is sandy, producing mainly potatoes and sugar beets, except in parts of the Elbe Valley, where it is rich enough for wheat and barley, and in the east, which is heavily forested.

The Central Belt

Lying between the level plains of the north and the dramatic mountains of the south are the roll-ing hills of Germany's central belt. The most rugged areas, covered with wide expanses of for-est, contain resorts and health centers—the spas so dear to German hearts and bodies. This is the area of Germany familiar to everyone as the setting of the fairy tales by the Grimm brothers. In the fertile valleys and plateaus there are flour-ishing vineyards, orchards and pasture lands for sheep, and in the region south of Kassel, great crops of sugar beets and potatoes.

The Southern Belt

The hills grow more rugged in southern Ger-many, culminating in a steep range of the Alps. There are prosperous cattle and dairy farms in the foothill country. Wheat and barley grow on the plateaus, much of the barley crop going to the area's numerous breweries to be made into beer. The steep, terraced hills along the Rhine and the Mosel Rivers produce some of the world's best white-wine grapes. Between the vast areas of dark evergreens in the Black For-est, southwest of Karlsruhe and Stuttgart, the valleys are carpeted with fields of grain.

VI

The Northern Style: Cold-Climate Cuisine

On the farm of Christian Gellert, near the north German village of Jork, crates of apples await delivery to a fruitgrowers' cooperative; in the background the Gellert family loads plums for market. The thatched roofs and half-timbered walls of the farm buildings are common throughout much of northern Germany.

The rolling plains of northern Germany are simple, even monotonous in their appearance. Facing the North and Baltic Seas, they make up a broad region that in Imperial times stretched from Holland in the west to Russia and Poland in the east. But the cooking of the north is more diversified than the soil, for it has been influenced by Dutch neighbors to the west, Danish and Swedish ones to the north and Polish and Russian ones to the east. Almost all north German cooking, native or derivative, is geared to a cold, damp climate. The northern fishermen and peasants lived on hefty soups of cabbage and bacon, combinations of pickled and smoked meat cooked with dried fruits, roast duck and goose, halibut, flounder, eel and herring. Yet not all of the cooking is as earthbound as this, for the region includes some of Germany's most sophisticated cities. The menus of Hamburg and Bremen shipowners have included delicately sauced sole and turbot, followed by rare roast beef in the English manner, washed down by the best Burgundy. And in Berlin, where the cuisine of France had been held in high esteem since the days of Frederick the Great, those who could afford it dined on truffled *foie gras* and voluptuous *tournedos*.

Within northern Germany, the easternmost provinces—Posen, West Prussia and East Prussia—had much in common in their food and in their way of living. All were agricultural provinces, made up of big estates farmed largely by Polish, Lett or Lithuanian labor. Many of these estates were held by the same families for generations, and they were well run, for the landed gentry loved their fields of sugar beets, potatoes, hops, barley, rye and oats. Life on these estates was patriarchal and, in matters of food, almost self-supporting.

The food of the region had been strongly influenced by that of Russia and Poland—which was all to the good, adding piquancy to the plain but substantial native cooking. The Slavs particularly left their mark in East Prussia, and East Prussia had, I think, the most interesting cooking of the entire region. Both sweet and sour cream, called *Schmand,* made soups and gravies smooth and piquant, as they do in Russian cooking. Slavic, too, was the custom of souring foods with vinegar or lemon juice, producing such ground-meat combinations as the famous *Königsberger Klopse (page 119).*

But the region had its own contributions to make. The widespread use of smoked bacon, of *Räucherspeck,* was typical of East Prussian cooking. It would have been almost a sin if a housewife failed to brown her hashed brown potatoes in it, or to include it in a pot of dumplings. It dominates a dish that brings nostalgia to all who grew up in East Prussia: *Graue Erbsen mit Speck,* a special kind of dried peas cooked with bacon and further flavored with onions, vinegar, pepper and a little sugar. The dusky flavor of smoked bacon and the tartness of sour cream are, I think, the elements characteristic of eastern German cooking. The two turned up together in festive roasts of veal or beef, browned in the bacon and sauced with the cream.

Hunting was the passion of the region. In the fall, when the birches and oaks turned golden against the cool emerald shade of the pines, you could hear the distant rattle of the beaters and the startled cries of fleeing jays and woodpeckers. When the early northern dusk gathered, the hunters returned with venison, to be grilled over a wood fire if it was young and tender, or more frequently, to be marinated in buttermilk and spices, then braised with juniper berries, stock and sour cream. Red cabbage *(page 63),* mashed potatoes and *Preiselbeerkompott,* or stewed lingonberries, were the classic accessories to *Elchkeule* (leg of elk) and *Wildschweinrücken* (saddle of wild boar). I once had the latter dish in a game warden's house in the Masurian Lakes district, where water and forest fused into a golden autumn haze. A dish of *Maränen,* the delicate fish of these lakes, related to the trout, had preceded it, cooked *au bleu* and served with a sauce of horseradish and whipped cream.

To the west of East Prussia are the provinces of Mecklenburg and Pomerania. Their rich farmland, planted in grains, sugar beets and potatoes, was also used for raising cattle, sheep, pigs—and geese. All Germany had good geese, but it was the Pomeranian birds that were acknowledged supreme. Farmers' wives raised geese in the competitive spirit of gardeners trying to grow the largest tomatoes or pumpkins. In the fall the geese were sent into the harvested fields to eat themselves fat and round for St. Martin's Day in November, when roast goose is the standard dish in all German lands. But the very best of these superb geese were not roasted. They were reserved for the ultimate in goose dishes: *Spickgans,* rosy, glistening pickled and smoked breast of goose, which is, I think, the best cold cut ever thought of by man.

Making *Spickgans* was a serious affair: the culinary reputations of the massive wives of the Pomeranian *Gutsherren,* or landed gentry, depended on it. Basically, the process was a simple one. A goose breast was cut into halves, and each half was rubbed with salt and pepper, a little saltpeter and a touch of sugar. The meat was left to stew in its own juices for a week or so, then rubbed free of clinging salt, dried off and lightly smoked a couple of times.

The real secret lay in the amounts of salt and saltpeter and in the kind of smoke. The seasonings had to be exactly right if they were not to produce too sharp a *Spickgans:* the smoke had to come from a fire of beechwood combined with a few juniper branches and a handful or so of peat. The combination of firewoods, the heat of the fire, the length of the smoking remained the *Gutsherrin's* secret, transmitted to her marriageable daughters.

Pomeranians enjoyed other dishes made with goose almost as much as this aristocrat of them all. The *Gänseklein* was made from bits of the bird cooked with celery, carrots and parsley; when the dish was half done, dried fruit such as apples, pears and prunes were added, and the whole was served with potato dumplings. The *Schwarzsauer von Gans* was a mixture of goose blood mixed with vinegar to prevent it from clotting, thickened with flour or groats and flavored with salt, sugar, nutmeg and cloves. Even pickled goose stomach, shredded and dressed with onion, thyme and vinegar, was enjoyed by the Pomeranian peasants, who ate it as a spread with dark bread.

In both Mecklenburg and Pomerania, the abundant fish taken from the Baltic Sea and inland lakes might turn up at any meal. I remember a visit to Rügenwaldermünde, one of the small seaports that turn into modest family resorts every summer. I was staying with distant relatives in a small hotel, famed for its roast breast of pork (and the pork was indeed superb, stuffed with prunes and apples and served with red cabbage). The meat was usually preceded by eel cooked *au bleu,* with boiled potatoes and cucumbers in sour cream containing plenty of dill *(page 117).* Eel was, in fact, a highly prized staple food, and smoked eel was often served either with well-buttered rye bread or with a dish of scrambled eggs and home-fried potatoes. Some fishermen smoked their own fat, juicy eels, hanging them on rafters over a peat fire set in a brick hearth. The smell of fish, smoke and tar was unforgettable. When I met it again years later in Denmark, it brought me back to myself at the age of 12, walking over glistening white sand dunes, through

Political Changes in the Northern Belt

The violent changes in Germany's borders in this century's two world wars affected the northern culinary belt most of all. In the west, part of Schleswig-Holstein north of Flensburg went to Denmark after World War I. In the east, the area on both sides of the Vistula River, including Danzig, was given to Poland, with Germany retaining a part of East Prussia beyond this "Polish Corridor." After World War II, East Prussia was divided between the U.S.S.R. and Poland, and the parts of Pomerania and Brandenburg that lie east of the Oder were also given to Poland. The rest of Brandenburg (except for part of Berlin) and most of Mecklenburg and Saxony went to East Germany.

107

hard grass that cut into my bare feet, toward the blue, motionless Baltic.

Characteristic of both the Baltic coast and the Waterkant, or North Sea coast to the west, was a fondness for pickled fish and pickled meat, especially pork. Herring was the fish most frequently pickled. Called by such names as *Matjes, Bismarck* and *Brathering,* pickled herring was served not only as a snack with rye bread and butter, but also as a full meal, with boiled potatoes and clabbered milk. Smoked fish also brought fame to the North Sea province of Schleswig-Holstein, particularly *Bücklinge* and *Kieler Sprotten. Bücklinge* are bloaters—large, fat herring slightly salted and smoked for only a short time, so as to retain their juiciness; they are the pride of the English breakfast table and they were equally beloved by the sturdy sons and daughters of the Waterkant. *Kieler Sprotten,* even tastier, are a variety of herring cured like bloaters; the best of them were made in Kiel, the port from which they took their name.

Two other Schleswig-Holstein delicacies are *Katenschinken* and *Katenwurst* —types of ham and sausage, respectively, that were originally smoked in peasants' huts called *Katen.* Taken with a glass or two of *Klaren,* the faintly caraway-flavored, clear *Schnaps* that is the water of life in those parts, *Katenschinken* dispels sorrow. It did that for me once in Eutin, a charming old town in the Holstein lake district with a romantic castle on a romantic lake in a romantic park of enormous beeches, and romantic little red-brick houses on winding cobbled streets. Let us skip over the reason for my sorrow; suffice it to say that a plateful of *Katenschinken* and rye bread, served with the proper refreshments in an old paneled inn, restored my morale. That was long ago; when I returned to Eutin a year or so ago, the town was full of mod and miniskirted teenagers on their way to a rock 'n' roll session in the former *orangerie* of the castle—but the *Katenschinken* and *Katenwurst,* the *Klarer* and the beer all tasted as good as ever.

Along the North Sea coast from Schleswig to Friesland were bountiful supplies of fish that found their way into the various *Labskaus,* nautical dishes originally cooked by seafarers aboard ship, that included onions and potatoes with fish, beef or both, and were flavored with anchovies or herring and served with sour pickles (*page 122*). But there was also more delicate seafood—sole, turbot, sea perch, tench and brill—that to my mind are upper-class fish. In port cities along the coast, elegant fish restaurants catered to the needs of rich and discriminating businessmen. Fish dishes were prepared with white wine, cream, eggs, shrimp and mussels, and served in the classical French manner with nothing but boiled potatoes.

Of all these cities, Hamburg was—and still is—the most famous for its excellent restaurants. There had always been a sophisticated, cosmopolitan air to that great city, reflected in the food eaten by the wealthy shipping people and distinguished city councilmen and senators. The finest symbol, perhaps, of this divine food is the *Mastgeflügel,* the fowl raised southeast of Hamburg in the district called the Vierlande. Chickens, particularly, were famous under the name of *Stubenküken*—literally, chicks raised in a small room, rather than a barnyard, to keep them plump, tender and flavorful. The classic way of cooking *Stubenküken* was to brown them gently in butter, then stew them in their own juice with diced smoked bacon, shallots and mushrooms. They were served in their own casserole with little new potatoes browned in butter. The fanciest version of this dish, *Bremer Kükenragout,* was not a ragoût proper but was so called because the sauce was a ragoût, cooked with white wine and a little lemon juice and containing mushrooms, stewed oysters or mussels, crayfish tails or veal sweetbreads, and perhaps even tiny dumplings and asparagus tips.

The Vierlande is famous not only for its high-quality birds but also for its architecture and its great flower and vegetable gardens. Its name means "four countries," and refers to four very old settlements established on drained marshes along the branches of the Elbe River. As you walk along the roads atop the dikes, farmhouses dating back to the 16th Century lie several feet below you—colorful and imposing half-timbered buildings in patterned rosy brick, with enormous A-line thatched roofs. Incongruously attached to the old farms are enormous expanses of modern greenhouses where tulips, daffodils, lilies of the valley, roses, carnations, asters and chrysanthemums grow for the flowershops of Hamburg; beyond them stretch rows upon neat rows of early carrots and leeks, peas and tomatoes, beans and asparagus, all destined to be eaten young, tender and out of season.

With the Vierlande one enters upon the inland regions of northern Germany, south of the Baltic and North Sea coasts. Regions such as Niedersachsen (essentially, the Kingdom of Hanover in Imperial days) and Brandenburg belong to northern Germany, yet their cooking has much in common with that of their neighbors to the south. This fact was clear to me when I recently traveled through Germany, searching for the cooking of the past and the present. The dishes of the southern parts of Niedersachsen, far from the North Sea, were clearly similar to those of Westphalia in central Germany. I shall discuss this cooking in the following chapter; suffice it here to say that it is earthbound, like the endless flat fields that stretch under a low, cloudy sky, and like the taciturn, solid people of the region, whose first demand of their food and drink is that it be plentiful and substantial.

But there are also romantic and evocative parts of this inland region of northern Germany. Among them is Lüneburg, one of the most beautiful cities in all Germany. Once a member of the Hanseatic League, Lüneburg is a city in which Gothic style mingles with Renaissance and Baroque. The stepped, red-brick mansions and half-timbered houses, the lofty churches and the decorated beams and wall paintings in the banquet hall of the medieval town hall should be seen by any visitor to Germany. South of the city stretches the Lüneburg Heath, once a ravishing wilderness of sand and moors, birches and heather, moor hens and nesting cranes that captured the imagination of all romantic Germans. In recent years much of the wilderness has given way to drained cropland, but sandy paths lined by silver birches still lead off into moor and heather to please the most solitary of wanderers, and there are still romantic villages and tiny towns clustered around little red-brick town halls. Typical of the foods of the region are dark and fragrant heather honeys, and the meat of the *Heidschnucken,* a breed of curly-horned sheep peculiar to the heath. I can report, however, that the taste of roast *Heidschnucken,* even when served in a restaurant in the vaulted cellars of the old town hall, is no different from that of other, less picturesque sheep.

On my last visit to Lüneburg, traveling south from Lübeck, I remember eating *Pinkel* with kale, a casserole dish hugely fancied in those latitudes. *Pinkel*

Continued on page 112

The Business and Pleasures of Buying and Selling

Much of the meat and seafood of northern Germany is sold amidst the clamorous bustle of traditional open-air markets. In many villages, such as Osterholz-Scharmbeck *(shown on these pages)*, a square is set aside for the buying, selling and trading of livestock. Cattle and horses change hands at annual sales; pigs, the most popular source of meat dishes, are brought in every week, and many a householder stocks his own table at the pig auction. In a typical transaction *(right)*, a buyer makes his selection of a young porker by heft and feel, and the purchase is concluded on the spot.

In the early days of such public livestock markets, buyers butchered their own pigs, and cured and processed their own pork. Nowadays, butchering, curing and processing are usually done by professionals, either on the farmer's premises or in one of the packing plants that abound in the region. As a grain-producing and livestock-raising area, northern Germany provides meat for other parts of the country, and as Germany's only coastal region, it furnishes all the nation's domestic seafood. From its packing plants roll carloads of lard, bacon, *Wurst* and fresh pork for the great cities and industrial areas of the country.

At left, the ritual of the *Handschlag*
(literally, a "strike of hands")
seals a verbal bargain between a
livestock buyer and seller. Below,
a satisfied buyer and his son walk
off with their purchase, oblivious
to their porker's protesting
wriggles and loud squeals.

The lively patter of an eel vendor amuses a crowd assembled in an Osterholz-Scharmbeck market square for an auction of pigs. Smoked eel is popular in northern Germany, where eels can be bought for as little as three for a dollar. Part of the pleasure of buying them lies in the rapid-fire spiels of the salesmen, who are sometimes the most popular "stand-up comedians" of their villages.

is a lightly smoked sausage made with groats, raw bacon, onions, salt and pepper. But *Pinkel* is not the only meat in this casserole, as I learned. I had been wandering around Hameln, home of the Pied Piper, and had in fact already sustained myself at the Pied Piper's legendary house, now a restaurant, with a snack of cold roast beef with remoulade sauce and potato salad. In my quest for regional specialties I passed by the attractive restaurants in the city's fashionable streets, wandering instead into the cobblestoned little streets lined with small, half-timbered houses where humbler citizens live jammed together like sardines in a box. Finally I spotted an unpretentious tavern that bore two signboards: *Frischer Pinkel mit Braunkohl* (fresh *Pinkel* with kale) and *Brägenwurst mit Grünkohl* (*Brägen* sausage with kale). In the smoky interior, earnest cardplayers at their evening game of skat barely lifted their heads as I came in. After ordering a beer, I told the substantial lady who waited on me to bring me both specialties of the house. This is what I got. The first casserole contained not only *Pinkel,* but a solid slice of smoked bacon, a large smoked pork chop, and a *Kochwurst,* a rich sausage five inches long. The meat of my second casserole was *Brägenwurst,* a lightly smoked, thinnish sausage made from flour, oats and pig's brains seasoned with onion, pepper and salt. The sausage, a curved 10-inch length of it, nestled in a bed of kale that had been cooked with lard, onions and a little ground pork. For the benefit of my studies, I ate a little of each, then recuperated from the experience with a digestive combination of *Lüttje Lagen,* or *Schnaps* and beer.

Sausage power did not end at Hameln. It reached its climax, I think, in Braunschweig, the city known in America as Brunswick, which is famous for *Braunschweiger* sausage, a lovely pinkish-brown, refined version of liv-

112

Smoked eel, eaten with the fingers and accompanied only by bread *(left)*, makes a tasty but rather messy meal. When the diners have eaten, their waiter traditionally pours *Schnaps* over their hands to wash off both the oil and the odor *(below)*.

erwurst. Not that *Braunschweiger* is the only sausage produced in the city; there are any number of others. They appear at their best in a *Schlachtplatte* (literally, "slaughter plate," from the fact that it was originally a by-product of a slaughtering day), a popular combination of meats and sausages. The *Braunschweiger* version was a nobly massive one, which inspired awe in strong men and led them to put away several *Korn* (the local *Schnaps*) and beers while tackling their *Männeressen* (best translated, perhaps, as "male fodder").

But there was a gentler gastronomic side to Braunschweig. Once, when I was in my teens, my parents left me there for a summer vacation with one of their friends while they went to Paris, and my parents' friend, the widow of a university professor, was fond of vegetables. It was in her house that I first became conscious of the beauties of asparagus, the sensuous, juicy, snow-white asparagus that is the crown of the German vegetable world. The widow served it frequently with butter and bread crumbs or with hollandaise sauce. I can still see her lifting a thick asparagus stem with the thumb and first finger of her large white and very well-kept hands, then lapping up its head with an abrupt thrust of her lips. (For those of you who wonder at eating asparagus with one's fingers, I must explain that eating it with a fork was then considered lower class.)

One other incident of my visit still sticks in my memory. On the day of my arrival, after my parents had left, the widow showed me over her apartment. She took me into a curious fairybook kitchen, all decorated tiles and stencil-decorated closets, with embroidered mottoes on the walls, embroidered display towels over the dish towels and embroidered doilies wherever a hand-embroidered doily could be made to rest. (I hasten to say that everything was *hand* embroidered, in colorful cross-stitch.) Even the brooms had their embroidered covers. To say the least, the kitchen impressed me greatly. "But we don't cook here, it would not be practical," said the widow—and led me into an adjoining room where an obviously rural maidservant officiated at a stove, in the semidark.

In those days, the beauty of medieval and Renaissance Braunschweig was largely intact; about a thousand half-timbered houses of those periods were still in use. World War II destroyed all but the core of the city, but as elsewhere in Germany, a new city has risen from the ashes. When I was there last, it was reassuring to see the restaurant advertisements in the local papers proclaiming bigger and better *Schlachtplatten* than ever.

In any country, every native son and daughter has a city of his own, and mine was Berlin. My memories of Berlin are the memories of a lifetime, overlaying one another like a cake made from pressed layers of experience. They go back to a dimly remembered day during the German inflation of the '20s when a shopping bag full of inflated marks bought me one piece of *Punschtorte*, the pink and chocolate cake that I adored. There are memories of thin, crisp *Kartoffelpuffer mit Apfelmus* (potato pancakes with applesauce, *page 118*), sprinkled with salt rather than sugar, and of *Graupensuppe mit Backpflaumen* (barley soup with prunes). I remember the evenings my father took me to Schlichter's, where the most delicate *Gebratene Kalbsleber auf Berliner Art* (pan-fried liver with apples and onions, *page 119*) and *Schweinebauch mit Mohrrüben* (pig's belly cooked with carrots and served with boiled potatoes in a light sauce) delighted such members of Berlin's theatrical intelligentsia as Berthold Brecht and Emil Jannings.

On the whole, Berlin is more significant as a cosmopolitan city than as a center of unique regional food. There you can get any German or foreign specialty in restaurants like Kranzler, Kempinski or the Ritz, cooked and served with great elegance. But the food of the people is basically simple and generally reminiscent of other German dishes. What is characteristic of Berlin food, perhaps, is the local predilection for ground or shredded meat dishes. The famous *Schabefleisch* or *Hackepeter* (local versions of *Beefsteak Tartar*, made with beef and pork, respectively), *Deutsches Beefsteak* and *Falscher Hase* (hamburgers and meatloaf, the latter a so-called "mock hare"), *Lungenhaschee* (hash made from lungs) and *Sülze* (head cheese)—these are dishes that Berliners have always greatly admired. And there is the *Sülzkotelett*, a pork chop under aspic *(page 120)*, generally eaten with home-fried potatoes.

Of the vegetables typical of Berlin, there were the *Teltower Rübchen*, a delicate little root once grown in a nearby suburb, but today a vegetable that can hardly be found. The asparagus from the sandy fields of Brandenburg was excellent, and it was part of an elegant chicken fricassee of French inspiration, *Hühner Frikassee mit Champignons und Spargel,* which dates back to the days when Huguenots fled from France to Berlin to escape religious persecution. No ordinary fricassee, this is a *blanquette* of chicken, with a sauce of white wine, egg yolks and cream, served with fresh mushrooms and asparagus tips (for an even more elaborate version, see *Recipe Booklet*). But the vegetable most beloved by ordinary Berliners is the cucumber, pickled as *Saure Gurke*, braised in butter and dill as *Schmorgurke*, or served as a salad dressed with sour cream and dill.

114

Berliners have always been fond of a quick bite, called a *Rascher Happe* or a *Happenpappen*. Before the war, the famous Aschinger stand-up restaurants dispensed hot dogs by the hundreds of thousands, with potato salad and beer or coffee. Only one Aschinger restaurant survives today in West Berlin, but there are numerous stands that serve more sophisticated fare, such as curry sausage and shashliks. Two other quick snacks deserve mention. One is *Soleier mit Mostrich*, hard-cooked eggs pickled in brine (the shells are pricked with a needle at top and bottom to allow the brine to penetrate) and eaten with mustard or a little French dressing. In the old days these eggs were part of the free lunch set up in Berlin beer taverns, and the large glass jar in which the eggs were pickling stood in a prominent place on every *Theke*, or bar. The second quick snack, called *Strammer Max*, "sturdy Max," is a well-buttered slice of dark bread topped with a thick slice of smoked or cooked ham, on which two fried eggs rest under a sprinkling of minced chives.

The best-known characteristic cakes of Berlin, called *Berliner Pfannkuchen*, are made with a yeast dough filled with plum or apricot jam and deep fried. They are essential for celebrating on New Year's Eve. Similar cakes called *Spritzkuchen* are ring-shaped, deep-fried crullers. Freshly made and cooked in good, fresh fat, they are even more irresistible than *Pfannkuchen*.

The Christmas cakes called *Baumkuchen*, to my mind the most subtle and original of all German cakes, are said to have originated in Berlin. Rising two or three feet tall, *Baumkuchen* are designed to resemble the trunk of a tree, and to contain the inner rings that a tree develops in its growth. The cake is constructed around a central shaft on which thin successive layers of a rich egg dough are spread and baked, one at a time. Finally the cake is glazed with sugar or chocolate. Thanks to the shaft, such a cake is in reality a large tube, but when it is cut horizontally in thin slices, its dozens of layers and their browned edges do remind one of a tree. I can't think of a better Christmas present than a pound or two of *Baumkuchen* to eat all by myself.

One can still get an old-fashioned Berlin meal in one of the small inns or beer places. In the Wedding, the working class district, you can go to a *Kneipe*, or tavern, for a plateful of *Rinderbrust mit Bouillonkartoffeln und Roten Rüben*, boiled ribs of beef served with potatoes cooked in bouillon, and red beet salad, or *Hoppelpoppel mit Salat*, a combination of sautéed cooked potatoes, meat leftovers and onions, folded over like an omelet *(page 122)*, with lettuce dressed with sour cream. In a middle-class restaurant, sitting on a terrace overlooking the forest-encircled lake called the Wannsee, you might start with potato soup, proceed through *Hammelfleisch mit Grünen Bohnen*, mutton cooked with green beans, and end up with a large *Schillerlocke*, a tube of puff paste filled with whipped cream and said to resemble the curls of the German poet Schiller. In both of these Berlin eating places you might accompany your meal with a *Molle*—that is, a glass of either Schultheiss or Patzenhofer lager, the two most popular Berlin beers—and take *einen Schuss Korn*, a clear *Schnaps*, as a chaser. Of all Berlin beers, however, the famed *Berliner Weisse* is certainly typical of the city. This is a pale, tart ale, low in alcoholic content, served in a vast goblet. It can be drunk as is, but it usually comes *mit Schuss*, a dash of pink raspberry or green woodruff syrup. The drink may sound awful, but it is not. What you get is a refreshing mild beverage that has little in common with ordinary beer—a beverage suitable for children, weak women or summer swelterers.

To serve 4 to 6

2 cups dried yellow peas
6 cups water
¼ pound lean bacon in one piece
1 cup finely chopped carrots
1 cup finely chopped celery
1 cup thinly sliced leeks, including
    2 inches of the green tops
½ cup finely chopped onions
⅛ teaspoon marjoram
2 tablespoons lard
1 medium-sized onion, peeled and
    thinly sliced
3 tablespoons melted butter

Erbspüree
YELLOW PEA PURÉE WITH BACON

Wash the peas thoroughly under cold running water and pick out and discard any blackened ones. In a heavy 4- to 5-quart saucepan, bring the water to a boil over high heat. Add the peas, bacon, carrots, celery, leeks, chopped onions and marjoram, and return to a boil. Reduce the heat to low and simmer, partially covered, for about 45 minutes, or until the peas are soft and have absorbed almost all of the liquid. Remove the bacon and drain it on paper towels. Then purée the peas and vegetables through a food mill or sieve set over a large bowl, and discard any pulp.

With a small, sharp knife, cut the bacon into ½-inch dice. In a heavy 8- to 10-inch skillet, melt the lard over moderate heat, add the bacon and cook, stirring frequently, until the dice are brown and crisp. With a slotted spoon transfer the bacon dice to paper towels to drain, and add the onion rings to the fat remaining in the skillet. Cook over moderate heat, turning the rings frequently, and regulating the heat so that they color evenly on both sides without burning.

Spoon the pea purée into a 2-quart baking dish, spreading it out evenly with a metal spatula. Strew the onion rings over the purée and sprinkle the bacon and then the melted butter on top. Bake in the middle of the oven for 20 minutes, or until the top is golden and lightly crusted. Serve at once, directly from the baking dish.

To serve 6

2 cups dried quick-cooking lentils
2 quarts cold water
¼ pound lean bacon in 1 piece
1 leek, white part plus 2 inches of
    green, finely chopped
1 large carrot, scraped and finely
    chopped
1 parsnip, scraped and finely
    chopped
1 celery stalk, finely chopped
2 tablespoons bacon fat
½ cup finely chopped onions
2 tablespoons flour
2 tablespoons cider vinegar
    (optional)
2 frankfurters, sliced into ¼-inch
    rounds
1 teaspoon salt
Freshly ground black pepper

Linsensuppe
LENTIL SOUP

Wash the lentils thoroughly under cold running water. In a heavy 4-quart casserole bring 2 quarts of water to a boil over high heat. Add the lentils, the piece of bacon, and the chopped leek, carrot, parsnip and celery. Return to a boil, reduce the heat to low, and simmer, partially covered, for 30 minutes.

Melt 2 tablespoons of bacon fat over moderate heat in a heavy 8- to 10-inch skillet and when it begins to splutter, add the chopped onions. Cook, stirring occasionally, for 8 to 10 minutes, or until the onions are soft and lightly colored. Sprinkle the flour over them, lower the heat and cook, stirring constantly, until the flour turns a golden brown. Watch carefully for any sign of burning and regulate the heat accordingly. Ladle about ½ cup of the simmering lentil soup into the browned flour and beat vigorously with a whisk until the mixture is smooth and thick. Stir in the vinegar, if you are using it. Then, with a spatula, scrape the entire contents of the skillet into the lentils and stir together thoroughly.

Cover the casserole and simmer over low heat for another 30 minutes, or until the lentils are tender but not mushy. Before serving, cut the bacon into small dice and return it to the soup with the sliced frankfurters. Simmer for 2 or 3 minutes to heat the meat through, then stir in the salt and a few gridings of black pepper.

If the soup is to be served as a main dish, increase the number of frankfurters as necessary.

Luscious legumes: lentils go into soup *(top left)*, yellow peas into a purée *(right)*, white beans into "blind hen" *(bottom)*.

Schmorgurken mit saurem Rahm und Dill
STEWED CUCUMBERS WITH SOUR CREAM AND DILL

With a small, sharp knife, peel the cucumbers and cut them in half lengthwise. Seed them by running the tip of a small spoon down them, from end to end. Cut the cucumber halves crosswise into 1-inch pieces and place them in a large bowl. Sprinkle them with salt, tossing them about with a spoon to spread it evenly. Let the cucumbers stand at room temperature for 30 minutes, then drain off all the liquid and pat them dry with paper towels. In a heavy 10- to 12-inch skillet, melt the butter over moderate heat. When the foam subsides, add the onions and cook, stirring frequently, for 8 to 10 minutes, or until they color lightly. Add the flour and cook, stirring constantly, until the flour turns a golden brown. Watch for any sign of burning and regulate the heat accordingly. Pour in the milk and, stirring constantly, bring to a boil. Reduce the heat to low and simmer for 1 or 2 minutes, until the mixture thickens slightly. Add the cucumbers and simmer, uncovered, for 15 minutes. When the cucumbers are tender but not pulpy, add the sour cream, parsley and dill. Taste for seasoning. Serve in a heated bowl.

To serve 6

6 medium-sized firm, fresh
   cucumbers (about 3 pounds)
2 teaspoons salt
2 tablespoons butter
½ cup finely chopped onions
2 tablespoons flour
2 cups milk
2 tablespoons sour cream
1 tablespoon finely chopped fresh
   parsley
1 tablespoon finely chopped fresh
   dill, or substitute 1 teaspoon dried
   dill weed

Königsberger Klopse differ from other meatballs in being poached. They always contain pork and at least one other kind of meat, very finely ground and combined with seasoning, eggs and bread crumbs. Dropped into boiling liquid, they are cooked like dumplings. Capers flavor the sauce shown being poured.

To make about 8 pancakes

6 medium potatoes (about 2
   pounds), preferably baking
   potatoes
2 eggs
¼ cup finely grated onion
⅓ cup flour
1 teaspoon salt
Bacon fat or lard
Applesauce or imported lingonberry
   (*Preiselbeeren*) preserves

Kartoffelpuffer mit Apfelmus
POTATO PANCAKES WITH APPLESAUCE

Peel the potatoes and as you proceed drop them into cold water to prevent their discoloring. In a large mixing bowl, beat the eggs enough to break them up, add the onion and gradually beat in the flour and salt. One at a time, pat the potatoes dry and grate them coarsely into a sieve or colander. Press each potato down firmly into the sieve to squeeze out as much moisture as possible, then immediately stir it into the egg and onion batter.

Preheat the oven to 250°. In a heavy 8- to 10-inch skillet melt 8 tablespoons of bacon fat or lard over high heat until it splutters. Pour in ⅓ cup of the potato mixture and, with a large spatula, flatten it into a pancake about 5 inches in diameter. Fry it over moderate heat for about 2 minutes on each side. When the pancake is golden brown on both sides and crisp around the edges, transfer it to a heated, ovenproof plate and keep it warm in the oven. Continue making similar pancakes with the remaining batter, adding more fat to the pan when necessary to keep it at a depth of ¼ inch. Serve the pancakes as soon as possible with applesauce or lingonberry preserves.

118

Gebratene Kalbsleber auf Berliner Art
CALF'S LIVER WITH APPLES AND ONION RINGS

Preheat the oven to 250°. In a heavy 10- to 12-inch skillet, melt 2 table-spoons of the butter over moderate heat. When the foam subsides, add the onion rings, a little salt and a few grindings of pepper. Stirring occasionally, cook the onion rings for about 10 minutes, or until they are light brown. With a slotted spoon, transfer them to a heatproof plate, cover them loosely with aluminum foil and place them in the preheated oven. Add 2 tablespoons of butter to the skillet and drop in half of the apple rings. Cook them until they are golden on both sides, add them to the plate with the onion rings and cook the remaining apple slices similarly in another 2 tablespoons of butter. Keep the apples and onions warm in the oven while you cook the liver.

Season the liver slices with salt and a few grindings of pepper. Dip the slices in flour, then vigorously shake off any excess. Add the remaining 2 tablespoons of butter to the skillet and melt the butter over moderate heat. When the foam subsides add the liver and cook it for 2 minutes on each side, or until the slices are light brown, turning them with kitchen tongs. Do not overcook. Remove the liver to a heated platter and scatter the apple and onion rings over it and serve at once.

Königsberger Klopse
POACHED MEATBALLS IN LEMON-AND-CAPER SAUCE

Melt 1 tablespoon of butter in a small skillet over moderate heat and in it cook the chopped onions for 5 minutes, or until they are transparent but not brown. Remove the skillet from the heat. Tear the bread into small pieces into a large bowl, add the cream and mix well. Add the onions, ground meat, anchovy fillets or anchovy paste, parsley, eggs, lemon peel, ½ teaspoon salt and black pepper. Knead vigorously with both hands until the ingredients are well combined, then put the mixture through the finest blade of a meat grinder. Moistening your hands lightly with cold water, shape the mixture into 8 large meatballs about 2 inches in diameter.

In a heavy 6- to 8-quart saucepan or soup pot, bring the water, whole onion, bay leaf and 1 teaspoon of salt to a boil over high heat. Boil, uncovered, for 10 minutes. Then reduce the heat to low and drop in the meatballs. Simmer, uncovered, for 20 minutes, or until the *Klopse* rise to the surface of the water. With a slotted spoon, transfer them to a deep heated platter and cover them with aluminum foil to prevent their darkening upon exposure to air. Strain the poaching liquid through a fine sieve into a bowl and put it aside.

In a heavy 10- to 12-inch skillet, melt 4 tablespoons of butter over moderate heat. When the foam subsides, stir in the flour. Pour in 3 cups of the poaching liquid and bring it to a boil, beating constantly with a whisk until the sauce thickens and is smooth. Reduce the heat to low, add the lemon juice and capers and simmer uncovered, stirring occasionally, for 15 minutes. In a small bowl break the egg yolks up with a fork, then stir into them ¼ cup of the simmering sauce. Whisk the mixture back into the skillet and stir in the sour cream. Taste for seasoning. Add the meatballs and simmer, basting from time to time, until they are thoroughly heated. To serve, return the meatballs to the platter, and pour the sauce over them.

To serve 3 or 4

8 tablespoons butter
2 medium-sized onions, cut into ⅛-inch slices and separated into rings
Salt
Freshly ground black pepper
5 medium-sized cooking apples (about 1½ pounds), peeled, cored and sliced crosswise into ¼-inch rings
1 pound calf's liver, cut into ¼-inch slices
Flour

To serve 4

MEATBALLS
1 tablespoon butter
½ cup finely chopped onions
2 slices homemade-type fresh white bread with crusts removed
2 tablespoons heavy cream
⅓ pound lean boneless beef, ⅓ pound lean boneless pork, and ⅓ pound lean boneless veal, ground together 3 times
3 flat anchovy fillets, drained, rinsed in cold water and coarsely chopped, or substitute 1 teaspoon anchovy paste
2 tablespoons finely chopped parsley
2 eggs
½ teaspoon finely grated lemon peel
½ teaspoon salt
¼ teaspoon freshly ground black pepper

POACHING LIQUID
2 quarts water
1 medium-sized onion, peeled and pierced with 1 whole clove
1 small bay leaf
1 teaspoon salt

SAUCE
4 tablespoons butter
4 tablespoons flour
3 tablespoons fresh lemon juice
1 tablespoon capers, drained
2 egg yolks
2 tablespoons sour cream

119

To serve 6

A 2-pound loin of pork, center cut,
  with the backbone (chine) sawed
  through but left attached and tied
  to the loin in 2 or 3 places
2 cups dry white wine
½ cup white wine vinegar
5½ cups cold water
1 medium-sized onion, peeled and
  pierced with 2 whole cloves
1 scraped carrot, cut into ¼-inch
  slices
2 celery stalks, including the leaves,
  coarsely chopped
10 parsley sprigs
1 bay leaf
1 teaspoon salt
¼ teaspoon freshly ground black
  pepper
2 envelopes unflavored gelatin
2 egg whites, beaten to a froth
Garnish as desired with thinly sliced
  and fancifully cut flowers made
  from any combination of cooked
  or raw carrots, drained and rinsed
  sweet gherkins, drained and rinsed
  pimientos, drained and rinsed
  pickled cauliflower, blanched
  scallion or leek tops, peeled
  cucumber, peeled and seeded
  tomato, and whites of hard-cooked
  eggs

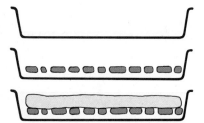

Fancy-looking molded aspics like the
pork cutlets opposite are surprisingly
simple to make. The trick is to use
layers of liquid aspic and let each
become firm before you add another.
First, pour a film of aspic into the
mold and refrigerate until firm (top).
Add the decorations (center). Place a
cutlet on top and pour in enough
aspic to cover it halfway. Refrigerate
until set, then fill the mold with
aspic and refrigerate again (bottom).
When all the layers are chilled, the
mold is ready to turn out and serve.

Sülzkotelett
PORK CHOPS IN ASPIC

In a deep, heavy casserole or a soup pot just large enough to hold the meat
comfortably, combine the pork loin, wine, vinegar and 5 cups of cold water.
Bring to a boil over high heat, meanwhile skimming off the foam and scum
that rise to the surface. Reduce the heat to low and add the onion, carrot, celery, parsley, bay leaf, salt and pepper. Cover the casserole and simmer the
pork for 1½ hours, or until it is tender and shows no resistance when pierced
with the tip of a sharp knife.

Transfer the pork to a plate and let it cool to room temperature. Then
cover it with aluminum foil or plastic wrap and refrigerate. (If you plan to
use the carrot slices to garnish the chops in the finished dish, reserve them
on the plate with the pork loin.)

Strain the cooking stock through a fine sieve into a large bowl, discarding
the vegetables and herbs. With a large spoon skim the surface of all fat.
There should be about 5 cups of stock. If more, boil briskly, uncovered,
until reduced to the required amount.

Prepare the aspic in the following fashion: Sprinkle the gelatin into the ½
cup of cold water and let it soften for 5 minutes. Then, in a 3- to 4-quart saucepan, combine it with the stock and add the beaten egg whites. Over high
heat, bring the stock to a boil, meanwhile stirring constantly with a whisk.
When the stock begins to froth and rise, remove the pan from the heat. Let
it rest for 5 minutes, then pour it into a large sieve lined with a damp kitch-
en towel and set over a large bowl. Allow the aspic to drain through without
disturbing it at any point, then taste for seasoning (it will probably need
more salt) and set it aside. Do not refrigerate.

Carefully carve the pork loin into 6 chops about ½ inch thick. Cut the
meat and fat away from the bones and trim the chops into neat, symmetrical
cutlets. Pour a layer about ⅛ inch thick of the aspic into each of 6 cutlet
molds or into a shallow baking dish large enough to hold the cutlets comfortably in one layer. Chill in the refrigerator until firmly set. Decorate the surface of the set aspic with the garnish of your choice and carefully place the
chops on top of it.

Pour enough liquid aspic into the mold or baking dish to come halfway
up the sides of the chops and refrigerate again until the aspic is firm. (This
step is necessary to prevent the chops from rising to the surface of the
molds when the remaining aspic is added.) When the chops are firmly an-
chored, cover them completely with liquid aspic and refrigerate for at least 4
hours, until firm. Any remaining aspic may be chilled in a flat pan or dish at
the same time and used chopped or cut into decorative shapes as a garnish
when the chops are served.

To unmold chops from individual molds, run a small, sharp knife around
the side of each mold, then dip the bottom into hot water for a few seconds.
Wipe the mold dry and turn it out on a chilled serving plate.

The chops in the baking dish may be served directly from the dish or you
may unmold them in the following fashion: Run a sharp knife around the
sides of the dish and dip the bottom in hot water for a few seconds. Place a
flat, shallow platter upside down over the dish and, grasping the platter and
dish firmly together, invert them. Rap them on a table and the aspic should
slide out easily.

120

Floral patterns of carrots, cucumbers, hard-cooked egg white, tomatoes and leek tops beautify these pork chops in aspic.

Labskaus

CORNED BEEF HASH WITH SALT HERRING

To serve 4 to 6

¼ pound filleted salt herring
9 medium-sized boiling potatoes
(about 3 pounds), unpeeled
6 tablespoons lard
1½ pounds cooked brisket of corned
beef, trimmed of fat and cut into
⅛-inch dice
2½ cups finely chopped onions
Freshly ground black pepper
Ground nutmeg

Place the herring fillets in a glass or enameled bowl and pour in enough water to cover them by about 1 inch. Refrigerate and soak for at least 12 hours, changing the water once or twice. Drain and rinse the fillets under cold running water, then pat them dry with paper towels. Remove any skin or bones and, with a large knife, chop the herring as finely as possible.

Drop the potatoes into a large pot of lightly salted boiling water, and boil them briskly, uncovered, until they show no resistance when pierced with the tip of a small, sharp knife. Drain and peel them, then force them through a ricer or food mill into a large bowl.

In a heavy 12-inch skillet, melt the 6 tablespoons of lard over moderate heat until a light haze forms above it. Add the herring, corned beef and onions, lower the heat and cook, stirring frequently, for 20 minutes, watching carefully for any sign of burning and regulating the heat accordingly. Stir in the potatoes, pepper and nutmeg and simmer only long enough to heat the mixture through. If the hash seems too dry and begins to stick to the pan, moisten it with a little water. Taste for seasoning, and mound the hash attractively on a large heated platter. *Labskaus* may be served with a poached egg on each portion and accompanied by pickled beets *(page 42)*.

Hoppelpoppel

EGGS WITH BACON, ONIONS AND POTATOES

To serve 2

3 medium-sized boiling potatoes
(about 1 pound), unpeeled
1½ cups coarsely diced lean bacon
½ cup finely chopped onions
4 eggs
1 tablespoon milk
2 tablespoons finely chopped parsley
½ teaspoon salt
Freshly ground black pepper

Drop the potatoes into enough lightly salted boiling water to cover them completely. Boil briskly, uncovered, until the potatoes show only the slightest resistance when pierced with the tip of a small, sharp knife. Be careful not to let them overcook.

Meanwhile, in a heavy 10- to 12-inch skillet, cook the bacon over moderate heat until brown and crisp. With a slotted spoon transfer the pieces of bacon to a double thickness of paper towels to drain. Pour all but 2 or 3 tablespoons of fat from the skillet, add the onions, and cook for 5 minutes, stirring them frequently, until they are soft and transparent but not brown. Set the skillet aside.

Drain the potatoes in a colander, then peel and cut them into ¼-inch slices. Add them to the onions in the skillet and cook over moderate heat for 8 to 10 minutes, turning the potatoes occasionally with a large spatula, until they are light brown. Then, in a small bowl, beat the eggs, milk, parsley, salt and a few grindings of pepper together with a fork until they are well blended. Strew the diced bacon over the potatoes and pour in the eggs. Tip the pan from side to side to spread the eggs evenly and cover the skillet. Reduce the heat to low and cook undisturbed for 5 or 6 minutes, shaking the pan gently every now and then to prevent the eggs from sticking. The *Hoppelpoppel* is done when the eggs are set, but still slightly moist. To serve, invert a heated serving plate over the skillet and, grasping skillet and plate firmly together, quickly turn them over. Serve at once.

NOTE: One cup of finely diced cooked ham may be substituted for the bacon. In that case, melt ¼ cup of lard or bacon fat in the skillet and cook the diced ham and the onions together for 5 minutes. Add the sliced potatoes and proceed with the recipe as described above.

122

Ente mit Äpfeln und Brot Füllung
ROAST DUCK WITH APPLE AND BREAD STUFFING

Preheat the oven to 425°. Wash the duck under cold running water and pat dry inside and out with paper towels. Rub the inside of the duck liberally with salt and pepper. For crisper skin, prick the surface around the thighs, the back, and the lower part of the breast with the tip of a sharp knife.

In a large bowl, combine the beef, pork, egg, crumbs, marjoram, 1 teaspoon of salt and a few grindings of pepper. Knead vigorously with both hands until the ingredients are well blended and the mixture is smooth. Then stir in the apples and spoon the stuffing loosely into the cavity. Close the opening by lacing it with skewers or sewing it with heavy thread. Fasten the neck skin to the back of the duck with a skewer and truss the bird securely.

Roast the duck, breast side up on a rack set in a large shallow pan, for 20 minutes, until it browns lightly. Pour off the fat from the roasting pan or draw it off with a bulb baster. Then reduce the heat to 350°, and roast for about 1 hour longer, removing the accumulated fat from the pan occasionally with a bulb baster. To test for doneness, pierce the thigh of the bird with the tip of a small, sharp knife. The juice should spurt out a clear yellow; if it is slightly pink, roast the bird for another 5 to 10 minutes. Transfer the duck to a heated platter and let it rest for 10 minutes before carving. Traditionally the duck is accompanied by red cabbage *(page 63)* and dumplings.

To serve 4

A 4½- to 5-pound duck
Salt
Freshly ground black pepper
¾ pound lean ground beef, preferably chuck
¾ pound lean ground pork
1 egg, lightly beaten
½ cup dried bread crumbs
½ teaspoon dried marjoram
2 medium-sized cooking apples, peeled, cored and cut into ½-inch cubes

Weingelee
WINE JELLY WITH FRUIT

In a small heatproof bowl, sprinkle the gelatin over 1 cup of the water. When the gelatin has softened for 2 or 3 minutes, set the bowl in a skillet of simmering water and cook over low heat, stirring constantly, until the gelatin dissolves. Remove the skillet from the heat, but leave the bowl of gelatin in the water. In a large bowl combine the wine, the remaining ½ cup of water, the lemon juice and sugar, and stir until the sugar dissolves. Thoroughly stir in the warm gelatin. Pour a ¼-inch layer of the mixture into a 5-cup mold, pack the mold into a bowl half filled with crushed ice or coarsely crushed ice cubes and refrigerate until firm. (Keep the remaining gelatin at room temperature so that it remains liquid and ready to use.)

Drain the fruit and spread the pieces between paper towels to dry them. Arrange a layer of various kinds of fruit on the surface of the set gelatin. Gradually pour over it enough liquid gelatin to reach almost but not quite to the top of the fruit. Chill again until set, then pour in enough gelatin to cover the fruit by ¼ inch. Chill. Repeat this process 4 or 5 more times, filling the mold with alternating layers of fruit and gelatin and refrigerating the mold after each step. Finally add enough gelatin to come to within ¼ inch of the top. Refrigerate for at least 6 hours, or until firm. (Any remaining gelatin may be chilled in a flat pan at the same time and used chopped or cut into decorative shapes as a garnish for the *Weingelee*.)

To unmold and serve, run a knife around the sides of the mold and dip the bottom in hot water for a few seconds. Wipe the mold dry, place a serving plate upside down over it, and, grasping plate and mold together, turn them over. Rap them on a table and the jelly should slide out easily. Chill until ready to serve. If you like, you may accompany *Weingelee* with whipped cream.

To serve 4 to 6

2 envelopes unflavored gelatin
1½ cups water
2 cups dry white wine
2 tablespoons fresh lemon juice
½ cup sugar
2 cups assorted fresh, canned or thoroughly defrosted frozen fruit such as peach halves or slices; pitted apricots or apricot halves; pear halves; pitted cherries, whole strawberries or strawberry halves; whole grapes or grape halves; pineapple wedges, banana slices or orange sections

VII

The Central Style: Rich and Filling

The most touching and heartfelt tribute ever paid to the foods of Westphalia, in central Germany *(map, page 127)*, can be seen in a 15th Century stained-glass window in the Wiesenkirche, a Gothic church in the little town of Soest. The window depicts the Last Supper, but in place of the traditional bread and wine, the anonymous artist substituted Westphalia's favorite ham, a pumpernickel bread and beer on the sacred table. The table itself resembles tables that can still be found in an old Westphalian inn.

Some five centuries after that window was created, and in just such an inn, I studied the men and women who were, like myself, putting away ham, pumpernickel and beer. I realized that I had seen the faces of these massive, deliberate people before, on the saints and patrons who figure in the Gothic murals at another of Soest's churches, the Petrikirche.

I thought of how well ham, pumpernickel and beer represent the earthbound qualities of Westphalia, where almost everyone, from the western mining district of the Ruhr to the northern and eastern farmlands, lives by the products of the soil. Close to the soil, too, is Westphalian architecture—in the medieval and Renaissance buildings of towns like Borken or Bocholt, the Romanesque cathedrals of Münster and Paderborn, the moated castles of Rauschenburg and Rauschhaus, all far more massive than corresponding buildings in other parts of Germany. Thick and massive, too, is the local dialect, almost unintelligible to outsiders. It is a dialect that finds its natural setting in the endless fields of rye, sugar beets, cabbage and turnips that make up the Westphalian countryside, and in the houses—small-windowed, shutterless, seldom softened by flowers—of Westphalian towns.

Hearty laughter sets the mood for the traditional Westphalian peasant breakfast, a feast of ham and *Schnaps,* in a historic farmhouse in the village of Telgte. The raw smoked ham—the kind that has made Westphalia famous—is served thin-sliced, garnished with pickles and accompanied by pumpernickel bread.

125

Pumpernickel, the coarse dark bread made from unsifted rye flour, is a bread that cries out for butter and cold cuts and cheese. It is a bread that gives strength to the eater, but only when it is made with pure rye flour, without the addition of suger-beet syrup. Good pumpernickel must leaven for 24 hours, then bake slowly for an equal length of time, so that the natural sugar in the rye flour will darken and sweeten the bread evenly.

Westphalian ham, traditionally made from pigs fed on the acorns of Westphalia's great oak forests, is lightly smoked and as savory as any *prosciutto* from Italy or *jambon* from France. The proper way of preparing a *Westfälische Schinkenplatte,* or ham platter, is to line a deep wooden plate with fresh lettuce leaves. Slices of cooked smoked ham rest on the lettuce; an even more abundant platter will also contain *Paprikaspeck*—smoked bacon, rosy with paprika—a few small, hard smoked sausages and golden butterballs. Along with the pumpernickel there ought to be a nip of *Steinhäger,* a fragrant *Schnaps* flavored with juniper berries, or a stein of the dark Westphalian beer made in Dortmund, home of the largest of all German breweries.

The pig has always reigned supreme in Westphalia. On a recent trip there, traveling along the flat country roads of the region, usually under a brooding sky, I stopped frequently at country *Gasthöfe,* many of which turned out to be owned by local pork butchers. In one of these inns near Paderborn I remember seeing a small army of pigs penned up in the back, squealing away for dear life, and my inner eye transformed them into the heavy, succulent, well-seasoned dishes that Wesphalians love. Many of those pork casseroles call for a stamina not given to all of us, but some are excellent in their sustaining way, especially when they are cooked with kale or broad beans. Broad beans, in fact, have found their bard in Westphalia, an anonymous poet who sang in the local dialect: "O hillige Graute-Baunen Tid, O Buk, wärd mi noch mal so wit!"—"Oh holy broad-bean time, oh stomach of mine, be twice as big!" Bean soup flavored with savory (the herb that flavors many German bean dishes); broad beans with bacon; kale with *Mettwurst* (smoked pork sausage) and bacon; kale with *Schinkenpfanne,* a thick pancake filled with potatoes and ham; and *Blindhuhn (page 138),* a casserole of beans, potatoes, carrots, onions and apples cooked with bacon—these are traditional pleasures that can still be enjoyed.

A Westphalian dish with a wider reputation is the famed *Pannhas,* a product of the autumnal *Schlachtfest,* or pig slaughter. A thick preparation of buckwheat flour cooked to a well-seasoned mush in the savory broth in which sausages have been simmered, *Pannhas* may be eaten hot and fresh or kept cold to be fried when needed. It is the father of our own Pennsylvania scrapple. Many of the Pennsylvania Dutch came to America from Westphalia; in the New World they made a sort of ersatz *Pannhas,* using native cornmeal in place of European buckwheat.

Pfefferpotthast (page 140), another old Westphalian favorite, originated in Dortmund. It is essentially a well-seasoned stew of beef short ribs, cooked with chopped onions, knob celery and carrots browned in bacon fat and served with potatoes. (To offset this heavy entrée, a side dish of beet salad [page 42] may be added in winter, or a mixed salad of tomatoes, cucumber and lettuce in summer.) The secret of the dish resides in the number of sauce-thickening onions, in the proportions of sliced lemons, capers, cloves and

bay leaf for flavoring, and in the ungodly amount of ground pepper that makes the dish hot. The last ingredient is crucial; *Pfefferpotthast* is the dish of choice for the banquets of Westphalian men's clubs, cardplayers, bowlers and hunting groups because, as they say, "It makes a good thirst."

A more delicate dish, which may have originated in a patrician's town house rather than a country kitchen, is *Münsterländer Töttchen*, a *ragoût fin* made of the meat of a calf's head cooked in a buttery sauce that is seasoned with onions, capers, a dash of vinegar and sherry or Madeira. But even the *Töttchen* has taken on a rural quality; it is customarily served with country bread and parsleyed potatoes and, like *Pfefferpotthast*, it should be on the peppery side, if only to justify the solace of a beer or a glass or two of the powerful *Schnaps* called *Münsterländer Korn*.

In addition to their pumpernickel, Westphalians have always baked a variety of interesting breads and pastries. *Pickert*, a bread made with wheat or potato flour and raised with yeast, is a gem of German peasant food, and so is *Appeltate*, a baked dessert of apples, almonds and raisins topped with an egg-and-cream batter. More ambitious is *der Westfälische* pudding, a pudding made with pumpernickel crumbs, eggs, sugar, grated chocolate, a dash of *Schnaps*, grated lemon rind, cinnamon, grated almonds and a handful of raisins. This complex affair may sound weird, but it is excellent, expecially with a side dish of vanilla sauce or one of apples or cranberries. And there are *Korinthenstuten*, wheat breads made with eggs and milk and dotted with raisins. On St. Nicholas Day, the sixth of December, the same bread takes the form of a *Stutenkerl*—a man with raisin eyes and raisin buttons, who keeps his hands in his pockets and dangles a long white clay pipe from his mouth.

Frankfurt, the chief city of Hesse, is famous as the birthplace of Goethe, and of such humbler products as *Frankfurter Würstchen*, progenitor of the American hot dog, and *Appelwoi*, a potent apple cider. This contrast between high culture and peasant heartiness somehow characterizes Frankfurt's range of local dishes. On the one hand there is the delicate *Kerbelsuppe*, to my mind the best of all German soups, made from fresh chervil cooked in bouillon and thickened with eggs and cream. On the other, there are dishes almost touching in their simplicity, such as *Rippchen mit Kraut*, smoked ribs cooked with sauerkraut. Goethe, of whom it has been said that he wrote

Political Changes in the Central Belt

Except for Silesia, the easternmost part of which went to Poland at the end of World War II, the central culinary belt remained German in the aftermath of both world wars. Thuringia and Saxony became part of East Germany after World War II, while Westphalia and Hesse were given to West Germany. The East-West line was determined generally by the positions that the Soviet and Western Allied military forces held at the end of the war.

127

some bad poetry but never ate a bad meal, loathed sauerkraut. His own taste ran to French dishes, for Frankfurt, a city of cosmopolitan bankers and merchants, has always looked west. And south, too: I am convinced that the city's greatest claim to gourmet cookery, its *Grüne Sosse (Recipe Booklet)*, or green herb sauce, must have come originally from Italy, brought back from the Italian tours that for centuries were obligatory for educated Germans.

Green herb sauces turn up in French and Spanish cooking, as well as Italian, but I consider the Frankfurt version vastly superior to all of them. For one thing, it is made up of an extraordinary variety of interesting herbs. Minced chives, parsley, chervil, borage, tarragon, savory, sorrel, watercress and a touch of dill go into it, with a little oil and vinegar and a touch of sugar. *Grüne Sosse* is the perfect mate for broiled fish and meats or (a favorite Frankfurt combination) hard-cooked eggs.

Among the meat dishes that have won fame wherever Germans cook is *Kasseler Rippenspeer (page 140)*, which may or may not be a dish of central German origin. Central Germans claim that its birthplace was the Hessian town of Kassel; Berliners insist that it was invented in their city by a butcher named Kassel in his now-legendary shop at Potsdamerstrasse 15. Whatever the truth of its origin may be, *Kasseler Rippenspeer* has earned its place as an all-German favorite. It consists of a cured and smoked loin of pork, usually reposing in a rosy blush on a bed of sauerkraut and accompanied by mashed potatoes. Alternatively—and I think preferably—it may be served with red cabbage and potato dumplings, which act as a sort of stomach liner for the meat's rich red-wine-and-sour-cream gravy.

Unlike their Westphalian neighbors, Hessians have always had a gentle hand with vegetables. Their forte, perhaps, is onions, which form the basis of many local dishes. In Bad Homburg, one of Hesse's lovely spas, I once had a superb dinner of smoked salmon, pork *Schnitzel*, and a vanilla ice cream spiked with bite-sized pieces of preserved ginger. The most memorable part of that meal, utterly delicious with the crisp, dry meat, was a dish of tiny onions sautéed in butter and stewed with a little bouillon and white wine. Equally good are the *Zwiebelkuchen*, open tarts with fillings of onions, bacon and a little cream, which you can pick up hot at the baker's for a picnic in the Taunus or Odenwald Mountains, or enjoy with a glass of wine in a country inn. Baked in both large and small forms, *Zwiebelkuchen* provide an interesting German equivalent for the popular French tart called a *quiche*.

There has always been a *gemütlich* tone to life in Hesse, particularly in the fall, when *Appelwoi* is drunk everywhe.e in much the way that *Heuriger*, or new wine, is drunk in Vienna. I had my first *Appelwoi* in Sachsenhausen, a Frankfurt suburb, where *Appelwoi* taverns crowd each other, each decorated with a huge fresh evergreen wreath to announce that the local nectar is ready. My escort and I sat down at bare scrubbed tables, and our waiter immediately brought us large fluted glasses of cider, dispensed by the owner from enormous stone jugs holding 10 to 15 quarts. Along with the glasses came plates, for it is customary—and wise—to temper *Appelwoi* with the famed *Frankfurt Handkäs mit Musik*, a soured cheese doused with an oniony French dressing and eaten with dark bread and butter. Steaming in large kettles were genuine *Frankfurter Würstchen*, five or six inches long, made with beef rather than pork and far tastier than our American hot dogs. Along with the other patrons, we sampled *Salzgebäck* (salty baked goods, such as pretzels and cheese sticks) from the baskets of well-upholstered peddlers—all of them ladies—who streamed in and out of the tavern and were not above lifting a glass of *Appelwoi* themselves when it was offered.

When Germans think of Thuringia, they think of the traditional Thuringian *Bratwurst*, the pork sausage grilled over open wood fires whose aroma permeates the meat and fills the air. They remember biting into the skin of these beauties—a skin far crisper than that of most sausages, because splashes of cold water during the final grillings make it deliciously brittle. They think, too, of the round *Thüringer Klösse*, dumplings made with potatoes rather than bread, flour or oats as in other parts of Germany.

Cooking old-fashioned Thuringian dumplings called for a skill and discrimination astonishing to outsiders. For one thing, they are made without eggs, a feat that requires the lightest touch if the dumplings are not to come out leaden. There were different schools of thought on the best ingredients to bind and strengthen the dumplings: some cooks used milk and semolina; others, potato starch. Some very special varieties of dumplings had their adherents. *Watteklösse*, called "cotton dumplings" for their ethereal quality, were made with cooked potatoes, potato starch and milk; *Grüne Klösse*, or green dumplings, were not green in color, but contained both raw (that is, green) and cooked potatoes. Local feelings ran high in that dumpling country, where standard kitchen equipment included such necessities of the dumpling-maker's craft as sets of potato presses and little cloth bags in which dumpling potatoes were squeezed dry.

The meats that were cooked with these dumplings matched them in variety and strength. *Topfbraten*, one of the aftermaths of slaughtering day, consisted of such parts of a pig as ears, kidneys, snout and heart, all cooked in a sauce thickened with gingerbread and plum butter. *Röstbratl* was a slice of pork grilled or roasted and basted with the dark local beer. Spread with mustard, it was eaten on dark peasant bread and washed down with beer or a crystal-clear *Schnaps* called *Nordhäuser Korn*. The regional variation upon *Beefsteak Tartar* consisted of ground pork, rather than the customary beef, seasoned with salt, pepper, minced onion and a little minced pickle; this mixture was spread with mustard and served on a fresh *Semmel*, or white roll.

Thuringia was a conservative land, well pleased with what had pleased her forefathers. Why bother with foreign culinary ways when the local dumplings were justly famous throughout Germany? And why learn new ways of baking when the local open fruit tarts were the juiciest in the *Vaterland?* The latter opinion was well founded. *Thüringer Obstkuchen*, for example, consisted of a thin layer of yeast dough, topped with a layer of sweet semolina or flour porridge that absorbed the juices of the fruits and kept the crust crisp. (Another way of getting the same effect was to cover the crust with bread crumbs or ground hazelnuts.) A thick layer of blueberries, cherries or plums was spread over the protective coating, and the fruit was topped with a custard consisting of egg yolks, cream, raisins and rum, and lightened with the beaten whites of the eggs.

Fruit tarts of this kind spread a heavenly smell when they are baking, and not long ago just such a smell attracted me to a baker's shop in Coburg (now part of Bavaria), at the edge of the Thüringer Wald, which covers the mountain ranges of the region. The food of Coburg was authentic; I could tell that simply from the Thuringian dialect of the baker's wife. I sat with her, waiting for the cakes to come out of the oven, in a shop that occupied part of the Renaissance house, with low arched ceilings and wooden paneling. The wait was worthwhile; never have I eaten a more delicious *Pflaumenkuchen,* juicy, tart and smooth.

Aromatic smoke from grilling sausages filled the air of Coburg's market square, surrounded by high early-Renaissance houses. Here the *Rostbratwürste* were grilled with special finesse over fires of pine cones. Trade was brisk, and I myself took a couple of the sausages dabbed with mustard and placed on a slice of rye bread. How warm they felt in my hands, chilled by the autumn wind, and how good they were, even to a stomach filled with *Pflaumenkuchen!*

There is more to Coburg than those Renaissance houses, with their painted big bays and ornamented façades. For centuries the city was the home of the ducal Saxe-Coburg-Gotha family, which exported kings, queens and assorted spouses to almost every royal house of Europe. Queen Victoria was part of that family, and her beloved Prince Albert was born near Coburg. The Ehrenburg, the royal residence built in 1543, contains the most Baroque of all Baroque halls, where enormous male caryatids hold torches in their outstretched arms, and you can still see the apartments where Queen Victoria stayed on her visits. High over the city looms the Feste Coburg, the greatest of all German fortresses, where Martin Luther wrote the hymn "A Mighty Fortress Is Our God." A museum in the fortress displays an astonishing collection of ceremonial coaches and sleighs dating from the 14th to the 18th Century, wonderfully carved, gilded and statuetted.

The former kingdom of Saxony, east of Thuringia, is now part of East Germany, and few Americans make their way to the Baroque architecture of Dresden or the Meissen porcelain factories. Even the great trade fair at Leipzig— the city that was the home of Johann Sebastian Bach and the birthplace of Richard Wagner, who spoke with a thick Leipzig accent to the end of his days —attracts few visitors from the West. As for bygone culinary treasures, the Saxony of earlier days was known for its superior cakes, different from the simpler, rural Thuringian ones but also based on doughs raised with yeast. The sweet Saxonian doughs, rich in almonds, raisins, currants and delicious glacé fruits, were exemplified in the *Dresdner Stollen (page 193)* that were baked at Christmas time. Equally famous were *Streuselkuchen (page 141)* and *Bienenstich,* both flat sheets of a sweet, egg-enriched yeast dough; the former was topped with crisp crumbs made with butter, sugar and flour, the latter with butter, sugar and sliced almonds. Happily, both these cakes still survive as German favorites; indeed, they have become standards of good home baking. Another Saxonian specialty was *Plinsen,* pancakes made with a combination of wheat and buckwheat flours, flavored with lemon rind and sour cream and raised with yeast. Over these light, flavorsome griddle cakes, Saxonians customarily poured a syrup made from sugar beets, one of the great crops of the region—a syrup that resembled the ones we Americans use with our own pancakes, but without the strong maple or molasses taste that characterizes our pancake syrups.

In general, the cooking of Saxony was far less hefty than that of Thuringia, though both cuisines shared a common emphasis on meat and dumplings. An example of the difference might be the Saxonians' fresh and imaginative way with liver. I don't generally care for liver, but in a Saxonian restaurant in Berlin I once had an intriguing dish consisting of a well-seasoned mixture of liver, ground together with smoked bacon, cooked with eggs and a few currants, and served with a sharp onion, wine and lemon-juice sauce. Other famous liver dishes of the region, somewhat more conventional in their approach to the meat, are *Leber im Grünen Bett* (liver sautéed in wine with a wealth of fresh herbs) and liver stewed in red wine with onions and currants.

Traditional Saxonian cooking was basically *Hausmannskost*, or homelike food. Typical of it were sweet-and-sour combinations, such as raisins and almonds cooked with beef or tongue, and pears cooked with pork and potatoes. Fresh or dried fruit was often substituted for vegetables, though one of the German dishes that has achieved international fame was originally a vegetable dish from Leipzig. The famous *Leipziger Allerlei* is a medley of young spring vegetables such as carrots, peas, cauliflower, asparagus and mushrooms, cooked separately and then combined in a light butter sauce thickened with a little flour and cream. The dish reflects the German habit of thickening vegetables with a sauce—a habit that, on the whole, I do not admire, but in this case it is under control. When the vegetables are fresh, small, tender and not overcooked, *Leipziger Allerlei* is an excellent side dish for chicken and other white meats.

The traditional food of Silesia, east of Saxony, was diversified, partly because the social and class contrasts of the region were especially pronounced. At one extreme were old aristocratic families on enormous estates and the rich owners of the great Silesian coal mines, who lived on a scale we nowadays associate with Polish and Russian princes. At the other were coal miners and linen weavers, who lived in abject poverty. For these people even bread was too costly; their staple food was boiled potatoes dressed with a little cottage cheese. A herring was a treat and so was butter. It was said that in the linen weavers' huts a salt herring dangled from the ceiling, and that each member of the family licked it at each meal to season his potatoes; in this way a single herring could last a whole family for as long as a year. It is hardly surprising that the famous folk song "Vom Schlesischen Bauernhimmel," which describes the paradise of the Silesian peasants, celebrated the pleasures of a stomach that for once was full.

At a higher level of elegance Silesian cooking gained enormously from that of Austria, Bohemia and Poland. Consider a few of the best-known Silesian dishes. *Schwärtelbraten,* a roast leg of pork cooked with sauerkraut and yeast dumplings and sauced with sour cream, might have been an Austrian dish. With Bohemia, Silesia shared a love for poppy seeds, as in the famed *Mohnstriezel (Recipe Booklet),* a Christmas yeast loaf filled with poppy seeds. Polish cooking was both reflected and immortalized in *Karpfen Polnischer Art,* the traditional Silesian Christmas Eve dish consisting of carp served with a rich, dark-brown sweet-and-sour sauce made with crumbled spice cakes, beer, onions, root vegetables, salt, sugar, vinegar and lemon juice. Like Polish cooks, Silesians specialized in soured dishes, in soups made with sorrel or sauerkraut, in cucumbers dressed with sour cream, and in

Almost every farmer in central Germany grows at least enough potatoes for his own family, and the children help with the harvesting. The workers in the foreground are removing dead stalks before putting the potatoes into large sifters to shake them free of soil. The couple in the background are sacking potatoes for sorting.

Bigos, a stew made with a varying mixture of meats, sauerkraut and potatoes. And in this great hunting country, both Polish and Silesian cooks produced superb dishes of game cooked with bacon, flavored with juniper berries, thyme and nutmeg, and sauced with sour cream.

The indigenous dishes of upper-class Silesian cooking are vividly described in *Gesegnete Mahlzeit*—literally, *Blessed Mealtime,* but actually the German equivalent of *bon appetit!*—a memoir of a lifetime of culinary experience by Beda von Müller, whose real name was Leo, Count Lanckoronski. This Silesian aristocrat was not only a gourmet of the most elegant and knowledgeable kind, but also a most amusing raconteur. His book of reminiscences is an entertaining and illuminating gastronomical and social history. He writes of delicious oyster patties and caviar toasts, of a concentrated pigeon broth made from home-bred birds that upper-class Silesians considered essential food for invalids, of the elaborately stuffed Silesian Christmas turkey and of all the other delicacies of a sophisticated cuisine. He describes many dumplings (including one kind made with apples), potato dishes like *Stampfkartoffeln* (mashed potatoes with diced bacon, eaten with cold buttermilk or sour milk

as a simple supper) and thick soup-stews made with lentils, beans or dried fruit and a little smoked pork or bacon. The best known of all these stews, and possibly the national dish of Silesia, was *Schlesisches Himmelreich,* or "Silesian heaven," a casserole of dried fruit and fresh or pickled pork, served with a thick spicy sauce that fairly cried aloud for the bread dumplings that generally accompanied it.

Silesians had a pronounced sweet tooth, perhaps because a thick brown syrup made from sugar beets was an inexpensive daily food in the region, and children ate bread and syrup for snacks or suppers. The local cakes were much like those of Saxony, but two Silesian Christmas pastries are worth special mention. *Thorner Kathrinchen* were spice-and-almond cookies baked in the shape of a woman; *Liegnitzer Bomben* were 3½-by-2½-inch glazed "bombs" made from a spicy, dark honey-cake dough. Finally, there were the aromatic fruit- or herb-flavored liqueurs of Silesia, such as *Kroatzbeere,* distilled from blackberries, and *Stonsdorfer,* named after a village in the picturesque Riesengebirge range. To end on a cheerful note, I will say that these pleasant potions can be had today anywhere in West Germany.

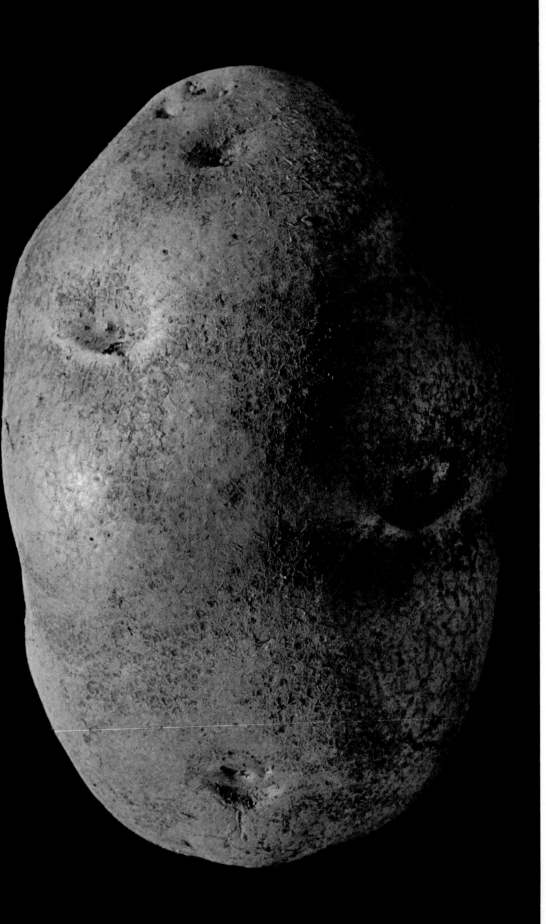

The King

Today *die Kartoffel* (the potato) is the king of German vegetables, but this was not always true. The Germans were among the last Europeans to learn to regard this New World import (the one at left is the famed Idaho) as an edible tuber. Once they had accepted it, however, they proceeded to apply to its use more ingenuity and inventiveness than had any of their neighbors. Mashed, sliced, diced, puréed, baked or turned into flour, potatoes are made by the Germans into an incredible variety of dishes and even into *Schnaps*. The dishes pictured at right are: *(top left)* triangular dessert dumplings *(page 139)* and, reading clockwise from them, hot potato salad *(page 42)*, potato pancakes *(page 118)*, potato soup and potato dumplings *(page 137)*. The Germans owe their appetite for potatoes to Frederick the Great. In 1744, almost two centuries after the potato had been brought to Europe from South America, Frederick distributed free seed potatoes to reluctant peasants and decreed that they should plant them, enforcing his edict by stationing armed soldiers in the fields. After this shotgun wedding, the parties to it lived happily together ever after.

To serve 4 to 6

9 tablespoons butter, softened
3 pounds kale
½ pound lean bacon, coarsely diced
½ cup beef or chicken stock, fresh
    or canned
2 teaspoons salt
¼ teaspoon ground nutmeg
9 medium-sized boiling potatoes
    (about 3 pounds), peeled and cut
    into ½-inch cubes
½ to ¾ cup milk
Freshly ground black pepper
2 egg yolks

Grünkohl mit Kartoffeln
BAKED KALE WITH POTATOES

With a pastry brush, coat the bottom and sides of an 8-by-10-inch baking dish with 1 tablespoon of softened butter. Set the dish aside.

Wash the kale thoroughly under cold running water. With a small, sharp knife, cut away the ends and the tough stems as well as any bruised or yellowed leaves. Drop the kale into enough lightly salted boiling water to cover it completely and boil briskly for 10 minutes. Drain thoroughly in a colander, and with the back of a spoon press it firmly to remove any excess liquid; then chop the kale coarsely.

In a heavy 4- to 5-quart saucepan, cook the bacon over moderate heat until it is crisp and brown. Add the kale, turning it about with a large spoon until the leaves are coated with the fat. Then stir in the stock, 1 teaspoon of the salt and nutmeg, and bring to a boil over high heat. Reduce the heat to low and simmer uncovered, stirring occasionally, for 20 minutes.

Meanwhile preheat the oven to 400°. Drop the potatoes into enough lightly salted boiling water to cover them completely, and boil them briskly, uncovered, until they are tender but not falling apart. Drain thoroughly, return them to the pan and shake them over low heat for 2 to 3 minutes until they are dry. Then force the potatoes through a food mill or ricer set over a bowl. A tablespoon at a time, beat 6 tablespoons of softened butter into the potatoes and then the milk a few tablespoons at a time, using as much of the milk as you need to make a purée thick enough to hold its shape in a spoon. Beat in the remaining teaspoon of salt, a few grindings of black pepper and the egg yolks, one at a time. Taste for seasoning.

Spread the cooked kale evenly over the bottom of the prepared baking dish, smooth the potatoes over it and dot the top with the remaining 2 tablespoons of butter cut into small pieces. Bake in the middle of the oven for 20 minutes, or until the surface of the potatoes is golden brown. Serve at once, directly from the baking dish.

To serve 4

6 medium-sized boiling potatoes
    (about 2 pounds), scrubbed but
    not peeled
1 cup finely chopped onions
⅔ cup chicken stock, fresh or
    canned
⅓ cup olive oil
1 tablespoon white wine vinegar
2 teaspoons prepared Düsseldorf-
    style mustard, or substitute 2
    teaspoons other hot, prepared
    mustard
2 teaspoons salt
1 teaspoon freshly ground black
    pepper
1 tablespoon fresh lemon juice

Leichter Kartoffelsalat
SUMMER POTATO SALAD

Drop the unpeeled potatoes into enough lightly salted boiling water to cover them completely. Boil them briskly until they show only the slightest resistance when pierced with the point of a small, sharp knife. Be careful not to let them overcook or they will fall apart when sliced. Drain the potatoes in a colander, then peel and cut them into ¼-inch slices. Set the potatoes aside in a bowl tightly covered with aluminum foil.

In a heavy 2- to 3-quart saucepan, combine the chopped onions, stock, oil, vinegar, prepared mustard, salt and pepper. Bring to a boil over high heat, stirring occasionally. Reduce the heat to low and simmer uncovered for 5 minutes. Remove the pan from the heat and stir in the lemon juice.

Pour the sauce over the potato slices, turning them about with a spatula to coat them evenly. Let the potatoes cool to room temperature, then taste for seasoning and serve.

Feine Kartoffelsuppe mit Gurken
POTATO SOUP WITH CUCUMBER

To serve 6

With a small, sharp knife, peel the cucumber and slice it lengthwise into halves. Scoop out the seeds by running the tip of a teaspoon down the center of each half. Cut the cucumber into ¼-inch dice and set aside.

In a heavy 3- to 4-quart saucepan, bring the potatoes and water to a boil over high heat. Reduce the heat to moderate, add the salt and pepper and cook uncovered until the potatoes are soft and can easily be mashed against the sides of the pan; then pour them and all the cooking liquid into a sieve set over a mixing bowl. With a large spoon force the potatoes through the sieve. (If you prefer, purée the potatoes in a food mill. But don't use a blender; it will make the mixture too smooth.) However you have puréed the potatoes, return them and their liquid to the saucepan and stir in the cream, milk, grated onion and cucumbers. Simmer over low heat for about 5 minutes, or until the cucumber is tender but still somewhat firm. Add the dill and taste for seasoning. Serve hot either from a heated tureen or in individual soup bowls.

1 medium-sized or 2 small cucumbers
6 medium-sized boiling potatoes (about 1½ pounds), peeled and cut into ½-inch dice
3 cups cold water
1½ teaspoons salt
¼ teaspoon freshly ground black pepper
1 cup heavy cream
1 cup milk
1 tablespoon grated onion
1 tablespoon finely chopped fresh dill, or substitute 1 teaspoon dried dill weed

Kartoffelklösse
POTATO DUMPLINGS

To make 15 to 20 dumplings

In a heavy 6- to 8-inch skillet, melt ½ cup of the butter over moderate heat. When the foam begins to subside, drop in the bread crumbs and cook, stirring constantly, until they are light brown. Set the toasted crumbs aside off the heat.

With a small, sharp knife, cut the bread into ½-inch squares (there should be about 1½ cups). Melt the remaining 2 tablespoons of butter in a heavy 8- to 10-inch skillet, add the bread and cook over moderate heat, stirring frequently, until the cubes are light brown on all sides. Add more butter, a tablespoon at a time, if necessary to prevent the bread from burning. Spread the croutons on a double thickness of paper towels to drain.

Combine the flour, farina, 1½ teaspoons of salt, the nutmeg and white pepper in a small bowl. Then, with a large spoon, beat them, a few tablespoons at a time, into the riced potatoes. Lightly beat the two eggs with a fork, and then beat them into the potato mixture. Continue to beat until the dough holds its shape lightly in a spoon. If it seems too thin, stir in a little more flour, a teaspoon at a time until the desired consistency is reached.

Lightly flour your hands and shape each dumpling in the following fashion: Scoop off about 2 tablespoons of dough and form it into a rough ball. Press a hole in the center with a fingertip, drop in 3 or 4 of the reserved croutons, then gather the outer edges of the opening together. Gently roll the dumpling into a ball again.

Bring 4 quarts of water and the remaining 2 teaspoons of salt to a bubbling boil in a deep 6- to 8-quart pot. Drop in all the dumplings, and stir gently once or twice to prevent them from sticking to one another or to the bottom of the pan. Simmer over moderate heat for 12 to 15 minutes, or until the dumplings rise to the surface of the water. Cook 1 minute longer, then remove the dumplings from the pot with a slotted spoon and arrange them on a large heated platter. Serve at once, sprinkled with the reserved toasted bread crumbs.

½ cup plus 2 tablespoons butter
1 cup fine dry white bread crumbs
2 or 3 slices fresh white homemade-type bread, crusts removed
½ cup all-purpose flour
½ cup regular farina, not the quick-cooking type
3½ teaspoons salt
⅛ teaspoon ground nutmeg
⅛ teaspoon white pepper
3½ cups hot or cold riced potatoes, made from 4 or 5 medium-sized baking potatoes (about 1½ pounds), boiled, peeled and forced through a ricer
2 eggs

Germans have never lost the taste they acquired in olden days for dried fruit. They combine several varieties (*at right*) to make an excellent compote (*opposite*) to serve with meat courses or as a light dessert.

To serve 4 to 6

1 quart cold water
1 cup dried white beans, preferably Great Northern or navy beans
½ pound slab of lean bacon cut lengthwise into 3 strips and crosswise into halves
1½ pounds cooking apples and 1½ pounds firm ripe pears, peeled, cored and cut into ¼-inch wedges, or use 3 pounds of cooking apples, peeled, cored and cut into ¼-inch wedges
1 pound fresh green string beans, trimmed, and cut into 2-inch lengths
1 cup coarsely diced scraped carrots
3 medium-sized boiling potatoes (about 1 pound), peeled and cut into ½-inch dice
Salt
Freshly ground black pepper

To serve 6 to 8

1½ pounds mixed dried fruits (about 5 cups)
2 cups sugar
A 2-inch length of cinnamon stick
Peel of 1 lemon, cut into ½-by-2-inch strips

Westfälisches Blindhuhn
BEANS WITH FRUIT AND VEGETABLES

In a heavy 4- to 6-quart saucepan or soup pot, bring 1 quart of water to a bubbling boil over high heat. Drop in the dried beans and boil uncovered for 2 minutes. Turn off the heat and let the beans soak for 1 hour. Then add the bacon, return the beans to a boil, and reduce the heat to low. Partially cover the pan and simmer as slowly as possible for about 1 hour, or until the beans are barely tender.

Add the apples, pears, green beans, carrots, potatoes, salt to taste and a few grindings of pepper to the beans. Partially cover the pan and simmer, stirring occasionally, for 30 minutes longer, or until the vegetables and fruit are tender and the beans fully cooked. Taste for seasoning and serve hot from a deep heated bowl.

Backobstkompott
DRIED FRUIT COMPOTE

Soak the fruit overnight, or for at least 12 hours in enough cold water to cover it by 1 inch. Drain the fruit in a colander. Measure the soaking liquid and if necessary add enough water to make 1 quart. Then pour it into a heavy 3- to 4-quart saucepan, add the sugar, cinnamon stick and lemon peel, and bring to a boil over moderate heat, stirring until the sugar dissolves. Drop in the drained fruit, reduce the heat to low and simmer, uncovered, stirring occasionally, for about 10 minutes, or until the fruit is tender and can be easily pierced with the tip of a fork. With a slotted spoon, transfer the fruit to a heatproof bowl. Then boil the syrup briskly over high heat for 5 minutes, or until it thickens slightly. Remove the pan from the heat and pour the syrup over the fruit. Serve the compote while it is still warm, or refrigerate until chilled. In Germany, *Backobstkompott* is usually served as an accompaniment to dumplings or meats. If you like, you may add ¼ cup of kirsch, brandy, rum or white wine to the fruit along with the syrup.

Kartoffelklösse mit Pflaumenmus
POTATO DESSERT DUMPLINGS WITH PRUNE-BUTTER FILLING

In a heavy 6- to 8-inch skillet, melt the butter over moderate heat. When the foam subsides, add the crumbs and cook, stirring constantly, until they are golden brown. Remove the skillet from the heat and set aside.

Drop the potatoes into enough lightly salted boiling water to cover them completely. Boil briskly for 20 or 30 minutes, or until the potatoes show no resistance when pierced with the point of a small, sharp knife. Drain and peel them, then force them through a ricer set over a mixing bowl. Beat in the ½ cup of flour and the egg yolks one at a time. Add the salt and nutmeg and continue to beat the potatoes, flour and egg yolks until a smooth dough is formed. Taste for seasoning. Refrigerate, covered with plastic wrap or foil, for about one hour.

Sprinkle a large baking sheet with 1 tablespoon of flour, tipping the sheet from side to side to spread the flour evenly. Place the chilled dough on the sheet and with a lightly floured pin roll it out into a rectangle 9 inches wide and 15 inches long. If at any point the dough becomes too sticky to handle, refrigerate it on the sheet until it is firm again.

With a ruler and a pastry wheel or small, sharp knife, measure and cut the dough into 3-inch squares. Drop 1 teaspoon of prune butter into the center of each square and brush all of the edges lightly with the beaten egg white. Fold each of the squares in half diagonally and pinch the edges lightly together to seal them.

Bring 4 quarts of water and 2 teaspoons of salt to a bubbling boil in a wide 6- to 8-quart pot. Drop in 4 or 5 of the dumplings and stir gently once or twice to prevent them from sticking to one another or to the bottom of the pot. Boil briskly for 3 to 4 minutes, until the dumplings rise to the surface, then remove them from the pot with a slotted spoon. As the dumplings are removed from the pot, batch by batch, arrange them side by side on a heated platter, sprinkle them with the reserved toasted bread crumbs and then with the plain sugar or cinnamon sugar. Serve at once.

To make 15 dumplings

½ cup butter
¼ cup fine dry white bread crumbs
6 medium-sized boiling potatoes (about 2 pounds), scrubbed but not peeled
½ cup flour
2 egg yolks
2 teaspoons salt
⅛ teaspoon ground nutmeg
1 tablespoon flour
15 teaspoons prune butter, or substitute 15 teaspoons apple butter
1 egg white, lightly beaten
¼ cup sugar, or ¼ cup sugar combined with ¼ teaspoon ground cinnamon

2 pounds beef short ribs, cut into
    2-inch pieces
Salt
Freshly ground black pepper
2 tablespoons lard
6 medium-sized onions (about 2
    pounds), sliced ⅛ inch thick
1 small bay leaf
¼ teaspoon ground cloves
4 cups cold water
3 tablespoons fresh rye bread
    crumbs, made in a blender from
    1 slice fresh dark rye bread
2 teaspoons capers, drained and
    rinsed in cold water
2 tablespoons fresh lemon juice
½ teaspoon finely grated fresh
    lemon peel

Westfälischer Pfefferpotthast
BEEF SHORT RIBS WITH SPICED LEMON-AND-CAPER SAUCE

Sprinkle the short ribs with salt and pepper. In a 3- to 4-quart flameproof casserole or Dutch oven, heat the lard over high heat, until it begins to splutter. Add the short ribs and brown them on all sides, regulating the heat so that the ribs brown quickly and evenly without burning. Remove the meat to a platter. Add the onions to the fat remaining in the casserole, and cook, stirring occasionally, for 5 minutes, or until they are soft and transparent but not brown. Add the bay leaf and cloves and pour in the water. Bring to a boil over high heat, scraping in any brown bits clinging to the bottom and sides of the pan.

Return the ribs to the casserole, cover and reduce the heat to its lowest point. Simmer for 1½ hours, or until the meat shows no resistance when pierced with the tip of a small, sharp knife. Then transfer the short ribs to a deep heated platter and cover with foil to keep them warm. Discard the bay leaf, and skim off the fat from the liquid remaining in the casserole. Stir in the bread crumbs, capers, lemon juice and lemon peel, and bring to a boil over high heat. Reduce the heat; simmer uncovered, for a minute or two. Taste for seasoning. The sauce should be quite peppery; add more pepper to taste if necessary. Then pour the sauce over the meat and serve at once.

To serve 4 to 6

2 tablespoons lard
1 cup coarsely chopped onions
1 cup coarsely chopped carrots
A 3½ to 4 pound smoked pork
    loin in one piece, with the
    backbone (chine) sawed
    through at ½-inch intervals, but
    left attached and tied to the
    loin in 2 or 3 places
4 whole juniper berries, coarsely
    crushed with a mortar and pestle
    or wrapped in a towel and
    crushed with a rolling pin
4 cups cold water
2 teaspoons cornstarch dissolved
    in 1 tablespoon cold water

Kasseler Rippenspeer
ROASTED SMOKED PORK LOIN

Preheat the oven to 350°. In a heavy 8- to 10-inch skillet, melt the lard over moderate heat. Add the onions and carrots and cook over moderate heat, stirring frequently for 8 to 10 minutes, or until the vegetables are soft and light brown. With a rubber spatula, scrape the entire contents of the skillet into a heavy casserole or roasting pan just large enough to hold the pork comfortably. Place the pork loin, fat side up, on top of the vegetables and strew the crushed juniper berries around the pork. Pour in the 4 cups of water and roast uncovered in the middle of the oven, basting occasionally with the cooking juices, for 1½ hours, or until the pork is golden brown. (If you prefer to use a meat thermometer, insert it into the pork loin before placing the loin in the casserole. Be sure the tip of the thermometer does not touch any bone. Roast the pork until the thermometer reaches a temperature of 175°.)

Cut away the strings and carve the pork into ½-inch-thick chops. Arrange the slices attractively in slightly overlapping layers on a large heated platter. Cover and set aside.

Strain the pan juices through a fine sieve set over a bowl, pressing down hard on the vegetables with the back of the spoon before discarding them. Skim as much fat as possible from the surface, then measure the juices. If there is more than 1½ cups, boil briskly over high heat until the juices are reduced to that amount; if there is less, add water. Bring the pan juices to a boil over moderate heat in a small saucepan. Give the cornstarch mixture a quick stir to recombine it and add it to the pan. Cook, stirring constantly, until the sauce clears and thickens slightly. Moisten the meat slices with a few spoonfuls of the sauce and serve the rest in a heated sauceboat.

Kasseler Rippenspeer is often served on a mound of either plain or pineapple sauerkraut *(page 24)*.

Streuselkuchen

SUGAR-CRUMB CAKE

Pour the lukewarm water into a small shallow mixing bowl and sprinkle it with the yeast and ¼ teaspoon of the sugar. Let the mixture stand for 2 or 3 minutes, then stir to dissolve the yeast completely. Set the bowl aside in a warm, draft-free place—such as a turned-off oven—for about 5 minutes, or until the mixture almost doubles in volume. Then stir in the lukewarm milk and the lemon peel.

In a large mixing bowl, beat the remaining ⅓ cup of sugar, the egg and the egg yolks together, and then stir in the yeast and milk mixture. Add the 3 cups of sifted flour, a cup or so at a time, beating well after each addition. Continue to beat until a soft dough is formed. Then beat in 6 tablespoons of the softened butter, 1 tablespoon at a time, and gather the dough into a compact ball.

Place the dough on a lightly floured surface and knead it by pushing it down with the heels of your hands, pressing it forward and folding it back on itself. Repeat this process for about 10 minutes, or until the dough is smooth and elastic. Gather it into a ball again, place it in a buttered bowl and dust the top lightly with flour. Cover the bowl with a towel and put it aside in a warm draft-free place for about 40 minutes, or until the dough doubles in bulk.

Preheat the oven to 375°. With a pastry brush, lightly coat the bottom and sides of an 11-by-17-inch jelly-roll pan with the remaining 1 tablespoon of soft butter. Set aside.

Prepare the *Streusel* topping by combining the ½ pound of chilled butter bits, 2 cups of flour, ⅔ cup sugar, and 1 teaspoon of cinnamon in a large bowl. Working quickly, rub the flour and fat together with your fingertips until they look like flakes of coarse meal.

When the dough has risen, punch it down and knead it on a lightly floured surface for 3 or 4 minutes. Then place it in the jelly-roll pan and stretch and smooth it out with your hands or a rolling pin until it covers the bottom of the pan.

Strew the *Streusel* mixture evenly over the top of the cake and sprinkle it with ¼ cup of melted butter. Bake in the middle of the oven for 45 minutes, or until the top is crusty. To serve, cut the cake into 2-inch squares and serve warm or at room temperature. Traditionally, *Streuselkuchen* is served at the German coffee table.

NOTE: To make *Pflaumenkuchen* or plum cake, prepare the dough as described above, but in place of the *Streusel,* cover the top with neat rows of firm ripe purple freestone plums, about 3 pounds.

Cut the plums almost in half, pit and spread them open. Overlapping the plums slightly, stand them flesh side up in parallel rows across the entire width of the cake. Sprinkle them evenly with 1 cup of sugar mixed with 1 teaspoon of cinnamon, and before baking dribble ¼ cup of melted butter evenly over the top of the cake.

Apfelkuchen, or apple cake, may be made in the same fashion. Peel, core and slice 6 medium-sized cooking apples, and toss them with 2 tablespoons of lemon juice, 1 cup of sugar and 1 teaspoon of cinnamon.

Arrange the apple slices in parallel rows side by side across the width of the cake, and before baking dribble ¼ cup of melted butter over them.

To make one 11-by-17-inch cake

CAKE

¼ cup lukewarm water (110° to 115°)
1 package or cake of active dry or compressed yeast
¼ teaspoon plus ⅓ cup sugar
¾ cup lukewarm milk (110° to 115°)
1 teaspoon finely grated lemon peel
1 egg, at room temperature
2 egg yolks, at room temperature
3 cups sifted all-purpose flour
7 tablespoons unsalted butter, softened

TOPPING

½ pound butter (2 sticks), cut into bits and thoroughly chilled
2 cups all-purpose flour
⅔ cup sugar
1 teaspoon ground cinnamon
¼ cup melted butter

VIII

The Southern Style: A Lighter Touch

A Bavarian dairy farmer hauls a sledload of cheeses, his summer's "harvest" in its most compact form, from an alpine shelter to a dairy in the valley. The cow behind him is one of a herd that he grazes in summer on rich pastures nestled in the mountain peaks.

Rhineland, goes the adage, is wineland. It is also the most civilized landscape in Germany. In the Rhineland proper *(map, page 145)*, vineyards climb in terrace after narrow terrace up the steep cliffs that rise from the banks of the Rhine and Mosel Rivers; to the south, in the Palatinate, they stretch unbroken to a hilly blue horizon. In picturesque wine towns patrician houses cluster like grapes, under castles both ruined and lived in, towering high over the rivers. On the Rhine, commercial craft from Germany and Belgium and Holland almost jostle for space, and as sleek, white passenger ships glide past the rocks of the Lorelei, their passengers invariably lift their voices in what is to my mind the most overrated of all songs. The green Mosel is quieter, and its vineyards rise even more steeply before they disappear into the woods that border their cliffs and hillsides.

Two thousand years ago the Romans planted the first grape cuttings in this region. We can still see Romans enjoying the fruit of their labors in a delightful Roman sculpture at the Landesmuseum in Trier, on the Mosel. It depicts a fully manned Roman ship transporting barrels of wine, and from the faces of the sailors on that ship we can be sure they felt little pain as they sailed down the river.

As with wine, so with food. The cooking of the region reflects a live-and-let-live attitude that one senses everywhere in the shimmery, golden air of the Rhineland. Most of the cooking is relatively simple and casual. Robust one-dish combinations of cabbage or turnips with smoked beef are traditional among the peasants of the Eifel and the Hunsrück, the Westerwald and the Taunus, all of them wooded mountain ranges that open into wide vistas, as the Green Mountains do in Vermont. The Rhineland is potato country, too, but potatoes are cooked there with far more imagination and grace than in northern and central Germany. Typical of the Rhineland's potato dishes are *Salzkartoffeln,* boiled potatoes shaken dry over the heat; *Schnippelkuchen,* a large, egg-enriched potato pancake; *Potthucke,* a pudding made from raw and cooked potatoes, eggs and milk, which is baked and then sliced and fried to a crisp in butter, and which goes wonderfully with ham and a green salad; and *Blech Grumbeeren,* diced potatoes baked with bacon.

One of these potato dishes is worth special mention. Some years ago as I drove on the lonely mountain roads of the Eifel to hear the vespers at Maria Laach, a Romanesque church and abbey completed before 1300, hunger forced me to stop at an unprepossessing village inn. There was no food to be had at the moment, I was informed, unless I wished to share the family's own *Himmel und Erde,* "heaven and earth," and of course I did. Perhaps the most famous of the old peasant dishes, *Himmel und Erde (page 164)* is made from equal quantities of potatoes and apples, and eaten with crisp slices of pan-fried blood sausage. In its sturdy simplicity the dish was surprisingly good, and it made the same impression upon me as did Maria Laach: an impression of great antiquity.

Equally old are the traditional dishes eaten in the lowlands along the riverbanks—dishes that often reflect the influence of French occupations of earlier centuries. In Trier, an old Roman city on the Mosel, where the fortified gateway called the Porta Nigra still stands as one of the most glorious of all Roman monuments, I once had a delicious dish of tiny eels. They had been dipped in lemon juice, wrapped in leaves of fresh sage and sautéed in butter. With the dish came a very dry apple cider called *Viez,* which has none of the cloying qualities of most ciders.

Anyone who goes to Germany should stop at Trier, where a whiff of France hangs in the air and Romanesque churches loom over the old streets. In Trier I found a superb restaurant that, unlike the great majority of first-class German restaurants, specializes in local dishes. The Kurtriersche Weinstube zum Domstein on the market square is primarily a wine shop, with a wine list that meticulously describes the characters of 14 open and about 140 bottled wines—all German. The owner's wife, a graduate of the German equivalent of France's *Cordon Bleu,* has resurrected many of the old dishes of the region. Among them I especially remember an excellent combination of leeks and smoked beef ribs, cooked with a rare consideration for our relatively delicate modern tastes and stomachs.

The Rhine no longer yields great quantities of salmon, but the memory of great salmon dishes survives. Scorching-hot grilled salmon with a dollop of tangy, ice-cold herb butter is one of my own memories of a restaurant at Winkel on the Rhine. It came with new potatoes and fresh green peas, just as it might have done in a Fourth of July dinner in New England, and the dry Schloss Vollrads wine from the great wine estate I had just visited was a perfect accompaniment to the dish.

Meats are excellent throughout the region. There is the ubiquitous Rhenish *Sauerbraten,* marinated in wine rather than buttermilk and served with a raisin sauce. More pleasant to my taste are two other Rhenish dishes: *Kalbsleber im Backteig,* small deep-fried fritters of sliced calf's liver, served with fresh

Political Changes
in the Southern Belt

Political boundaries in Germany's
southern culinary belt were least
affected by the two world wars.
Except for the much-disputed
territory of Alsace-Lorraine (at lower
left on this map), boundary changes
were negligible. Alsace-Lorraine was
given to France after World War I,
was occupied by Germany in 1940
and then was restored to France at
the end of World War II.

peas; and *Schweinsfilet mit Äpfeln*, a fillet of pork spread with mustard, dipped in egg and bread crumbs, browned in butter and baked in the oven with marjoram-flavored apples and sour cream.

My highest praise, however, must go to the Rhenish way with game birds and venison. *Gefüllter Fasan*, a pheasant stuffed with a mixture of ground chicken liver, eggs, mushrooms, onions, chervil, parsley, tarragon, grated lemon rind and a dash of brandy, wrapped in bacon and baked in the oven with frequent bastings of white wine—this dish represents one kind of culinary paradise to me. (A recipe for a very similar dish appears on page 83.) So does the Rhenish roast partridge stuffed with fresh green grapes and sauced with sour cream *(page 86)*. Best of all, perhaps, was a dish I reveled in during a visit to the Eifel: a marinated roast of wild boar, flamed with juniper *Schnaps* and flavored with juniper berries and marjoram. During the cooking the roast had been basted with hot, onion-flavored red wine, and this wine, with the addition of a little sour cream, formed the sauce in which the roast was served. Marjoram-flavored mashed potatoes and a tart applesauce accompanied the roast.

Obviously these are not simple rural dishes, and they are served not in rural *Gasthöfe* but in elegantly appointed and staffed de luxe restaurants. Handsome, high-style living is a tradition in the great cities of the region, and nowhere is this more true today than at Bonn, the capital of West Germany, with its concentration of high civil servants and diplomats. In nearby Bad Godesberg, where most of the diplomats live, there are truly fabulous restaurants such as the famous Michaeli Stuben. You must knock at the door and be greeted by the host before gaining admittance to this establishment, but here the resemblance to speak-easy days in New York ends.

On a recent visit to the Michaeli Stuben I had a strong but delicious red pepper soup with sauerkraut and cream. For my main course I wavered between *Was Mutti Gerne Isst* ("What Mom likes to eat"), a steak with chicken livers and ham, covered with a spicy cream sauce and served with French-fried potatoes and salad, and a dish called *Wotan's Lustbissen* ("a bite for Wo-

Continued on page 154

A Time to Make Wine and Make Merry

In southern Germany autumn is the season for harvesting grapes and making wine, and then for celebrating a hard task well done. Along the Rhine and Mosel Rivers and in the other wine-growing regions of Germany, where centuries-old vineyards flourish on the steep hillsides (as at Bernkastel, *left*), fall festivals deriving from immemorial tradition are held to pay homage to wine. The mood of the celebrants was expressed in the 16th Century painting above, one of 12 on the face of the famous clock in the Münster Cathedral in Westphalia, each representing a traditional agricultural activity appropriate for the current month. Under the picture there is a Latin inscription that means "With joyous care, October gathers the laughing grapes."

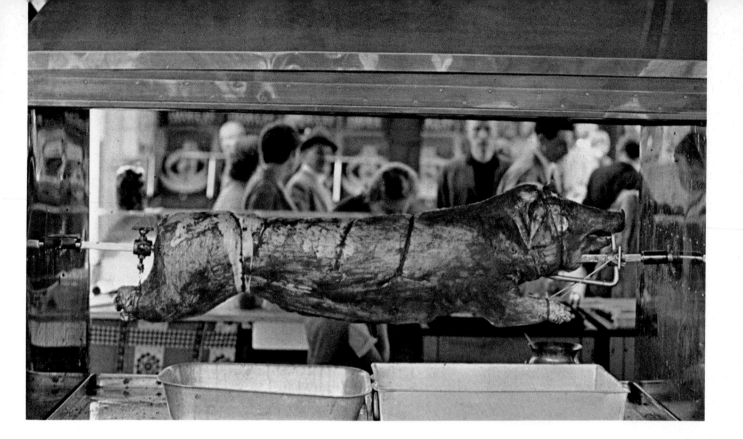

Wine Festivals: Great Days for Gorging

One of the oldest of the German wine festivals is held in mid-September in Bad Dürkheim, a picturesque village in the Rhine Valley. Here, in tents and pavilions, visitors from all over Germany sample dozens of the new season's wines, served by the generous tumblerful. The festival turns the village into an exuberant fair, with rides for the children and hearty food for everybody. The woman at left enjoys a piece of chicken while her companion nibbles at a kabob, to the music of a strolling street band. Above, a barbecued pig awaits the vendor's carving knife. The small boy devouring a chocolate-covered sugar puff has a further treat in store. The huge chocolate-coated heart that almost conceals him is made of *Lebkuchen* (gingerbread) and sold with a neck string attached. The motto written in icing proclaims: "Love me only or leave love alone." The wine, food, music and general gaiety attract most of the visitors, but the Dürkheim fair also has its practical side. Not far from the fun-seekers, wine dealers and manufacturers of wine-making equipment conduct business.

A Time for Pigs to Turn into Wursts

"Everybody rejoices when November kills its pig." So says the Latin inscription under the painting depicting the agricultural activity appropriate to November on the great clock in Münster cathedral. The artist showed a family, helped by a relative, doing its own butchering as was the custom in the 16th Century. After the butchering was completed and the *Wurst* was made, the family and the neighbors got together for a *Schlachtfest*, a convivial meal at which they sampled the freshly made *Wurst* and dined on the parts of the pig that could not be processed. Nowadays farmers either take their pigs to a commercial plant to be slaughtered and processed or call in professional butchers to do the work. The *Wurst*-maker at right is working with his own equipment in the sunny backyard of one of his customers, a farmer in the Bavarian Alps, filling a casing with a *Wurst* paste he has made himself using his own recipe.

A Galaxy of wursts (*see next page*)

Best of the Wursts

Most of Germany's great variety of sausages can be eaten either hot or cold. But some—like *Bratwurst (number 14)*—must be pan-fried before eating, and a few—like the *Schlachtwurst (1, 3 and 22)* and the *Touristenwurst (12)* are eaten only when cold. The names and chief ingredients of the various kinds of *Wurst* on the preceding pages are:

1. *Schlachtwurst*, ¾ beef, ¼ pork.
2. *Frische Leberwurst*, pork and pork liver.
3. *Schlachtwurst (see 1).*
4. *Kalbsleberwurst*, calf, pork and pork liver.
5. *Speck Blutwurst*, solid pork fat, blood and pork.
6. *Fleischwurst*, beef, pork and veal.
7. *Braunschweiger Leberwurst*, pork and pork liver.
8. *Thüringer Blutwurst*, lean pork and blood.
9. *Bierwurst*, solid pork fat, pork and beef.
10. *Holsteiner Kochwurst*, ½ pork, ½ beef.
11. *Hildesheimer Streichleberwurst*, pork and pork liver.
12. *Touristenwurst*, ¾ beef, ¼ pork.
13. *Kassler Leberwurst*, diced, lean pork and pork liver.
14. *Koch-Bratwurst*, pork and seasoning only.
15. *Speck Blutwurst (see 5).*
16. *Hamburger gekochte Mettwurst*, coarse, lean pork.
17. *Trüffel Leberwurst*, pork, pork liver and truffle.
18. *Blut Schwartemagen*, lean pork and blood.
19. *Blut Zungenwurst*, diced, solid pork fat, pork tongue and blood.
20. *Stuttgarter Presskopf*, pork, veal and beef.
21. *Speck Blutwurst (see 5).*
22. *Schlachtwurst (see 1).*
23. *Braunschweiger Leberwurst (see 7).*
24. *Sülze* (headcheese), coarsely sliced pork and gelatin.
25. *Kalbsroulade*, pork, veal, diced pork fat, pistachios.
26. *Gekochte Schinkenwurst*, beef and coarse, lean pork.

tan's pleasure"), two slices of beef fillet, mushrooms, smoked ham, red and green sweet peppers, cream sauce and rice. The latter won a prize from the *Bonner Marmiten*, a club of elegant gentlemen who love to cook delicious meals for one another, but as a more-or-less domestic type I chose *Mutti* over *Wotan*—and then could not cope with half of the bonanza spread before me.

As I review my account of that great meal, I realize that I have omitted dessert, as I have done in so many of my descriptions of meals in this book. The reason is simple: I don't particularly care for dessert after a meal. When I do eat cake or pudding, I'd much rather have it for breakfast or tea. But I do like the cookies of the Rhineland, such as a fried *Mutzenmandeln;* the *Hohlhippchen*, which are crisp cones filled with butter cream or whipped cream; and the *Stuten* and *Blatz*, the first made with raisins, the second without them. Both occupy an intermediate place between bread and cake and are eaten with apple butter. The most famous of these regional cookies, seldom baked at home because they are centuries-old specialties of the local bakers, are the *Spekulatius*, crisp, cinnamon-flavored butter cookies shaped in special molds, and the *Aachener Printen*, one of the best and most ancient of all German brown cookies, made without the usual honey.

To my taste the food of Baden is the best in Germany—but much of it is not particularly German. Baden borders on the province of Alsace, which has slipped back and forth between Germany and France throughout its history, and the culinary ties between the two are close. Snails cooked with herb butter, frogs' legs in a cream sauce, superb trout cooked *au bleu* or *à la meunière*, Black Forest smoked ham and bacon, partridge cooked with bacon and white wine and served with sauerkraut simmered in the same wine, Black Forest venison stew marinated and cooked in red wine, and a fabulous old-fashioned wild boar pie—these are some of the delights of this land of civilized good living. The delicious plums of Baden are made into *Pflaumenwasser*, an excellent clear brandy. They are also used in compotes, the best of which is simplicity itself: heavily sugared, juicy plums are simmered in a slow oven, literally stewing in their own juice.

Finally there is Baden's *Schwarzwälder Kirschtorte*, or Black Forest cherry cake, one of the most famous of all German cakes. A recipe for one version of this great dessert appears on page 160. Another equally popular version consists of three different kinds of white and chocolate cake layers, sprinkled with the cherry brandy called kirsch and filled with custard, a sour cherry compote (the cherries *must* be sour for the right contrast of flavors) and whipped cream. The top of this creation is covered with more cream and pleasantly decorated with more cherries and curls of bitter chocolate. Strong-minded and heartier lovers of kirsch may prefer the powerful local breakfast of kirsch, smoked bacon, rye bread and coffee, especially when the kirsch is poured into the coffee.

In Württemberg a traveler in search of food will meet all the members of the family of *Spätzle* (literally, "little sparrows"), tiny dumplings made from the white flour of the local wheat *(page 164)*. There are *Maultaschen*, the local form of ravioli or kreplach; liver *Spätzle;* cheese *Spätzle;* and *Knöpfle Spätzle*, made in the old-fashioned way by snipping the egg-and-milk dough into boiling water. *Spätzle* are the potatoes of Württemberg, and they taste best with the thick creamy gravies that the local people make so well. But they are also good with sour kidneys, which are soaked for 30 minutes in several changes of water to remove their harsh taste, then stewed in bouillon, wine vinegar, wine and a little lemon rind. *Spätzle* go well, too, with minced veal and with such humble dishes as lentils cooked with bacon—or, most simply, with cabbage, a dish that is a rural favorite.

In both Baden and Württemberg, *Spätzle* and a salad are considered a meal; in fact, few meals are served without a salad that may contain all or some of these ingredients: field lettuce, curly endive, dandelion greens, watercress, sorrel and chervil. But salads provide only one of the vegetable delights of the region. Some of the best asparagus in Germany, thick, white and tender as butter, grows in Tettnang not far from Lake Constance. In the spring an asparagus mania overcomes natives and visitors alike, and everyone repairs to restaurants that list 20 or more specialties made with this king of vegetables. The best I ever had was one of the simplest, a bowl of asparagus covered with a tart, thin hollandaise sauce, with which I ate a *Speckpfannkuchen,* a plate-sized egg pancake with bits of bacon in the batter. Another interesting vegetable of this vegetable-loving region (it is, significantly, one of the few parts of Germany in which vegetables are generally cooked well) is hops. Most of us think of hops simply as a flavoring for beer or ale, but they are delicious in a butter sauce or as a salad with a very light dressing of unsweetened whipped cream flavored with lemon juice.

To many Americans, Bavaria is little more than Munich and the Alps—which is a pity. The northern part of the state is rich in magnificent architecture and art as well as superb wines and beers. It is, in fact, a region where esthetics and gastronomy often go together. I encountered one such combination in Pommersfelden, not far from Würzburg. Pommersfelden is the site of Weissenstein, one of the greatest of Germany's Baroque castles, its four-story stairway decorated with an almost unbelievable wealth of stucco curlicues. In a nearby village was a little country inn, modernized with checkered brown-and-green tablecloths and stainless-steel trays of flatware. My young waitress had an enormous beehive hairdo that somehow seemed belied by her apple cheeks and the full, warm figure she had squeezed into a waitress' black dress and white apron. I started my meal with a homemade *Griess Suppe mit Ei,* a semolina soup with an egg beaten into it. Then I bit into heavenly *Bratwürste,* or grilled veal sausages, six on a plate with the accompaniment of home-fried potatoes and a mild sauerkraut sprinkled with a few caraway seeds. I don't think I have ever had better *Bratwürste,* not even in Nürnberg, their place of origin.

The people of northern Bavaria like the products of the pig, boiled as *Kesselfleisch,* roasted to a golden crispness in a *Schwärtelbraten* or made as *Schweinswürstl mit Kraut*—a dish of coarse, marjoram-flavored pork sausages with cabbage that I once ate with pleasure in the shadow of medieval Bamberg Cathedral. Other popular Bavarian sausages are the well-seasoned *Milzwurst,* made with veal and pieces of milt and browned in butter, and *Wollwurst,* which is veal so finely ground that it becomes a smooth, white mass, also cooked in butter. Then there are all the other *Würste* that sustain life as a main dish or a snack, eaten with a crisp roll or a huge pretzel, with mustard or *Kren* (horseradish) on the side, and accompanied by the smoky beer of Bamberg, the blond beer of Würzburg or the rich, dark beer of Kulmbach.

What most of us think of as typical Bavarian food is eaten in Munich and the Alpine regions. "Meat is the best vegetable," say these Bavarians, and their favorite meats are pork and *Kalbshaxe (page 165)*, the veal counterpart to the pig's knuckle favored in other parts of Germany. The size of a Bavarian *Kalbshaxe*, braised or roasted to a crisp gold, has to be seen to be believed, and so does the speed with which the natives put it away, usually with potato dumplings and a mixed green salad. Other dishes remind one of the cooking of southern Bavaria's neighbor, Austria: stuffed breast of veal; the meat of a calf's head boiled and then breaded and fried; *Kalbsbeuscherl*, the lung, heart and milt of a calf, made into a goulash; and the voluptuous cream sauces that go with most of these meats. One of the passions of the Bavarians—a passion they share with Austrians—is *Schweinernes*, all parts of the beloved pig, fresh, pickled or smoked. A favorite Bavarian meat is *Gselchtes*, mildly smoked ham and bacon, which Bavarians often eat as a snack along with the delicious coarse, dark peasant bread, a stein of beer and a chaser of *Enzian Schnaps*, made from the root of the gentian, a wild Alpine flowering plant. *Gselchtes* is also cooked with kraut and served with *Knödl*, a kind of Bavarian dumpling.

These *Knödl* resemble the dumplings of Austria. There are *Semmelknödl* made with stale rolls, which become *Speckknödl* when they contain bits of bacon, and *Leberknödl* when there is liver in them. *Leberknödl* are perhaps the most popular, either large as a main dish, or small as a garnish for consommé. *Knödl* also go well with meat, sauerkraut or a salad; they are eaten cold or sliced and fried as an accompaniment for stewed fruit. They are, in fact, nothing less than a culinary way of life—and an excellent one when the cook has a light hand.

Another category of Bavarian (and Austrian) food, called *Mehlspeis*, includes all the good things made with white flour. Among them are *Dampfnudeln (page 162)*, which are not noodles at all but yeast dumplings baked with a little butter and milk in a tightly covered pot so that they rise to twice their original size. *Dampfnudeln* may be served with vanilla sauce or stewed fruit as a dessert, or they may make a whole supper, along with *Milchkaffee* (a mixture of equal parts of coffee and milk). *Schmarrn*, another dish shared with Austria, are egg pancakes made with flour, rice, semolina or stale bread, and torn apart with two forks after being cooked. These scrambled pancakes have entered the local idiom: unimportant or trivial remarks are "not worth a *Schmarrn*," and a busybody will be told that something is "not his *Schmarrn* business." Finally there are the *Strudel* of Bavaria. These rolls of thin pastry may be filled with fish or cabbage, and very good they are in this fashion. More conventionally they contain apples, cottage cheese or plums—or, at their best, poppy seeds or cherries.

There are good reasons for the popularity of these substantial dumplings and pancakes and *Strudel*, which started life as peasant fare and later conquered the cities. For one thing they are inexpensive. For another they are ideal for meatless Fridays, rigorously observed in Catholic Bavaria.

In Munich, all food is beer food, and Munich beer is famous. It comes in several seasonal variations. The famous dark *Bockbier*, for example, is a strong beer brewed in the winter for consumption the following spring. Another winter-brewed beer, *Märzenbier*, is popular at Munich's great autumn festival, the Oktoberfest (where it is often called *Oktoberbier*), and is also drunk in the spring (the word *März* means "March"). In the summer connoisseurs turn to Bavarian *Weissbier*, light in color and quality and usually accompanied by a slice of lemon *(pictures, pages 56 and 57)*. At any time of year the full impact of beer and beer *Gemütlichkeit* can be had in an evening at the Schwemme, the ground floor of Munich's Hofbräuhaus.

Beer is also part of the *Brotzeit*, the Munich expression for "snack time," and *Brotzeit* calls for *Schmankerl*, an untranslatable term applied to any number of appealing little tidbits. All sausages, but particularly *Weisswürste*, are *Schmankerl*. So is a thick slice of juicy cheese that comes from the Bavarian dairying district called the Allgäu and is eaten on buttered bread with a seasoning of salt and pepper and garnish of *Radi*, Munich's vegetable symbol. A *Radi* is a salted white radish cut into the thinnest of slices; eaten alone or as a garnish for cheese, sausage or other foods, it is inseparable from beer.

Equally popular for snacks is *Leberkäs*. Literally translated, the word means "liver cheese," but *Leberkäs* has nothing to do with cheese and need not be made with liver. Generally it is made from finely ground beef, pork and bacon, with a flavoring of salt, pepper, onion, marjoram and nutmeg; the whole is shaped into an oblong loaf. Butchers make *Leberkäs* not only in Munich but throughout southern Bavaria, Austria or the German-speaking parts of Switzerland. In all these regions you will see handwritten signs in butchers' shop windows: "Hot *Leberkäs* at 10 o'clock"—or at 2 o'clock, or even twice a day. The signs are important, for though *Leberkäs* may be eaten cold, it is at its best when fresh and hot. Connoisseurs of *Leberkäs* eat it in thick slices that have a delicious crust at the bottom and top, with a good mustard and fresh dark bread or a big pretzel, all washed down with a *Halbe Helle*—a half liter of light beer. This was my own *Schmankerl* at Munich's famous Franziskanerbräu, opposite the post office, where it was served to me with a ritual and flourish that warmed my heart. Somehow, the humble dish and the ceremonious service combined to make a fitting farewell to my tour—a tour at once culinary, historical and geographic—of the three great schools of German cooking.

Bounty from the Forest Floor

Southern Germany's Black Forest is a paradise for mushroom hunters. Women and children, who expertly search for the fungi in the forests from June through October, supply most of the mushrooms on the local German market. In the storybook picture at left, a young mushroom gatherer explores a likely-looking patch—deep in the forest, hidden away under dead branches and leaves—as her grandmother watches. Mushrooms are popular as an ingredient in German meat and egg dishes and are also prized as a delicacy on their own. Of the four popular varieties shown below, the *Pfifferling* (usually called the chanterelle in English-speaking countries) is excellent with meats; the *Steinpilz* (yellow boletus) is often sautéed and eaten as a vegetable; the *Speisemorchel* (morel) is favored with scrambled eggs and omelets; and the *Waldegerling* (common, or field, mushroom) is used for a wide variety of dishes, including chicken fricassee *(Recipe Booklet)*.

PFIFFERLING

STEINPILZ

SPEISEMORCHEL

WALDEGERLING

159

To serve 8 to 10

CHOCOLATE CURLS
8 ounces semisweet bar chocolate

CAKE
1 tablespoon butter, softened
6 tablespoons flour
10 tablespoons sweet butter
6 eggs, at room temperature
1 teaspoon vanilla extract
1 cup sugar
½ cup sifted flour
½ cup unsweetened cocoa

SYRUP
¾ cup sugar
1 cup cold water
⅓ cup kirsch

FILLING AND TOPPING
3 cups chilled heavy cream
½ cup confectioners' sugar
¼ cup kirsch
1 cup poached pitted fresh red
   cherries or 1 cup drained and
   rinsed canned sour red cherries
Fresh sweet red cherries with stems,
   or substitute maraschino cherries
   with stems, drained and rinsed

Nothing more wonderful can befall
cherries from the Black Forest than
to end up as a component of the
incomparable cake, *Schwarzwälder
Kirschtorte*, or as the essential
ingredient in kirsch, the clear
aromatic brandy more properly called
Kirschwasser. Both Black Forest
specialties are ideal for the afternoon
coffee table; the cake, moistened
with the fragrant kirsch and covered
with chocolate curls, whipped cream
and more cherries, is shown with an
old Meissen coffee cup and a glass
of the brandy.

Schwarzwälder Kirschtorte
BLACK FOREST CHERRY CAKE

To make chocolate curls to garnish the cake, the bar or chunks of chocolate
should be at room temperature but not soft. Hold the chocolate over wax
paper or foil and shave the bar or square into thin curls with a sharp narrow-
bladed vegetable peeler. Draw the peeler along the wide surface of the
chocolate for large curls, and along the narrow side for small ones. Handle
the chocolate as little as possible. Refrigerate or freeze the curls until you are
ready to use them.

Preheat the oven to 350°. With a pastry brush or paper towel, lightly coat

the bottoms and sides of three 7-inch round cake pans with soft butter using about 1 tablespoon of butter in all. Sprinkle 2 tablespoons of flour into each pan, tip them from side to side to spread the flour evenly, then invert the pans and rap them sharply on a table to remove any excess flour. Set the pans aside.

Clarify 10 tablespoons of butter in a small saucepan by melting it slowly over low heat without letting it brown. Let it rest for a minute off the heat, then skim off the foam. Spoon the clear butter into a bowl and set aside. Discard the milky solids at the bottom of the pan.

In an electric mixer, beat the eggs, vanilla and 1 cup of sugar together at high speed for at least 10 minutes, or until the mixture is thick and fluffy. (By hand with a rotary beater, this may take as long as 20 minutes of uninterrupted beating.) *Continued on next page*

Combine the ½ cup of sifted flour and the unsweetened cocoa in a sifter. A little at a time sift the mixture over the eggs, folding it in gently with a rubber spatula. Finally, add the clarified butter 2 tablespoons at a time. Do not overmix. Gently pour the batter into the prepared cake pans dividing it evenly among the three of them.

Bake in the middle of the oven for 10 to 15 minutes, or until a cake tester inserted into the center of each cake comes out clean. Remove the cakes from the oven and let them cool in the pans for about 5 minutes. Then run a sharp knife around the edge of each cake and turn them out on racks to cool completely.

Meanwhile, prepare the kirsch syrup in the following fashion: Combine ¾ cup of sugar and 1 cup of cold water in a small saucepan and bring to a boil over moderate heat, stirring only until the sugar dissolves. Boil briskly, uncovered, for 5 minutes, then remove the pan from the heat and when the syrup has cooled to lukewarm stir in the kirsch.

Transfer the cakes to a long strip of wax paper and prick each layer lightly in several places with the tines of a long fork. Sprinkle the layers evenly with the syrup and let them rest for at least 5 minutes.

If you are using fresh cherries for the filling, poach them in the following fashion: Remove their stems and pits, then combine them with 2 cups of water and ¾ cup of sugar in a small saucepan. Bring to a boil over high heat, then reduce the heat to low, simmer for 5 minutes, or until the cherries are tender. Drain them in a colander, discarding the syrup, and pat the cherries completely dry with paper towels. Canned cherries need only be rinsed in cold water and patted completely dry with paper towels.

In a large chilled bowl, beat the cream with a whisk or a rotary or electric beater until it thickens lightly. Then sift ½ cup of confectioners' sugar over the cream and continue beating until the cream forms firm peaks on the beater when it is lifted out of the bowl. Pour in the ¼ cup kirsch in a thin stream, and beat only until the kirsch is absorbed.

To assemble the cake, place one of the three layers in the center of a serving plate. With a spatula, spread the top with a ½-inch-thick layer of whipped cream and strew the cup of fresh or canned cherries over it leaving about ½ inch of cream free of cherries around the perimeter. Gently set a second layer on top of the cherries and spread it with ½ inch of whipped cream. Then set the third layer in place. Spread the top and sides of the cake with the remaining cream.

With your fingers, gently press chocolate curls into the cream on the sides of the cake and arrange a few chocolate curls and fresh or maraschino cherries attractively on top.

Dampfnudeln

DESSERT DUMPLINGS WITH VANILLA SAUCE

In a small, shallow bowl, sprinkle the yeast and 1 tablespoon of the sugar over the ¼ cup of lukewarm water. Let the mixture stand for 2 or 3 minutes, then stir it to dissolve the yeast. Set the bowl in a warm, draft-free place—such as a turned-off oven—for 4 or 5 minutes, or until the yeast bubbles and doubles in volume.

In a mixing bowl, combine the lukewarm milk, melted butter, the re-

To make 10 to 12 dumplings

DUMPLINGS

1½ teaspoons active dry yeast (½ envelope)

2 tablespoons sugar

¼ cup lukewarm water (110° to 115°)

¾ cup lukewarm milk (110° to 115°)

2 tablespoons butter, melted

¼ teaspoon salt

¾ cup sifted all-purpose flour

162

maining 1 tablespoon of sugar, and ¼ teaspoon of salt. Add the yeast and then the flour, beating until a smooth dough is formed. Gather the dough into a ball, and knead it vigorously on a lightly floured surface for about 5 minutes, or until it is smooth and elastic. Then return the dough to the bowl, dust it lightly with flour, and cover with a kitchen towel. Set the dough in a warm, draft-free place for about 45 minutes, or until it has doubled in bulk. Punch the dough down with one blow of your fist. Divide the dough into 10 or 12 equal pieces and with lightly floured hands shape them into balls. Place them 2 inches apart on a baking sheet, and set them aside in the same warm place to double in bulk again. Then, in a heavy 10-inch skillet 2½ inches deep or a flameproof casserole of similar size, melt 2 tablespoons of butter over moderate heat. When the foam subsides, stir in 2 tablespoons of sugar and ½ cup of cold milk. Bring to a boil, then arrange the dumplings side by side in the skillet and cover it tightly. Reduce the heat to low and simmer undisturbed for 15 minutes, or until the dumplings have absorbed all the liquid. Remove from the heat and set the dumplings aside in the covered skillet to keep them warm.

While the dumplings are poaching, make the vanilla sauce. Beat the egg yolks and sugar together with a wire whisk or a rotary or electric beater for 3 or 4 minutes, or until the yolks are thick and pale yellow. Bring 2 cups of cold milk to a boil in a heavy 2- to 3-quart saucepan and then, beating constantly with a whisk, pour the milk in a thin stream over the yolks. Pour the mixture back into the saucepan and cook over low heat, stirring constantly with a spoon, until the sauce is thick enough to coat the spoon lightly. Do not let the sauce come to a boil or it may curdle. Remove the pan from the heat and stir in the vanilla.

To serve, arrange the dumplings, bottom sides up, on a heated platter or individual serving plates and spoon the vanilla sauce over them.

POACHING LIQUID
2 tablespoons butter
2 tablespoons sugar
½ cup cold milk

VANILLA SAUCE
4 egg yolks, lightly beaten
½ cup sugar
2 cups cold milk
1 teaspoon vanilla extract

Apfelbettelmann
APPLE AND PUMPERNICKEL CRUMB DESSERT

Preheat the oven to 350° and coat the inner surfaces of a 6- to 8-cup soufflé or baking dish with 2 tablespoons of the softened butter. Melt 5 tablespoons of the butter and set aside.

In a large mixing bowl, soak the currants in the rum for 30 minutes. Then add the bread crumbs, chopped nuts, ½ cup of the sugar, melted butter, lemon peel and cinnamon, and stir until all the ingredients are well combined. With a small, sharp knife, quarter, peel and core the apples, and cut them lengthwise into ¼-inch slices. Drop the slices into another bowl and sprinkle them with the remaining ¼ cup of sugar, turning the slices about with a wooden spoon to coat them evenly. With a spatula, spread about one third of the bread-crumb mixture on the bottom of the baking dish and strew about one half of the apple slices evenly over it. Repeat with another layer of the bread-crumb mixture and cover with the remaining apples. Spread the remaining bread-crumb mixture over the apples and dot the crumbs with the remaining 2 tablespoons of butter. Bake in the middle of the oven for 30 to 40 minutes, or until the apples are tender and show no resistance when pierced with the tip of a sharp knife. Serve at once directly from the baking dish. If you like you may sprinkle the top with cinnamon and sugar.

To serve 4

9 tablespoons butter, softened
½ cup currants
5 tablespoons rum
1½ cups fine pumpernickel bread crumbs, made in the blender from fresh German-style dark pumpernickel bread
½ cup coarsely chopped almonds or hazelnuts
¾ cup sugar
1 teaspoon finely grated lemon peel
1½ teaspoons ground cinnamon
4 medium-sized tart cooking apples

To serve 4

1 pound boneless beef chuck, cut
    into 1-inch cubes
1 pound beef marrow bones, sawed,
    not chopped, into 1-inch pieces
2 quarts cold water
1 large onion, peeled and pierced
    with 2 whole cloves
1 small bay leaf
1 teaspoon salt
Freshly ground black pepper
1 cup coarsely diced peeled celery
    root
½ cup coarsely diced scraped carrots
½ cup coarsely diced scraped
    parsnips
1 cup coarsely diced leeks, including
    2 inches of the green top
2½ cups coarsely diced potatoes
One recipe *Spätzle (below)*
1 tablespoon finely chopped parsley

To make about 4 cups

3 cups all-purpose flour
1 teaspoon salt
¼ teaspoon ground nutmeg
4 eggs
1 cup milk
1 cup fine dry bread crumbs
    (optional)
¼ pound (1 stick) butter (optional)

To serve 8

1 tablespoon sugar
2 teaspoons salt
½ teaspoon freshly ground black
    pepper
2 cups cold water
9 medium-sized boiling potatoes
    (about 3 pounds), peeled and cut
    into 1-inch cubes
1 pound tart cooking apples, peeled,
    cored and quartered
½ pound lean bacon, cut into ¼-
    inch dice
2 medium-sized onions, peeled and
    sliced ⅛-inch thick and separated
    into rings
1 teaspoon cider vinegar

Gaisburger Marsch
VEGETABLE-BEEF SOUP WITH TINY DUMPLINGS

In a heavy 5- to 6-quart flameproof casserole or soup pot, bring the beef, bones and water to a boil over high heat, skimming off the foam and scum as they rise to the surface. Reduce the heat to the lowest possible point, add the onion pierced with cloves, bay leaf, salt and a few grindings of pepper, and simmer, partially covered, for 1½ hours, skimming whenever necessary. Then remove the onion and bay leaf, discard them, and transfer the bones to a plate.

With a small spoon or the tip of a knife, scoop out the marrow from the bones, add it to the soup and discard the bones. Add the celery root, carrots, parsnips, leeks and potatoes and simmer, undisturbed for 30 minutes, or until the vegetables and meat are tender. Stir the *Spätzle* into the simmering soup and cook for 1 or 2 minutes longer to heat them through. Then add the parsley, taste for seasoning, and serve either from a large heated tureen or in individual soup bowls.

Spätzle
TINY DUMPLINGS

In a large mixing bowl, combine the flour, ½ teaspoon of the salt and the nutmeg. Break up the eggs with a fork and beat them into the flour mixture. Pour in the milk in a thin stream, stirring constantly with a large spoon, and continue to stir until the dough is smooth.

Bring 2 quarts of water and the remaining ½ teaspoon of salt to a boil in a heavy 4- to 5-quart saucepan. Set a large colander, preferably one with large holes, over the saucepan and with a spoon press the dough a few tablespoons at a time through the colander directly into the boiling water. Stir the *Spätzle* gently to prevent them from sticking to each other, then boil briskly for 5 to 8 minutes, or until they are tender. Taste to make sure. Drain the *Spätzle* thoroughly in a sieve or colander. When *Spätzle* are served as a separate dish with roasted meats, such as *Sauerbraten (page 22)*, they are traditionally presented sprinkled with toasted bread crumbs. To toast the crumbs, melt ¼ pound of butter in a heavy 6- to 8-inch skillet over moderate heat. When the foam almost subsides, drop in 1 cup of bread crumbs and cook, stirring constantly, until the crumbs are golden brown.

Himmel und Erde
POTATOES WITH APPLES

In a heavy 12-inch skillet combine the sugar, 1 teaspoon of the salt and the black pepper in 2 cups of water. Then drop in the potatoes and apples and bring the water to a boil over high heat. Reduce the heat to moderate and cover the skillet tightly. Simmer, undisturbed, until the potatoes are tender but not falling apart.

Meanwhile, in an 8- to 10-inch skillet, cook the bacon over moderate heat until brown and crisp. With a slotted spoon, spread it out on a double thickness of paper towels to drain. Add the onions to the fat remaining in the skillet and cook over moderate heat, stirring frequently, for 8 to 10 minutes, or until the rings are soft and light brown.

Just before serving, stir the remaining teaspoon of salt and the teaspoon of vinegar into the potatoes and apples, and taste for seasoning. Then transfer the entire contents of the skillet to a heated bowl and serve topped with the onion rings and bacon.

Griessklösse
FARINA DUMPLINGS

In a heavy 2- to 3-quart saucepan heat the milk, ½ teaspoon of the salt, the nutmeg and the butter over moderate heat until the butter dissolves and the milk comes to a boil. Pour in the farina slowly, so the milk never stops boiling, stirring it constantly with a wooden spoon. Reduce the heat to low and simmer, stirring frequently, until the farina thickens enough to hold its shape in the spoon. Remove the pan from the heat and beat in the eggs, one at a time. When the farina is cool enough to handle, shape it into round dumplings about 1½ inches in diameter.

Bring 2 quarts of water and 2 teaspoons of salt to a boil in a large saucepan or soup pot and drop in as many dumplings as the pot will hold comfortably. Stir once or twice to prevent the dumplings from sticking to one another or to the bottom of the pan. Reduce the heat to low and simmer, undisturbed, for 15 to 20 minutes. Then, with a slotted spoon, transfer the dumplings to a heated platter. Serve them as a hot dessert, sprinkled with cinnamon-sugar or accompanied by applesauce or stewed fruit *(page 138)*. They may instead be topped with melted butter to accompany a roast or stew. Or they may be made smaller to garnish a soup.

To make about 2 dozen dumplings

3 cups milk
2½ teaspoons salt
⅛ teaspoon ground nutmeg
3 tablespoons butter
1½ cups regular farina, not the quick-cooking type
3 eggs
Cinnamon-sugar, applesauce, or stewed fruit compote *(page 138)*

Kalbshaxe mit Gewürzgurkensosse
VEAL SHANKS IN PICKLE SAUCE

In a heavy 8-quart casserole or soup pot, combine the veal shanks, onion, carrot, leek, parsley, vinegar, clove, bay leaf, peppercorns, and 1 teaspoon salt. Pour in enough water to just cover the shanks. Bring to a boil over high heat, skimming off the foam and scum that rise to the surface. Reduce the heat to its lowest point, cover the casserole, and simmer for 1 hour, or until the meat shows no resistance when pierced with the tip of a small, sharp knife. With tongs, transfer the shanks to a plate. Strain the cooking stock through a fine sieve set over a large bowl, skim off all fat and set the stock aside. When the veal shanks are cool enough to handle, trim off the fat with a small knife and cut the meat away from the bones. Discard the bones, and cut the meat into 1-inch pieces.

In a heavy 10- to 12-inch skillet, melt the butter over moderate heat. When the foam subsides, add ½ cup of the chopped onions and cook, stirring frequently for 5 minutes, or until they are soft and transparent but not brown. Stir in the flour and cook for another minute or so. Gradually pour in 3 cups of the reserved stock, stirring constantly with a whisk until the sauce is lightly thickened and smooth. Add the chopped pickle, ½ teaspoon salt and a few grindings of pepper, and simmer, uncovered, for 10 minutes, stirring occasionally. Then add the veal and simmer for another 5 minutes, or only long enough to heat it through. Serve at once from a deep, heated platter or serving bowl.

To serve 4 to 6

2 meaty veal shanks (about 4 to 5 pounds), each sawed into 2 or 3 pieces
1 medium onion peeled and cut into ¼-inch slices
1 carrot, scraped and cut into ¼-inch slices
1 leek, white part only, thoroughly washed and cut into ⅛-inch slices
2 parsley sprigs
2 tablespoons cider vinegar
1 whole clove
1 small bay leaf
3 whole black peppercorns
1 teaspoon salt

SAUCE
4 tablespoons butter
½ cup finely chopped onions
3 tablespoons flour
1 cup finely chopped dill pickle
½ teaspoon salt
Freshly ground black pepper

IX

Baking Raised to a Fine Art

Cookies called *Springerle*,
seen here in a pattern of
cookie molds and finished
cookies, proclaim the
Christmas season with
enchanting designs of
yuletide symbols and
traditional figures such as
St. Nicholas *(center right)*.
The festive sweets are made
of simple egg, sugar and
flour dough flavored with
anise and lemon.

Of all the German ways of preparing food, baking has always been the most interesting and important. Intimately linked with both the economic and spiritual lives of the nation, it has played an almost mystical role throughout German history. Bread was honored in pagan times as the staff of life and also as a sacred symbol; in Christian times it has been thought of as more than a food because of its connection with the bread of the Eucharist. Its uses and abuses have been a constant theme of German prose and poetry. One of Grimm's fairy tales tells of a mother whose beloved child died. Wishing to bury the child in the noblest funeral clothes, she baked a pair of shoes with the finest and whitest flour. But in the other world, as in this one, it was a sin to tread upon bread, and the dead child could not find peace in his grave until his mother took the shoes of bread off his feet and put ordinary ones on.

In our age of waste, when we toss stale bread into the garbage can, it may be hard to understand why Germans have cared so desperately for it. Bread has always been the basic food of the German people and it still is. The lack of bread during the First and Second World Wars and the postwar periods haunts the affluent Germans of today, even though they rarely speak of it.

Standing alone, the word "bread" means wheat bread, for wheat has always been the most important of all grains to Western man; we qualify other breads with the name of their grain—rye, corn, barley. Wheat is the only grain that can make a bread both soft and light. Without wheat, there cannot be fine bread—and this is why the art of decorative baking has flourished mainly in the wheat-growing regions of central and southern Germany.

In northern Germany, where the climate is best suited to rye and barley, we find solid dark loaves and flat breads, nourishing enough, but plain indeed compared to the fancy bakings of the southern regions.

Until the modern science of nutrition made dark breads fashionable, white bread was a status symbol. In earlier days in Germany, the rich ate white bread when they could; generally speaking, the poor ate dark rye bread. White bread was baked almost exclusively in the cities; more often than not, rural bakers were prevented by guild restrictions from baking white bread. Such restrictions were easy to impose, for in Germany, as in most of Central and Southern Europe, comparatively little bread was baked at home. In such places as Scandinavia or the American frontier, farms were scattered and people widely dispersed; in Germany and Italy, people huddled together in villages and towns to repel enemy attacks. Thus, most Germans have always spent their lives in enormously overcrowded surroundings, without privacy or the means for such elaborate housekeeping as home baking.

To make matters worse, Central and Southern Europe have always suffered a chronic shortage of fuel, particularly in periods when men used wood for everything from masts for ships to the utensils of everyday life. In search of wood, the ancient Romans almost deforested Italy; in Germany, governmental edicts protected the forests from that fate and turned them into well-cared-for preserves (the *Förster*, or forest warden, is a man of almost mystical strength and authority in German tradition). Obviously, centralizing bread-baking in communal ovens or professional bakeries helped to save fuel. It also facilitated the application of guild or governmental regulations.

The daily bread of earlier Germans did not differ radically from our own. A 1466 portrait of a Nürnberg baker shows both big, round, dark loaves and small, oblong, white ones, as well as what we now would call finger rolls and pretzels. Such daily breads were a far cry from the fancy bakings of medieval and modern Germany. On festive occasions, bread was a feast for the eyes as well as the palate. The baker became a sculptor, molding his dough into complex forms and patterns, almost always with ancient, symbolic meanings. These are the famous German *Gebildbrote*, or "picture breads," which take the shapes of horses, birds, deer, fish and serpents, flowers, sheaves of wheat, wreaths and stars. There are also sculptured breads in the shapes of men and women, and breads bearing superimposed designs of such Christian symbols as the loaves and fishes.

Modern picture breads may derive from symbolic offerings to the gods and the ritual cults of the dead; certainly breads were so used in ancient times in regions as disparate as Egypt, Rome and Northern Europe. In this way bread took the place of sacrificial beasts, which the poor could ill afford. A braided bread may have stood for an offering of hair; a bread in the form of a wheel for the sun; another in the form of a wreath for eternity; and a *Kipfel,* or crescent roll, for the moon. Thus the *croissant*, which graces the breakfast tables of all Europe, may be a religious symbol far older than popular legend suggests. According to tradition, crescent rolls were first produced by the bakers of Vienna, who expressed their rejoicing in the Western victory over the Turks in 1683 with a roll in the shape of the Muhammadan crescent. But the cult of the moon is far older than any conflict of Turk and Christian. At the monastery of St. Gall in Switzerland, bakings called *panis lu-*

natis (bread of the moon) were made as early as the Eighth Century. And on Christmas Day in 1217, long before the Turks stood before Vienna, the bakers of that city paid homage to Duke Leopold of Babenberg with an offering of crescent-shaped rolls.

However pagan their origin, sculptured and decorated breads became part of Germany's enduring cuisine. Baked and eaten on the various feast days of the year, they never quite lost their sacred character. The pretzel, one of the ancient shapes, may once have been a symbol of the solar cycle, and it was clearly held in special reverence as late as 1256, when the authorities of Landshut decreed that a baker who did not bake his pretzels from fine, white flour would be severely punished. At Christmas time in Germany today there are still bread Santas and braided breads in the shape of stars; at Easter, a bunny made of bread still lays a colored egg from under his tail. Godparents still give their godchildren gifts of large, intricate breads in the shapes of men and women. The varieties of these breads are too numerous to list here, and so are the minor variations that distinguish them by region or even by town, but they are a common German inheritance. To this day they must be baked with white wheat flour.

How and why did cookies first become distinguished from bread? The line between them is shadowy, for many of their characteristics are shared. But one fact is significant: Cookies can be shaped and molded in many more different forms than bread, because they are made with relatively unleavened doughs that are far easier to control than the yeast doughs of bread. Yeast doughs tend to rise in every direction, as anybody who has ever tried to bake bread in fancy shapes well knows. Even the professional bakers of Germany, who prepare breads in elaborate human shapes, animals, houses and whole scenes (I once saw a baked Garden of Eden), must often do their work many times over before it is perfect.

Not even the earliest cookies, however, were totally unleavened. The "baking powder" of old was powdered hartshorn, made from the antlers of harts and deer. The modern equivalent of hartshorn is powdered ammonium carbonate, still used for cookie baking in Germany and Scandinavia for the lovely, very crisp texture it imparts. Ammonium carbonate can be bought in American drugstores and substituted for equal quantities of baking powder in a cookie recipe.

Another way of distinguishing cakes and cookies from bread is by sweetness, but there are exceptions to this rule. In earlier days, unsweetened cake dough made from white flour and eggs was cut into snippets and fried in deep lard. Formed as a twist, bow or disc, a *Schmalzgebackenes*, "something fried in lard," was known under a number of different names—*Flädli, Strübli, Kücheli, Krapfen* and many more. Such pastries are still made in the rural parts of southern Germany, but they are not so plentiful as in earlier times, when heaped platters of the glistening, crisp, unsweet *Schmalzgebackenes* were brought forth at church fairs and on market days, at weddings and christenings—wherever and whenever people had something to celebrate.

On the whole, however, it was sweetness that meant festivity and joy to the Germans of old. It is interesting that after two world wars brought hunger to modern Germany, the national taste veered even more sharply to sweet things, as if to compensate for the insufficiency of the wartime diet.

In a 16th Century drawing, a satisfied baker in a Nürnberg monastery admires the designs he has imprinted on spicy *Lebkuchen* (gingerbread) by pressing the dough into intricately carved molds. Nürnberg, renowned then as a spice-trade center, is still famous for its spice and honey cakes and, in fact, is known as the gingerbread capital of the world.

Continued on page 173

Homemade Bread from a Village Oven

Every two weeks Frau Klaus of Mettingen, Germany, carries unbaked loaves of sourdough bread and sweet pastries through the streets of her small village. She is heading for the communal baking house—an institution that grew up at a time when professional guildsmen were in sole charge of a community's ovens. Joined by her daughter-in-law *(opposite)*, Frau Klaus personally tends the fat, round loaves as they bake deep inside the wood-heated oven. The resulting bread, made with both white wheat and dark rye flours, turns out to be coarsely textured and a rich brown when she cuts it *(right)*. Although identified simply as *Holzofen-Bauernbrot* (wood-oven peasant bread), this particular bread may be unique. Frau Klaus, like a number of old-fashioned cooks, has never recorded the recipe.

The large number of candy shops in Germany testifies to this fact, and so does the increased sugar content of much German wine. Many a German wine maker has said to me that his father would have rejected the wine being made today as far too sweet.

The earliest sweeteners known in Germany were honey and dried fruits, rather than sugar. We can hardly imagine a world without an abundance of sugar, but sugar was scarce in Europe until the 17th Century when the sugar plantations of the Caribbean islands began to export large quantities. Until then, sugar had trickled into Europe as an immensely precious commodity from the Near East, brought by the Crusaders and by Arab traders. (The very word "sugar" comes from the Arabic *sukkar*, which in turn derived from the Sanskrit word *sarkara*—"gravel" or "pebble"—the name by which sugar was known in India many centuries before the coming of Christ.)

It is understandable, then, that honey cakes and fruit breads are the oldest forms of Germany's sweet bakings, or *Süssgebäck*. *Hutzelbrot*, a plain fruit bread in an archaic but delicious form, is made and loved to this day in southern Germany, but the most popular fruit breads are the various *Stollen* made for Christmas, the time of greatest rejoicing. The most famous was developed in Dresden *(page 193)*; correctly made, it consists of just enough dryish dough to hold together a treasure of the strongly flavored tidbits of Christmas—almonds, raisins, currants and gaily colored *glacéed* fruit.

A kind of cultural history of the regions of Germany could be written in terms of their honey cakes and honey-sweetened cookies. These pastries were not made for eating alone; they also served as ceremonial and sentimental gifts and sometimes sported portraits of the donors. The craftsmen who carved the molds were talented sculptors, expressing the German pride in beautiful things; they never meant their cakes and cookies, rich with precious spices, fruits and honey, to be gobbled down thoughtlessly. And the bakers who produced the pastry hearts and the angels, the wreaths and all the other festive shapes—they were artists, too, proud of their craft and practicing it for people with high artistic standards.

The richness of this heritage can still be seen in the old German baking molds, made of wood, ceramics or metal, that are preserved in museums or recalled in histories like *Liebeskutsche, Reitersmann, Nikolaus und Kinderbringer* by Albert Walzer. Its very title *(The Lovers' Coach, the Horseman, St. Nicholas and the Bringer of Children)* suggests the variety of the bakers' art. The molds depict babies swaddled together, symbolic figures mounted on roosters, storks swinging babies from their beaks, scenes of courtly gallantry, Eve standing under the Tree of Knowledge from which Adam hangs upside down, harvest scenes, sentimental lovers' mottoes—all in the styles of successive artistic periods, from early Gothic through the Renaissance, Baroque, Rococo and 19th Century Biedermeier. Small softwood molds served for marzipan and delicate egg bakings, while large molds for the robust dough of the honey cakes were made from clay, pewter or the solid wood of fruit and nut trees. The cakes and cookies that came from these molds were gratefully accepted by the highest or most humbly born as graceful, desirable presents, just as handsome sweets are welcomed by the Germans of today.

Not all Germany's favorite cakes and cookies were made from the dark, spicy honey doughs. There were also the pale yellow *Springerle* cookies *(page*

Bread is the undisputed staff of life in Germany; it is plentiful and is varied enough to satisfy a people who eat it in some form at almost every meal. At present more than 200 different kinds of bread are produced in West Germany alone; and although many of these are regional, there is a generous assortment in all parts of the country. In the photograph on the opposite page, typical German rolls appear in baskets in the center foreground and at the center left. Various dark breads are also in the foreground and at the top of the photograph. White breads, including the decorative "picture breads," are shown at the center and upper-right-hand sections. The numbers superimposed on the breads are listed below with the names and descriptions of the breads.

ROLLS
1. *Kümmelbrötchen*, an all-purpose roll topped with caraway seeds.
2. *Mohnbrötchen*, a poppy-seed roll usually eaten at breakfast.
3. *Semmel*, a breakfast roll.
4. *Römischer*, a roll with caraway seeds.
5. *Kaisersemmel*, a variation of *Semmel (3)*.
6. *Eiweckerl*, perhaps the most common breakfast roll of all.
7. *Salzweckerl*, a salted snack roll.

DARK BREADS
8. *Schrotbrot*, a whole-wheat bread.
9. *Vollkornbrot*, made from whole rye or rye-and-wheat kernels that are cracked or rough-ground. The loaf at the lower right is dusted with oatmeal.
10. *Grahambrot*, cracked-wheat bread named for and based on the recipe of the 19th Century American food faddist, the Rev. Sylvester Graham.
11. *Roggenbrot* (rye bread), also known in southern Germany as *Bauernbrot*. The loaf at the left is dusted with flour.
12. *Schwarzwälderbrot* (Black Forest bread), a rye bread borrowed from Switzerland.
13. Pumpernickel, a rye bread from Westphalia.
14. *Leinsambrot*, a rye bread with linseeds.
15. *Graubrot*, a mixture of rye and wheat eaten in northern Germany.
16. *Roggenmischbrot*, made from a mixture of flours, mostly rye.

PLAIN WHITE BREADS
17. *Buttermilchbrot* (buttermilk bread).
18. *Stangenbrot*, open-face sandwich bread.
19 and 20. *Weissbrot* (white bread).
21. *Weissbrot* with almonds.

PICTURE BREADS *(Gebildbrote)*
22. *Salamander* (salamanders).
23. *Schildkrötchen* (little turtles).
24. *Zopf*, braid bread.
25. *Sonnenrad* (sun wheel).
26. *Zopf* with almonds.
27. *Geige* (violin).
28. *Mohnzopf*, braid bread with poppy seeds.
29. *Salzzopf*, salt-topped braid bread.
30. *Brezeln* (pretzels).
31. *Hörnchen* (little horns, or crescents).

SALT STICKS
32. *Salzstangen*.

CRACKERS
33. *Knäckebrot*, cracked-wheat bread.

182), of which only the simplest molded shapes are made today in America. In Swabia, their original home, *Springerle* molds developed into huge affairs adorned with large human figures—ladies in crinolines, top-hatted gentlemen, horsemen and soldiers. Though we now know *Springerle* only in their natural yellow color, it was the fashion at the beginning of the 19th Century to tint them in every detail, as photographs were tinted before the days of color photography. Another form of baking that flourished in 19th Century Germany used the vegetable gum tragacanth, flour or potato starch, water and sugar, and was frequently flavored with rose water. This kind of dough decorated *Torten* and candies, but it was also shaped by hand or molded into rectangular picture cookies. These so-called *Tragantfiguren* are among the prettiest of all German bakings.

But the cakes most closely associated with the fine art of German baking are the honey cakes *(page 181)* and spice cakes *(Recipe Booklet)*, or *Lebkuchen*. Spice and honey cakes were made in many German cities and sold from special stalls at fairs, carnivals and markets, just as hot dogs are sold in America. The best-known cakes and cookies—the *Printen* from Aachen, the tall, round *Bomben* from Breslau and Liegnitz, the *Kathrinchen* from Thorn, the *Pfefferbrot* from Köln, the *Spekulatius* of the Rhineland—competed with one another for customers in earlier days as they do now. But Nürnberg topped all its rivals to win a fame that has endured to this day.

As the meeting point of the great European trade routes, Nürnberg was a center of the spice trade. Ginger, pepper, cloves and even saffron were readily available for the dark-brown, fragrant cakes. Nürnberg was also near famous beekeeping districts scattered in extensive forests around the city, and thus had easy access to another basic ingredient of its sweet product. The bakers of Nürnberg honey cakes were organized in special guilds, which enjoyed privileges denied to all other bakers; in fact, the working quarters of the honey-cake bakers were strictly segregated from those who made bread.

Through the centuries the cakes were baked in many shapes. For inexpensive everyday consumption there were plain, flat *Zelten*, sold in bundles or wrapped in gaudily colored papers. For religious holidays, there were saints and Santas; for temporal ones, horsemen and windmills, babes and animals. Decoration was an especially important aspect of *Lebkuchen*, and reflected the basic artistic styles of the times. Piped sugar, white or colored, defined and emphasized the cakes' shapes. During the Romantic period, gaily colored pictures like those on old-fashioned Christmas cards, with angels, cooing doves or roses, were affixed to the shiny brown *Lebkuchen*. For birthdays, weddings, or christenings there were *Lebkuchen* with piped-on names or with wise sayings in much the style of modern fortune cookies.

Many of the most popular *Lebkuchen*, designed as lovers' gifts, were heart-shaped, and a book could be written about their decorations and inscriptions. Some held little mirrors at their centers, with suitable mottoes inscribed around the rims; others entrusted a soldier to God's care, so that he might be saved for his sweetheart. In his short story "Romeo und Julia auf dem Dorfe" ("A Village Romeo and Juliet"), the 19th Century Swiss author Gottfried Keller, tells a tale of two doomed lovers that could have taken place anywhere in rural Germany. At one point in the story, the heroine gives her sweetheart a *Lebkuchen* heart with this inscription (I translate the words for

174

their meaning rather than their literal rustic lyricism): "A sweet almond kernel is in this heart, but my love for you is sweeter than the almond." The back of the heart reads: "When you have eaten this heart, do not forget this saying: 'My brown eye will break ere my love will break.'"

As popular as *Lebkuchen* in both early and modern times, is marzipan, a delicious paste of almonds and sugar, flavored with rose water or orange. It has created a whole German art of lovely shapes, decoration and packaging. Marzipan is not a German invention, nor was it developed in France or Scandinavia, where it is also popular. It is, in fact, not a European invention at all, but the gift of the Near East, where almond trees and sugar cane have been cultivated for thousands of years. The Persians knew it as early as 965, and the people of the West learned of the delicious sweetmeats through the Crusades and the Arab conquests, just as they learned of melons, rice and spices. The Holy Roman Emperor Charles IV received gifts of gilded marzipan loaves in Siena in 1368. In Germany, domestically produced marzipan is first mentioned in the 15th Century, and from that time on it was an essential dessert course at the tables of the great. Lübeck, the trading center and seaport of the Hanseatic League, soon became the most famous center for the manufacture of marzipan, and has remained so to this day.

From the beginning, the shapes of German marzipan were elaborate. Not only animals, flowers, vegetables, trees and human figures, but whole pieces representing historical, martial or mythological scenes were formed from the sweet, pliable paste. At the Convocation of Speyer in 1526, the centerpiece for one banquet was a molded marzipan gilded and decorated with a princely coat of arms and surrounded by a border in the shape of a picket fence that was also made of marzipan.

Marzipan was rarely served in its natural off-white color. The pieces were colored, either in delicate, romantic pastel shades, or realistically, to imitate the color of potatoes and radishes, apples and cherries in the tiny marzipan fruits and vegetables that became part of the German Christmas. For centuries, marzipan was *the* sweetmeat, the dessert of all who could afford it. While the incredible elaboration of past centuries has disappeared from today's marzipan, it is still the most charming of all confections.

Charming, too, are the boxes in which German marzipan was shipped all over the world. Many old ones are preserved in the museums of German cities, and like all the baked goods I have described in this chapter they reflect the art and spirit of their times. One of the prettiest I have ever seen dates from 1872. It bears the words: "Lübecker Marzipan / A Sweet Picture Book for Our Little People"; and on its top is a view of Lübeck and a picture of a baker holding a large loaf of marzipan and surrounded by "little people"—four eager children, dressed in the Victorian costumes of the day.

The Elegant Pastries of Afternoon Coffee Time

Afternoon *Kaffee-Trinken* is a social ritual Germans cherish, partly because the custom includes eating the richest, most beautiful pastries that *Hausfrauen* and professional cooks can concoct. If she wishes, a woman may join her friends for coffee at a *Konditorei* (*page 59*), where the assortment of pastries matches every whim. But the most gracious *Kaffee-Trinken* takes place in the relaxed atmosphere of one's own living room around a *Kaffeetisch* laid with flowers, choice porcelain and a variety of cakes and cookies. In the cheerful setting above, freesias blend with an exquisite 18th Century Meissen service.

On the right, an *Obsttorte* (fruit tart) contributes another burst of color with its glazed fruits encircled by toasted almonds. Lending mellow tones at the left is a *Frankfurter Kranz* (Frankfurt wreath, *page 180*), which combines rum-flavored dough and cream filling with a finish of praline crumbs. To complete the coffee-time delights, a plate of cookies is tucked between the crystal bases of the cake stands: decorative *S-Gebäck* (*page 194*), chocolate *Haselnussmakronen* (hazelnut macaroons, *page 182*), sugared *Mandel-Halbmonde* (almond crescents, *page 194*) and *Spritzgebäck* (*page 183*).

CHAPTER IX RECIPES

To make one 10-inch round loaf

¼ cup lukewarm water (110° to 115°)

3 packages or cakes of active dry or compressed yeast

2 teaspoons sugar

½ cup lukewarm milk (110° to 115°)

4 cups sifted all-purpose flour

2 eggs, at room temperature

¼ pound unsalted butter, cut into ¼-inch pieces and softened to room temperature

1 tablespoon salt

1 tablespoon caraway seeds

Cornmeal

Weissbrot mit Kümmel

WHITE BREAD WITH CARAWAY SEEDS

Pour the lukewarm water into a small, shallow bowl and sprinkle the yeast and ½ teaspoon of the sugar over it. Let the yeast and sugar stand 2 or 3 minutes, then stir together to dissolve them completely. Set in a warm, draft-free place, such as an unlighted oven, for 3 to 5 minutes, or until the mixture almost doubles in volume.

Transfer the yeast to a large mixing bowl and stir in the milk. Beat in 3 cups of the sifted flour about ¼ cup at a time. Then beat in the eggs one at a time, and finally beat in the bits of butter. Continue to beat until the dough can be gathered into a compact ball.

Place the ball on a lightly floured board and knead in the remaining cup of flour, a few tablespoons at a time, pushing the dough down with the heels of your hands, pressing it forward and folding it back on itself. Knead until all the flour is incorporated and the dough is stiff and quite dry. Shape it into a rough ball, place it in a mixing bowl, and add enough cold water to cover it by several inches. In 10 to 15 minutes, the top of the dough should rise above the surface of the water.

Remove the dough from the water and pat the surface as dry as you can with paper towels. Return it to a floured board, punch it down, and sprinkle with the remaining 1½ teaspoons of sugar, the salt and the caraway seeds. Lightly flouring the dough from time to time, knead it for about 10 minutes, or until smooth and elastic. Pat and shape the dough into a round loaf about 8 inches in diameter, mounded slightly in the center.

Sprinkle a baking sheet lightly with cornmeal, place the dough in the center of the sheet and cover it loosely with a kitchen towel. Let the dough rise in a warm draft-free place for about 30 minutes, or until it doubles in bulk. Preheat the oven to 375°.

Bake the bread in the middle of the preheated oven for about 1 hour. The crust should be a light golden color. Remove the bread from the baking sheet and cool it on a rack before serving.

To serve 8 to 10

PASTRY

2 cups all-purpose flour

¼ cup sugar

2 egg yolks

1 hard-cooked egg yolk, forced through a fine sieve

½ pound (2 sticks) unsalted butter, melted and cooled

Obsttorte

MIXED FRUIT TART

Sift the flour and sugar into a large bowl and make a well in the center. Drop in the raw egg yolks and the sieved, cooked yolk. Mix them together with your fingertips or a large spoon. When the ingredients are well combined, mix in the melted butter a few tablespoons at a time, and continue to mix until the dough is smooth and pliable. On a lightly floured surface pat and shape the dough into a roll about 6 inches long and 2½ inches in diameter, wrap it in wax paper and refrigerate for at least 30 minutes.

Preheat the oven to 325°. With a sharp knife, carefully slice the pastry roll into rounds about ¼ inch thick. Arrange the rounds in a single layer in a 9-inch springform cake pan. With your fingers, gently pat the rounds and smooth the edges so that they completely cover the bottom of the pan and no empty spaces show between them. Stand the remaining slices around the sides of the pan, pressing them down about ½ inch into the bottom layer to secure them to the base and to create a scalloped effect around the top. Refrigerate for 10 minutes, then prick the surface of the dough all over with the tines of a fork without penetrating through to the bottom of the pan. Bake in the middle of the oven for 40 minutes, or until the pastry is firm and light brown. Transfer the pastry shell to a cake rack and let it cool completely before removing the sides of the pan.

In a heatproof measuring cup or small bowl, sprinkle the gelatin over the fruit juice. When the gelatin has softened for 2 or 3 minutes, set the cup in a small skillet of simmering water and cook over low heat, stirring constantly, until the gelatin dissolves completely. Remove the cup from the skillet and let the gelatin cool slightly.

With a pastry brush, lightly coat the bottom of the pastry shell with the gelatin to seal it and let it set for about 5 minutes. Then with paper towels, pat the pieces of fruit you plan to use completely dry. Arrange the fruit on the gelatin, in decorative concentric circles, overlapping the pieces slightly to cover the bottom of the shell completely and filling the shell to within about ¼ inch of the top. The number of layers you will need depends on the size and shape of the fruit.

Glaze the final layer with a thin coating of gelatin. If the gelatin becomes too thick to brush smoothly over the fruit, return it to the warm water for several minutes. Set the tart aside.

Preheat the oven to 350°. Spread the almonds in a shallow baking pan and bake or toast, turning them frequently, for 5 minutes, or until they are light brown. With a wire whisk or a rotary or electric beater, beat the egg white until it thickens slightly. Sprinkle the sugar over it and beat until the white forms firm peaks on the beater when it is lifted out of the bowl.

With a small metal spatula coat the outside of the pastry shell evenly with the meringue and press the almond slices against it to secure them. The entire outer surface should finally be covered with almonds.

Beat the cream with a whisk or a rotary or electric beater until it thickens slightly, then sprinkle with confectioners' sugar and vanilla, and continue beating until the mixture forms stiff peaks on the beater when it is lifted out of the bowl. Transfer the whipped cream to a bowl and serve it separately with the tart.

FILLING

1 envelope unflavored gelatin

1¼ cups canned fruit juice, preferably a mixture of juices drained from canned fruit

5 to 6 cups combined fresh and drained, canned fruit such as strawberries, raspberries, orange sections, apple wedges, canned peach halves or slices, pitted green plums, pear halves, pitted apricots, pineapple slices

ALMOND COATING

1½ cups thinly sliced blanched almonds

1 egg white

1 tablespoon superfine sugar

TOPPING

1 cup chilled heavy cream

1 tablespoon confectioners' sugar

A few drops of vanilla extract

To make an *Obsttorte* pastry shell, shape the dough into a 2½-inch roll, chill and cut into ¼-inch slices.

Fit one layer of the slices into a 9-inch springform pan and press them together to cover the bottom.

Stand the remaining pastry slices around the edge of the pan, pressing them firmly into the corners.

THE CAKE

1 tablespoon butter, softened
2 tablespoons flour
¼ pound plus 4 tablespoons
   unsalted butter (1½ sticks),
   softened
1 cup sugar
1 cup all-purpose flour
1½ teaspoons finely grated lemon
   peel
6 eggs, at room temperature
¾ cup cornstarch
1 tablespoon double-acting baking
   powder
¾ cup rum

FILLING

10 egg yolks, at room temperature
1 pound unsalted butter (4 sticks),
   softened
1⅓ cups sugar
⅛ teaspoon cream of tartar
⅔ cup water
½ cup rum

TOPPING

1 tablespoon butter
1 cup sugar
½ cup cold water
1 cup blanched almonds

Frankfurter Kranz

LAYER CAKE WITH BUTTER-CREAM FILLING AND PRALINE TOPPING

Frankfurter Kranz is a frankly extravagant cake that uses more than a dozen eggs, almost a pound and a half of butter, and over a cup of rum. Even in Germany, it is a special treat served only on the most elegant occasions.

Preheat the oven to 325°. With a pastry brush or paper towel, coat the bottom, sides and tube of a 9-inch tube cake pan with 1 tablespoon of soft butter. Sprinkle the butter with 2 tablespoons of flour, tip it from side to side to spread the flour evenly, then invert the pan and rap the bottom sharply to remove the excess flour.

In a large bowl, cream ¼ pound plus 4 tablespoons of butter, 1 cup of sugar, 1 tablespoon of the flour and the lemon peel together by mashing and beating them against the sides of the bowl with a large spoon. Then beat in the eggs, one at a time, and continue to beat until smooth. Combine the remaining flour, cornstarch and baking powder, and sift them into the butter a little at a time, beating well after each addition.

Pour the batter into the cake pan and bake in the middle of the oven for 40 minutes, or until a cake tester inserted in the center comes out clean. Let the cake cool in the pan for 10 minutes. Then run a knife around the inside edges of the pan, place a wire cake rack on top and, grasping rack and pan firmly together, turn them over. The cake should slide easily out of the pan. When the cake has cooled completely, slice it crosswise with a large, sharp knife into three equal layers. (It is easiest to cut if baked a day in advance.) Spread the layers on a long strip of foil or wax paper and sprinkle each layer with ¼ cup of rum.

To make the butter-cream filling, beat the 10 egg yolks in a large bowl with a whisk or a rotary or electric beater until they are thick and lemon colored. Set the beaten yolks aside. Cream the pound of soft butter by mashing and beating it against the sides of a bowl with a large spoon until it is light and fluffy. Set it aside.

Bring 1⅓ cups of sugar, ⅛ teaspoon cream of tartar and ⅔ cup of water to a boil over moderate heat in a small saucepan, stirring only until the sugar dissolves. Increase the heat to high and boil the syrup briskly without stirring until it reaches a temperature of 236° on a candy thermometer, or until a drop spooned into cold water immediately forms a soft ball.

Pour the syrup in a thin stream into the reserved egg yolks, beating constantly with a whisk or a rotary or electric beater. Continue beating for 4 or 5 minutes longer, or until the mixture is thick and smooth. Gradually add ½ cup of rum, and continue to beat until the mixture has cooled to room temperature and is thick. Now beat in the reserved butter, a tablespoon or so at a time, and when it is completely absorbed, cover the bowl with wax paper or plastic wrap and refrigerate the butter cream for at least 30 minutes, or until it can be spread easily.

Meanwhile prepare the praline topping in the following fashion: With a pastry brush or paper towel, coat a baking sheet with 1 tablespoon of butter and set it aside. In a small saucepan, bring 1 cup of sugar and ½ cup of water to a boil over moderate heat, stirring until the sugar dissolves. Increase the heat to high and boil briskly, undisturbed, until the syrup reaches a temperature of 236° on a candy thermometer, or a drop of syrup spooned into cold water immediately forms a soft ball. Stir in the nuts and cook until the syrup reaches a temperature of 310° on a candy thermometer, or until the syrup caramelizes and turns a rich golden brown.

Pour the syrup evenly onto the baking sheet. When it is cool and firm, break the praline into small pieces and pulverize it in a blender for a few seconds or crush it with a mortar and pestle. Spread it out on wax paper.

To assemble the cake, place the bottom layer in the center of a large cake plate and, with a spatula, spread it with about ½ inch of butter cream. Set the second layer on top and spread it with another ½-inch layer of butter cream. Finally set the top layer of cake in place and mask the top and sides with the remaining butter cream (if you like, reserve some butter cream to decorate the cake). Gently press the crushed praline over the sides of the cake and sprinkle the remainder over the top. Any extra butter cream may be piped on top of the cake through a pastry tube fitted with a decorative tip.

Honigkuchen
HONEY CAKE

Preheat the oven to 350°. If you would like to top the cake with nuts, spread the 1 cup of slivered almonds evenly over a baking sheet or in a large, shallow baking dish and toast them in the oven, stirring and turning them frequently, for about 10 minutes, or until they are light brown. Watch carefully for signs of burning. Set aside.

If you would prefer to glaze the cake instead of covering it with almonds, prepare the glaze by stirring the confectioners' sugar, almond extract and lemon juice or rum together in a small bowl. Stirring constantly, add about 2 tablespoons of cold water, 1 teaspoon at a time, until the glaze is smooth and thin enough to be spread easily.

With a pastry brush or paper towel, coat the bottom and sides of an 11-by-17-inch jelly-roll pan with the 1 tablespoon of soft butter. Sprinkle 2 tablespoons of the flour over the butter and tip the pan from side to side to spread it evenly. Then invert the pan and rap the bottom sharply to remove any excess flour. Set aside.

In a large bowl, stir together the 5 cups of flour, baking powder, ground almonds, chopped citron, cocoa, cloves, cinnamon, cardamom, lemon peel and almond extract. In a heavy 5-quart saucepan or casserole, bring the honey, sugar and water to a boil over moderate heat, stirring only until the sugar dissolves. Reduce the heat to low and simmer, uncovered, for 5 minutes. Pour the hot honey mixture over the flour mixture and beat them together with a large spoon until a smooth dough is formed.

With your fingers, pat and spread the dough out evenly in the prepared pan. Bake in the middle of the oven for 20 minutes, or until top is firm to the touch. Remove the pan from the oven and, if you are using almonds, strew them over the cake immediately, pressing them gently into the surface. Let the cake rest for 4 or 5 minutes, then cut it into rectangles or fancy shapes of whatever size you like and transfer the pieces to a wire rack to cool. If glazing the cake, brush the top with almond glaze before it is cut.

Honigkuchen should be wrapped in foil or placed in a cookie jar or tin and allowed to mellow for several days before it is served. It can be kept in a tightly covered jar for 2 or 3 months.

To make one 11-by-17-inch cake

1 cup blanched slivered almonds (optional)

ALMOND GLAZE (OPTIONAL)
1 cup confectioners' sugar
½ teaspoon almond extract
1 teaspoon fresh lemon juice, or 1 teaspoon rum
2 tablespoons cold water

CAKE
1 tablespoon butter, softened
5 cups plus 2 tablespoons all-purpose flour
1½ teaspoons double-acting baking powder
¼ cup blanched almonds, pulverized in an electric blender or with a nut grinder or a mortar and pestle
3 tablespoons finely chopped candied citron
1 tablespoon unsweetened cocoa
1 teaspoon ground cloves
1 teaspoon ground cinnamon
2 teaspoons ground cardamom
1 teaspoon finely grated lemon peel
½ teaspoon almond extract
1 cup honey
1 cup sugar
½ cup cold water

To make 2 to 3 dozen cookies,
    depending on size of forms used

2 tablespoons butter, softened
1 cup anise seeds
2 eggs
1¼ cups sugar
1 teaspoon finely grated lemon peel
A drop of vanilla extract
3 cups sifted all-purpose flour

Springerle
MOLDED ANISE-SEED COOKIES

With a pastry brush or paper towel, coat two large baking sheets with a tablespoon of butter each. Sprinkle the butter evenly with the anise seeds and set the pans aside.

In a large bowl, beat the eggs with a whisk or a rotary or electric beater until they are thick and lemon-colored. Gradually add the sugar and continue beating until the mixture is thick enough to fall back on itself in a slowly dissolving ribbon when the beater is lifted from the bowl. Beat in the lemon peel and vanilla, and then the flour, a cup or so at a time.

Shape the dough into a ball and place it on a lightly floured board. If it feels sticky, work additional flour into it with your fingers, adding a tablespoon at a time. Then knead the dough with lightly floured hands for 10 minutes or so, until it is smooth and pliable.

Sprinkle the board with flour again, pinch off about half of the dough and roll it out into a rectangle about ¼ inch thick. Sprinkle a *Springerle* mold or *Springerle* rolling pin evenly with 2 tablespoons of flour, and rap it sharply on a table to remove the excess. Then press the mold down or roll the pin firmly across the dough, to print the pattern on it as deeply and clearly as possible. Cut the cookie squares apart with a small, sharp knife and place them an inch apart on the prepared baking sheets, pressing them gently into the anise seeds. Roll and cut the rest of the dough similarly. You must work quickly because the dough dries rapidly. Set the cookies aside uncovered at room temperature for 24 hours.

Preheat the oven to 250° and bake the cookies for 20 to 30 minutes, or until they are firm but not brown. With a large metal spatula, transfer the cookies to a cake rack to cool. Then set them aside uncovered for a few days to soften. They may be stored for several weeks in tightly sealed jars or tins.

NOTE: Save the anise seeds remaining on the baking sheets and scatter them over the bottom of the cookie jar or tin. Their flavor will permeate the cookies as they stand.

To make about 20 cookies

2 teaspoons butter, softened
2 egg whites
¾ cup sugar
1½ cups shelled hazelnuts
    (preferably blanched), pulverized
    in an electric blender or with a
    nut grinder or mortar and pestle
6 tablespoons unsweetened cocoa
2 teaspoons finely grated lemon peel
A pinch of salt
1 teaspoon vanilla extract

Haselnussmakronen
HAZELNUT MACAROONS

With a pastry brush or paper towel, coat a large baking sheet with 2 teaspoons of soft butter and set it aside. In a large bowl, beat the egg whites with a wire whisk or a rotary or electric beater until they foam and thicken slightly. Sprinkle the sugar over them and continue to beat until the whites form stiff, unwavering peaks on the beater when it is lifted out of the bowl. Combine the ground hazelnuts, cocoa, lemon peel, salt and vanilla in a small bowl and, with a rubber spatula, gently but thoroughly fold the mixture into the whites, using an over-under cutting motion rather than a stirring motion. To make the cookies, drop the dough by the tablespoon onto the prepared baking sheet, spacing them about an inch apart. Let the cookies rest at room temperature for 1 hour before baking.

Preheat the oven to 300°. Bake the cookies in the middle of the oven for 30 minutes, or until they are firm. With a spatula, carefully transfer the cookies to a cake rack to cool. *Haselnussmakronen* can be stored for several weeks in tightly sealed jars or tins.

182

Spritzgebäck
PRESSED HAZELNUT COOKIES

Preheat the oven to 350°. In a large bowl, cream the butter and sugar together by mashing them against the sides of the bowl with a large spoon until light and fluffy. Then beat in the eggs one at a time, add the vanilla and continue beating until smooth. Sift the flour into the mixture ½ cup at a time, beating well after each addition. Finally, beat in the ground nuts.

Place the dough in a pastry bag or cookie press fitted with a medium-sized star tip. Pipe the dough out on ungreased baking sheets forming rounds and rings about 1½ inches in diameter, or S-shapes and crescents about 2 inches long, and spacing the cookies 1 inch apart. Bake in the middle of the oven for about 10 minutes, or until the cookies are firm and light brown. With a spatula, transfer them immediately to a cake rack to cool. The *Spritzgebäck* can be stored for several weeks in tightly sealed jars or tins.

To make about 5 dozen cookies

½ pound butter (2 sticks), softened
1 cup sugar
2 eggs
1 teaspoon vanilla extract
2 cups sifted all-purpose flour
1 cup shelled hazelnuts, pulverized in an electric blender or with a nut grinder or mortar and pestle

Schokoladen Brezeln
CHOCOLATE PRETZELS

In a large mixing bowl, cream the butter and ¼ cup of sugar together by beating and mashing them against the sides of the bowl with a large spoon until light and fluffy. Dissolve the cocoa in the hot water, let it cool to room temperature, and beat it into the butter-sugar mixture. Then beat in the flour, a cup at a time, and when it has all been absorbed, add the egg and vanilla. Pat and shape the dough into a cylinder about 7 inches long and 2 inches in diameter. Wrap in wax paper and refrigerate for 30 minutes, or until firm.

Preheat the oven to 350°. Slice the dough crosswise into ⅜-inch rounds and roll each slice between your hands to make a rope-like strip about 14 inches long and ¼ inch in diameter. Shape each rope into a pretzel as shown below. Arrange the pretzels 1 inch apart on ungreased baking sheets and bake in the middle of the oven for 10 minutes, or until they are firm to the touch. Transfer the pretzels to a cake rack to cool.

To make the glaze, combine the milk, ⅔ cup of sugar, sweet chocolate, unsweetened chocolate and corn syrup in a small, heavy saucepan or the top of a double boiler. Cook over low heat or simmering water, stirring constantly, until the sugar is dissolved and the chocolate melted. Stir in 1 teaspoon of butter, remove the pan from the heat and cool to lukewarm. With tongs, dip the pretzels into the glaze one at a time to coat them thoroughly. Dry them for at least 15 minutes on a cake rack set over wax paper.

To make 25 pretzels

¼ pound (1 stick) unsalted butter, softened
¼ cup sugar
¼ cup unsweetened cocoa
3 tablespoons hot water
2 cups all-purpose flour
1 egg, lightly beaten
1 teaspoon vanilla extract

GLAZE
½ cup milk
⅔ cup sugar
2 ounces sweet chocolate
2 ounces unsweetened chocolate
½ cup light corn syrup
1 teaspoon butter

To make chocolate pretzels, shape the dough into a roll 2 inches in diameter, chill, then slice it into rounds *(left)*. Roll each round between your hands to make a ¼-inch rope about 14 inches long. Drape the rope on a board into a loop with its ends crossed so that it looks like a small script "e." Twist the ends of rope again under the loop *(center)*. Spread the tips apart, bring the loop over to them and pinch the tips to the loop *(right)*.

X

Festive Revelry and Nostalgic Holidays

Brightly tinted marzipan, molded in the shapes of fruits and figurines, is an essential ingredient of a traditional German Christmas. Used as Christmas-tree ornaments as well as a confection, the candy is made of sugar, almond paste and egg white. It probably originated in ancient Persia.

For many a tourist and for almost every native, Germany is *the* land of *Volksfeste*, or popular festivals. They come in a bewildering variety of forms and functions—religious and secular, historical and modern, local and international—and all of them are accompanied by food and drink. One or another German town or cathedral seems always to be celebrating an anniversary with memorial plays or gorgeous processions against a backdrop of historic buildings. Beer and wine festivals are held in the spring and fall. There are special children's festivals like the one in the picturesque medieval town of Dinkelsbühl, and music festivals like the great Wagner weeks at Bayreuth. There is a festival for the plum harvest at Bühl in Baden, and an onion fair at Boppard on the Rhine. The festival of the Billy Goat Auction at Deidesheim dates back to 1404. *Rennwoche*, racing week, at Hamburg or Baden-Baden is a high spot for international racing fans. And throughout the year there are jollifications held by the social organizations of which the Germans are so fond, with appropriate infusions of beer, wine and song.

Religious festivals are equally numerous and diverse. Saints are celebrated on their calendar days with costumed processions, and on Corpus Christi flowered barges cross the Bavarian lake called Chiemsee. Pagan rituals and Christian observances merge in spring festivals designed to banish the winter; on June 24, *Johannistag* (St. John's Day), young men leap over great bonfires to celebrate the summer solstice. At the fall harvest festivals, too, the secular and the religious merge, and thanks are given in churches decorated with sheaves of wheat and the fruits of field and garden.

The most impressive mixture of pagan revelry and Christian rite is the pre-

Continued on page 188

In one of seven huge tents erected by leading breweries to celebrate Munich's Oktoberfest, beer and *Gemütlichkeit* flow furiously as revelers sway arm in arm, singing and stamping their feet to the *oom-pa-pa's* of a Bavarian band. About 10 million visitors drop in on Munich in late September during this 16-day orgy of beer and food; in an average *Fest* they consume four million quarts of beer, a million sausages, almost 400,000 roast chickens, 50 tons of fish and scores of whole oxen roasted on spits.

Lenten carnival, or *Fasching,* celebrated throughout the Catholic parts of Germany, especially in such cities as Köln and Munich. It is a relic of the Middle Ages, when a strict religion enforced the harsh penances of Lent but permitted one final letting-off of steam before the praying and fasting began. In it we can still see the total involvement of all the townspeople that characterized the great German festivals of the past, for the carnivals of these cities are designed for their citizens rather than the tourist trade.

Certainly they are not designed for the prude. As a visitor to both the Köln *Fasching* and the New Orleans Mardi Gras, I can report that the latter is but a pale shadow of the former. For three days the affairs of everyday life come to a standstill while mummers and maskers roam the streets with floats and broadsheets. Drinking and dancing fill the nights, as abandoned in an elegant hotel as in a humble wine shop. One German judge is said to have declared that marital infidelity does not matter at carnival time.

The palm for uninhibited secular festivals, however, must go to Munich's Oktoberfest, which lasts for 16 days in late September and early October. Founded in 1810 to celebrate the marriage of Crown Prince Ludwig of Bavaria, it now draws as many as 10 million visitors from Germany and abroad. What they get is a beery bash to end all beery bashes, relieved only by mountains of food and by such amusement park delights as Ferris wheels and roller coasters, shooting and gambling booths, carrousels and pony rides.

An adequate account of a typical Oktoberfest would call for the pen of a Rabelais or the brush of a Breughel. Munich's great fairground, the Theresienwiese (named after Ludwig's bride, Therese), is crowded with gigantic beer tents, furnished with long tables and dedicated to fraternal drinking to the sound of Bavarian bands. Within these tents, huge steins of foaming beer are hefted by sharp-tongued, indefatigable waitresses in peasant costumes, who need all their stamina. Outside, oxen are roasted whole over open fires; in addition, *Steckerlfisch* (a variety of small fish impaled on a wooden spit and roasted over a fiery trench), *Brathändl* (spit-roasted chicken) and innumerable *Würste* help to provide solid foundations for the beer.

The carousings of the Oktoberfest represent a special taste, and whether they are enjoyed or not depends upon the beholder. At the Oktoberfest of a recent year, there were 100 brawls and 50 *Bierleichen,* or "beer corpses"—people who passed out so cold that they had to be carted away. The Red Cross gave first aid to some 1,700 celebrants.

Every fall, on a smaller scale, the grape harvest is celebrated with equal abandon in hundreds of picturesque little wine towns scattered through western Germany. The ancient inns along the Rhine reverberate to the strains of sentimental ballads, and as the evening progresses the German exercise called *Schunkeln* can be observed in depth. To perform it, congenial and uninhibited souls, both male and female, sit round a table, link arms and sway to and fro as they sing loudly and with feeling. The best known of these wine fairs is probably the Dürkheim Fair, also called the Sausage Fair. There, in a recent year, more than 50,000 gallons of wine wetted the throats of some 500,000 visitors. The sausages consumed in this eight-day fair would stretch for 60 miles; 545 pigs, 91 cattle and 55 calves were slaughtered in their preparation.

Not all German festivals have a bacchanalian tone. At Easter time *der Osterhase,* the Easter Bunny, hides his colored eggs in the house and garden for

The Advent calendar.

children to find. In the Whitsun Festival, seven Sundays after Easter, old and young take to the country in a traditional family outing, the *Pfingstausflug,* to celebrate the spring flowers and the new green on tree and in meadow. And then there are the Christmas fairs, of which Nürnberg's ancient *Christkindlmarkt* (Christ Child market) is perhaps the best. The streets of the lovely old town are crammed with stalls piled with the shiny bells and balls, angels and stars that adorn the German Christmas tree. Along with them there are the toys for which Nürnberg has been famous for centuries. Even in this age of plastic and metal playthings children still love the painted wooden toys of Nürnberg: the jumping jacks, *Hampelmänner* dancing on their strings, the soldiers, the animals of Noah's Ark and the dolls and doll houses that have enchanted children for hundreds of years. The wintry air, thick with snow or the promise of snow, is fragrant with the scent of Nürnberg *Lebkuchen* and *Pfefferkuchen,* the town's famous honey and spice cakes.

Despite all the clutter of modern technology, a German Christmas is still an old-fashioned, nostalgic occasion. Protestants and Catholics may worship differently, but to all who speak German, wherever they are, Christmas means two things—*das Christkind,* or Christ Child, and *der heilige Abend,* or Christmas Eve. Christmas day, called *der erste Weihnachtstag,* may be the day of the big dinner and the family visits, but the real Christmas takes place the evening before, when *das Christkind* brings the presents that accompany the brilliantly decorated Christmas tree.

Advent and Christmas have always been the most holy of all seasons in German-speaking lands. The awe and reverence of the time are best expressed, I think, in words from Shakespeare's *Hamlet:*

> Some say that ever 'gainst that season comes
> Wherein our Saviour's birth is celebrated,
> The bird of dawning singeth all night long.
> And then, they say, no spirit dare stir abroad,
> The nights are wholesome, then no planets strike,
> No fairy takes nor witch hath power to charm,
> So hallowed and so gracious is the time.

In the distant and not-so-distant German past, Christmas customs were rich and strange. Good spirits were propitiated and bad ones exorcised by masked mummers; seven spices were baked into the honey cakes, in memory of the seven days in which God created the world; rosemary was brought into the house to ward off evil spells. Few of these rites survive, yet even in modern Germany, Christmas remains a deeply religious holiday. Eating and drinking are festive and generous but not exuberant, and the main emphasis is on the great figures and symbols of the Christian faith.

Thus, in Germany, the Christ Child rather than Santa Claus is the bringer of Christmas gifts, though an anonymous *Weihnachtsmann* (Christmas man) may assist *das Christkind* in bringing the gifts. Santa Claus—who is, of course, the German Saint Nicholas—comes into his own weeks earlier, on December 6, Saint Nicholas Day, which used to be one of the great festivals of central Europe. Even today on Saint Nicholas Eve children hang a stocking or a boot before their door or window. If they have been good all year, they will find it full of sweets, apples and nuts next morning; if they have been bad, a switch is their lot. Saint Nicholas himself may also visit a household on the eve-

Hanging the Christmas greens.

ning of his day—but not to bring gifts. He asks how the children have be-haved and hears their prayers or their catechism, then rewards them personally from his big sack or punishes them with a few strokes of the switch.

Modern Germany may not be a profoundly religious country, but during Advent much of the Christmas anticipation of the past invariably returns. In Germany, as in Scandinavia, an Advent wreath is hung in the dining room or set upon the table. The wreath bears four candles for the four Sundays be-fore Christmas, and each is lit on the appropriate day; by Christmas Day all four are ablaze. Everywhere children mark off the 24 days before Christmas on Advent calendars, opening in turn each of the dated little paper flaps to see the picture underneath. The last flap, opened on Christmas Eve, usually re-veals a Christmas tree in all its shimmering glory.

Long before there were Christmas trees, green boughs were brought in from the winter woods and hung on house, stable and barn at the time of the winter solstice. The custom, one of the many in which pagan and Chris-tian rites intermingle, still survives; to this day a proper German home is dec-orated with Christmas greens, if nothing more than twigs of greens wedged behind the corner of a mirror. But the greens are often far more elaborate. I re-member my mother's weaving armfuls of fir and spruce into great swags that went over the doorways; other greens were placed behind pictures and among books, or stood in big bunches on chests and dressers. Like our Christ-mas tree, they were not taken down until January 6, when we celebrated *Dreikönigstag*, or Epiphany.

Far more exciting than the greens, of course, is *der Weihnachtsbaum*, the Christmas tree, ablaze with candles (and nowadays, increasingly, with elec-tric lights), hung as of old with apples and gilded nuts and with glittering dec-orations that are saved from year to year. Curiously, the tree is not nearly so old as many of the other Christmas customs of German lands. The first men-tion of it occurs in an Alsatian chronicle of 1605, which in the quaint German of its time tells of fir trees set up in the rooms of Strasbourg and hung with paper roses, apples, flat cakes, gilded candies and sugar. By 1659, however, Li-selotte von der Pfalz, daughter of a count of the Palatinate and sister-in-law of King Louis XIV of France, could describe a Christmas room not very dif-ferent from one today. The Germans, she said, had a practice called *Christkindel* (Baby Jesus). "Tables are fixed up like altars and outfitted for each child with all sorts of things, such as new clothes, silver, dolls, sugar candy and so forth. Boxwood trees are set on the tables, and a candle is fas-tened on each branch; it looks very lovely and I would still like to see it."

I think you had to have been a child in Germany to know the full glory of *der Weihnachtsbaum*. On the day before Christmas you dressed in your best clothes. Perhaps your father took you out for a walk or, on Christmas Eve it-self, to a candlelight service to sing carols of the Middle Ages—songs of Mary rocking her babe and of the rose that blossomed in the winter's night. Then you came home to a darkened house, and were told to wait until the little silver bell rang three times. For weeks, one of the rooms had been tightly locked—because, you were told, *das Christkind* needed a place to rest during his visits to your house. Sometimes he left behind him strands of silver "angels' hair"—the tinsel on the Christmas tree. If your parents were clever, they had already smuggled the Christmas tree into the

The sudden sight of Christmas.

190

house, though a trail of pine needles and the sweet scent of the tree may have given them away.

There you sat in the dark room, your heart in your mouth, waiting, waiting for the bell to ring. And then the bell did ring, the doors burst open, and all you saw was the Christmas tree, shining in all its candles like one great light—and you were too shy to enter the room immediately.

In Germany, presents are not piled up under the Christmas tree, as they are in America, but stacked in individual heaps on little tables. An important part of the presents is *der bunte Teller*, a brightly colored dish laden with apples and nuts, raisins and all the cookies baked over the past weeks. In our family we did not open the presents as soon as we came into the festive room. First, by candlelight, my father read the Christmas Gospel. Then we sang "Holy Night" and "O Tannenbaum." Next we all embraced and kissed, wishing each other a Merry Christmas. Finally we opened our presents —and shared the bliss of a heart's desire fulfilled on Christmas Eve.

All I really remember about our Christmas Eve suppers was that for the only time in the year I was allowed to get up from the table whenever I pleased to play with my new toys. We did not have carp, though carp has been the traditional dish of Christmas Eve since the Middle Ages, when carp ponds were maintained in the monasteries. Even today in some parts of the country, people will start fattening their Christmas carp as early as St. Bartholomew's Day on August 24.

But the real eating of a German Christmas takes place at *Mittagessen* on Christmas Day. Roast hare or a roast goose stuffed with chestnuts or with apples and onions used to be the mainstay of the festive meal, though they never held the secure place that we give our Thanksgiving turkeys. Today German families make their Christmas dinners of anything they like. On a recent visit I asked many householders what would be a festive Christmas meat, and received varying answers. Goose, turkey, venison, wild boar, chicken, roast beef, roast pork, roast veal and even *Schnitzel* made the grade.

Other foods, however, are firmly fixed by custom. *Apfel, Nuss und Mandelkern* (apple, nut and almond), says an old rhyme, are the foods for Christmas. Symbolically the apple stands for the Tree of Knowledge in Paradise; nuts and almonds, with their hard shells and sweet kernels, stand for the mysteries and difficulties of life as expressed in the proverb, "God gives the nuts, but man must crack them by himself." Apples go on the Christmas tree, and so do the nuts, gilded and silvered. Nuts and almonds go into the sweet bakings and marzipan that are the soul of German Christmas foods.

I have described these bakings, many of them dating back to the Middle Ages, in previous chapters. Some of them are associated with specific cities: *Thorner Kathrinchen, Nürnberger Lebkuchen, Dresdner Stollen (page 193), Liegnitzer Bomben, Aachener Printen*, and the marzipan of Königsberg or Lübeck. Others are made everywhere in Germany: the *Springerle (page 182), Aniskuchen, Mandelbrezeln* and all the other cookies whose sweet spicy fragrance fills the years of a German childhood and, more than anything else, brings those years back to us. German housewives no longer go in for the baking binges of the past, which began in early fall with honey and spice cakes, but they still do bake these sweet things, for without *Hausgebackenes* (home-baked things) Christmas wouldn't be Christmas—and without Christmas, Germany wouldn't be Germany.

The "bright dish" of Christmas.

Pfeffernüsse
SPICE COOKIES

To make about 30 cookies

Soft butter
4 cups all-purpose flour
1 teaspoon double-acting baking
    powder
1 teaspoon ground cloves
½ teaspoon ground allspice
½ teaspoon ground cinnamon
¾ cup honey
1 cup dark corn syrup
¾ cup sugar
2 tablespoons butter
1 tablespoon lard

Preheat the oven to 400°. Coat two large baking sheets lightly with butter. Combine the flour, baking powder, cloves, allspice and cinnamon in a bowl, and set aside. In a deep, heavy 5- to 6-quart saucepan, bring the honey, corn syrup and sugar to a boil over moderate heat, stirring until the sugar dissolves. Reduce the heat to low and simmer, uncovered, for 5 minutes. Remove the pan from the heat, add the butter and lard, and stir until melted. Beat in the flour mixture, a cup or so at a time. When the batter is smooth, drop it by teaspoonfuls onto the baking sheets, leaving an inch or so between the cookies. Bake in the middle of the oven for about 15 minutes, or until the cookies are firm to the touch and light brown. Transfer them to a cake rack to cool, and proceed with the remaining batches, coating the baking sheets with a little butter each time. If you like, you may brush the cookies while still warm with the almond glaze for *Honigkuchen (page 181)*. *Pfeffernüsse* can be stored for 6 to 8 weeks in tightly sealed jars or tins.

The fruit-filled *Dresdner Stollen*, which improves with age, is a Christmas cake exchanged throughout Germany as a season's gift.

Dresdner Stollen

DRESDEN CHRISTMAS FRUIT BREAD

Combine the raisins, currants, candied citrus peel, angelica and cherries in a bowl. Pour the rum over them, tossing the fruit about to coat the pieces evenly. Soak for at least 1 hour.

Pour the lukewarm water into a small bowl and sprinkle it with the yeast and a pinch of sugar. Let the mixture stand for 2 or 3 minutes, then stir to dissolve the yeast completely. Set the bowl in a warm, draft-free place (such as a turned-off oven) for about 5 minutes, or until the mixture almost doubles in volume.

Meanwhile, drain the fruit, reserving the rum, and carefully pat the pieces completely dry with paper towels. Place the fruit in a bowl, sprinkle it with 2 tablespoons of the flour, and turn it about with a spoon until the flour is completely absorbed. Set aside.

In a heavy 1½- to 2-quart saucepan, combine the milk, ½ cup of the sugar and the salt. Heat to lukewarm (110° to 115°), stirring constantly until the sugar dissolves. Off the heat, stir in the reserved rum, the almond extract and fresh lemon peel, and finally the yeast mixture.

Place 5 cups of the flour in a large bowl and with a fork stir in the yeast mixture, a cup or so at a time. Beat the eggs until frothy and stir them into the dough, then beat in the bits of softened butter. Gather the dough into a ball and place it on a board sprinkled with the remaining ½ cup of flour. Knead the dough, by pushing it down with the heels of your hands, pressing it forward and folding it back on itself. Continue the kneading for about 15 minutes, or until all the flour is incorporated and the dough is smooth and elastic. Flour your hands lightly from time to time. Now press the fruit and almonds into the dough, ⅓ cup or so at a time, but do not knead or handle it too much or the dough will discolor. Coat a deep bowl with 1 teaspoon of melted butter and drop in the dough. Brush the top of the dough with another 2 teaspoons of melted butter, drape a towel over the bowl and set it in a warm, draft-free place for 2 hours, or until the dough doubles in bulk.

Punch the dough down and divide it into two equal pieces. Let them rest for 10 minutes, then roll the pieces out into strips about 12 inches long, 8 inches wide and ½ inch thick. Brush each strip with 2 tablespoons of the remaining butter and sprinkle each with 2 tablespoons of the remaining sugar. Fold each strip lengthwise in the following fashion: bring one long side over to the center of the strip and press the edge down lightly. Then fold the other long side across it, overlapping the seam down the center by about 1 inch. Press the edge gently to keep it in place. With lightly floured hands, taper the ends of the loaf slightly and pat the sides gently together to mound it in the center. The finished loaf should be about 3½ to 4 inches wide and 13 inches long.

With a pastry brush, and 1 tablespoon of melted butter, coat the bottom of an 11-by-17-inch jelly-roll pan. Place the loaves on the pan and brush them with the remaining 2 tablespoons of melted butter. Set the loaves aside in a warm draft-free place for about 1 hour, or until doubled in bulk. Preheat the oven to 375°. Then bake the bread in the middle of the oven for 45 minutes, or until golden brown and crusty. Transfer the loaves to wire racks to cool completely. Just before serving, sprinkle the loaves with the sifted confectioners' sugar.

To make two 13-inch loaves

½ cup seedless raisins
½ cup dried currants
1 cup mixed candied citrus peel
¼ cup candied angelica, cut into ¼-inch dice
½ cup candied cherries, cut in half
½ cup rum
¼ cup lukewarm water (110° to 115°)
2 packages or cakes of dry or compressed yeast
¾ cup plus a pinch of sugar
5½ cups plus 2 tablespoons all-purpose flour
1 cup milk
½ teaspoon salt
½ teaspoon almond extract
½ teaspoon finely grated fresh lemon peel
2 eggs, at room temperature
¾ cup unsalted butter, cut into ¼-inch bits and softened
8 tablespoons melted unsalted butter
1 cup blanched slivered almonds
¼ cup confectioners' sugar, sifted

To make about 3 dozen

TOPPING

¼ cup blanched almonds, finely
  chopped
⅓ cup sugar
1 teaspoon ground cinnamon

COOKIES

½ pound (2 sticks) unsalted butter,
  softened
¾ cup sugar
4 hard-cooked egg yolks, sieved
2 raw egg yolks
2 teaspoons finely grated lemon peel
3 cups all-purpose flour, sifted before
  measuring
1 egg white

To make about 7 dozen cookies

½ pound (2 sticks) plus 2 teaspoons
  unsalted butter, softened
1 cup sugar
7 egg yolks
1 teaspoon finely grated lemon peel
4 cups all-purpose flour
1 egg white
Decorating sugar

Mandel-Halbmonde
ALMOND CRESCENT COOKIES

Stir the chopped almonds, the ⅓ cup of sugar and the cinnamon together in a small bowl and set aside. Preheat the oven to 325°.

In an electric mixer equipped with a pastry arm, beat the butter and the ¾ cup of sugar together at high speed until the mixture is light and fluffy. Then beat in the hard-cooked egg yolks, raw egg yolks and lemon peel. Reduce the speed to medium and sift in the flour, beating until the mixture is smooth. (To make the dough by hand, cream the butter and sugar together by mashing and beating them against the sides of the bowl with a large spoon until light and fluffy. Then beat in the hard-cooked egg yolks, raw yolks and lemon peel, and continue to beat until smooth. Sift the flour into the mixture a little at a time, beating well after each addition.)

In a small bowl, beat the egg white with a whisk or a rotary or electric beater until it is stiff enough to form unwavering peaks on the beater when it is lifted out of the bowl. Shape each cookie in the following fashion: Pinch off about 2 tablespoons of dough and roll it between the palms of your hands to make a cylinder about 2½ inches long. Curve the ends of the cylinder together, flatten it a little and taper the ends to form a crescent. Then dip the crescent into egg white and roll it in the almond mixture. Place the cookie on an ungreased baking sheet. Make the remaining cookies similarly, arranging them on the sheet 1 inch apart. (Use 2 baking sheets if necessary.)

Bake in the middle of the oven for about 10 minutes, or until the cookies are firm. With a metal spatula, transfer to cake racks to cool. *Mandel-Halbmonde* can be stored for several weeks in tightly sealed jars or tins.

S-Gebäck
S-SHAPED BUTTER COOKIES

In a large bowl, cream the ½ pound of butter and the cup of sugar together by mashing and beating them against the sides of the bowl with a large spoon until light and fluffy. Then beat in the egg yolks one at a time, add the lemon peel and continue beating until smooth. Sift the flour into the mixture, ½ cup at a time, beating well after each addition.

Pat and shape the dough into a long roll about 2 inches in diameter, wrap it in wax paper, and refrigerate it for at least 30 minutes, or until firm.

Preheat the oven to 400°. With a pastry brush and the remaining 2 teaspoons of soft butter, lightly coat two large baking sheets. Set aside. Slice the dough into rounds about ⅓ inch thick. To shape each cookie, roll a slice of dough between your hands to form a rope about ½ inch thick and 4 to 5 inches long. Gently press the rope flat on a pastry board to make a strip about ¾ inch wide and ¼ inch thick. Then with your fingers, form the strip into an S shape. Arrange the cookies an inch apart on the baking sheets and refrigerate for 10 minutes.

In a large bowl, beat the egg white with a whisk or a rotary or electric beater until it is frothy and lightly thickened. Brush the top of each cookie lightly with the white and sprinkle it with a little of the decorating sugar. Bake in the middle of the oven for about 10 minutes, or until the cookie is firm but only faintly colored. With a spatula, transfer the cookies to cake racks to cool. *S-Gebäck* can be stored for several weeks in tightly sealed jars or tins.

Lebkuchen Häuschen
GINGERBREAD HOUSE

NOTE: This recipe makes enough dough for one 11-by-17-inch gingerbread cake. You will need three of these cakes to make the house shown on the cover and in the diagrams on pages 196 and 197. You may bake the cakes in three batches (they become firmer and easier to handle as they age, so it is possible to do the baking over a period of several days as long as you cut them as soon as they are baked). Or you may double or triple this recipe and make the cakes in one or two batches; in that event, you will need a very large mixing bowl and extra pans. The icing recipe is intended to make enough for the whole house, but generous decorations may require more.

Cut out the cardboard templates for the house and its base as shown in the diagrams on page 196. Set them aside. With a pastry brush or paper towel, lightly coat an 11-by-17-inch jelly-roll pan with 1 tablespoon of soft butter. Sprinkle ¼ cup of flour into the pan, and tip it from side to side to coat it evenly. Then turn it over and knock out the excess. Set the pan aside.

Sift 6 cups of flour, baking powder, cinnamon, cloves, nutmeg, cardamom and salt together into a large mixing bowl and set them aside.

Preheat the oven to 325°. In a heavy 4- to 5-quart saucepan, bring the honey, sugar and butter to a boil over high heat, stirring with a large spoon until the sugar is dissolved and the butter melted. Remove the pan from the heat, mix in the lemon juice and lemon peel, and cool to room temperature. Beat in 2 cups of the flour-and-spice mixture, add the egg and egg yolk, and then beat in the remaining 4 cups of flour-and-spice mixture. Flour your hands lightly and knead until the dough is smooth, pliable and still slightly sticky. If it is too moist to handle, beat in more flour by the tablespoon.

Place the dough in the jelly-roll pan, and with a lightly floured pin, press and roll it out as evenly as possible, forcing it into the corners with your fingers. Bake for 35 minutes, or until the cake is firm and the top brown. Let the cake cool in the pan for 4 or 5 minutes, then using the templates as your guide, cut it into the requisite shapes with a pastry wheel or small knife. Do not be tempted to cut the house pieces freehand; they must fit together precisely to make a stable structure. Set the pieces aside on wax paper until they cool completely. Bake and cut the remaining cakes in the same fashion.

In a large bowl, beat the egg whites with a whisk or a rotary or electric beater until they are frothy and slightly thickened. Sift the confectioners' sugar into the whites ½ cup at a time, beating thoroughly after each addition. Continue to beat for about 5 minutes, or until a stiff icing is formed. Fill a pastry bag fitted with a round decorative tip with a cup of the icing.

While the pieces of gingerbread are still spread out flat, decorate the front, back and sides of the house with windows, shutters, doors and the like to approximate the gingerbread house shown on the cover, or to suit your own fancy. When the icing is completely dry, assemble the base and walls of the house according to the directions on page 197, using the icing as cement to hold the pieces together. Let the walls stand undisturbed until the icing is completely set. With the remaining icing, cement the roof and chimney pieces in place, and after the icing is set, decorate the roof and chimney. Make more icing if necessary. For more elaborate decoration, coat candies and cookies on one side with the icing and press them gently onto the walls and roof. As a final touch, sift a snowlike coating of sugar over the base.

GINGERBREAD
1 tablespoon butter, softened
6¼ cups all-purpose flour
6 tablespoons double-acting baking powder
1½ teaspoons ground cinnamon
1 teaspoon ground cloves
¼ teaspoon ground nutmeg
¼ teaspoon ground cardamom
⅛ teaspoon salt
¾ cup honey
1¾ cups sugar
¼ cup butter
⅓ cup fresh lemon juice
1 tablespoon finely grated lemon peel
1 egg
1 egg yolk

DECORATION
2 egg whites
2½ cups confectioners' sugar
Candies and cookies for decorating the house
1 to 2 cups sugar for decorating the base

A Gingerbread House That Can Stand for Years

A gingerbread house like the one on the cover is as much fun to make as it is to look at, and you may be as whimsical as you like with its decoration. But to make a house that will stand proudly through the Christmas holidays for years to come, the gingerbread must be cut with precision and the pieces fitted firmly together.

The first step is to make patterns for the pieces from stiff cardboard, following the dimensions and shapes in the diagrams at right. (Where pieces are identical, one pattern will do.) Now bake three 11-by-17-inch gingerbread cakes according to the recipe on page 195. While the cakes are still in the pans, lay the patterns on the cakes and cut the warm gingerbread with a pastry wheel or a small, sharp knife. If you like, cut out a door and a window or two as well. With a wide metal spatula, slide the cakes onto wax paper to cool. (There will be gingerbread left over, including one piece big enough to be cut into gingerbread figures.) Then outline door and window frames, shutters and other trim on the walls with the egg-white-and-sugar icing described on page 195.

After the wall trim decorations are dry, set the base on a cutting board or a large piece of heavy cardboard to enable you to move the house from place to place when it is finished. Assemble the house, using icing to cement the pieces together.

First ice the bottom of one end wall—the back of the house—and the bottom and one end of a side wall; fit them together and place them carefully on the base. Ice the bottom and two sides of a corner post and place it between them. Hold the pieces upright for 3 or 4 minutes, until the icing has set. Ice the opposite end of the side wall and the bottom of the other end wall, and fit that wall onto the house for

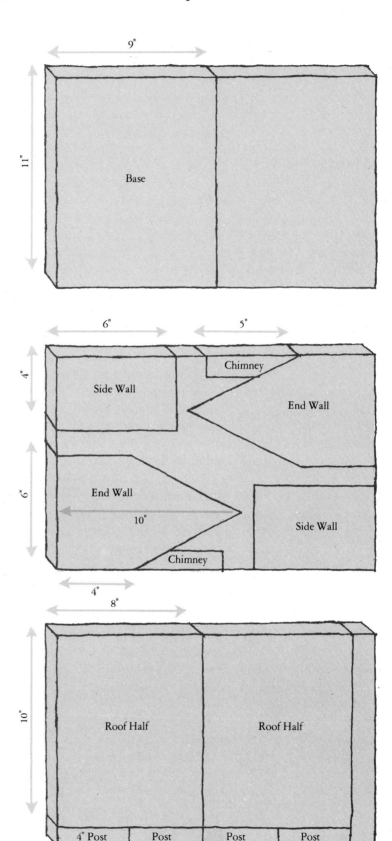

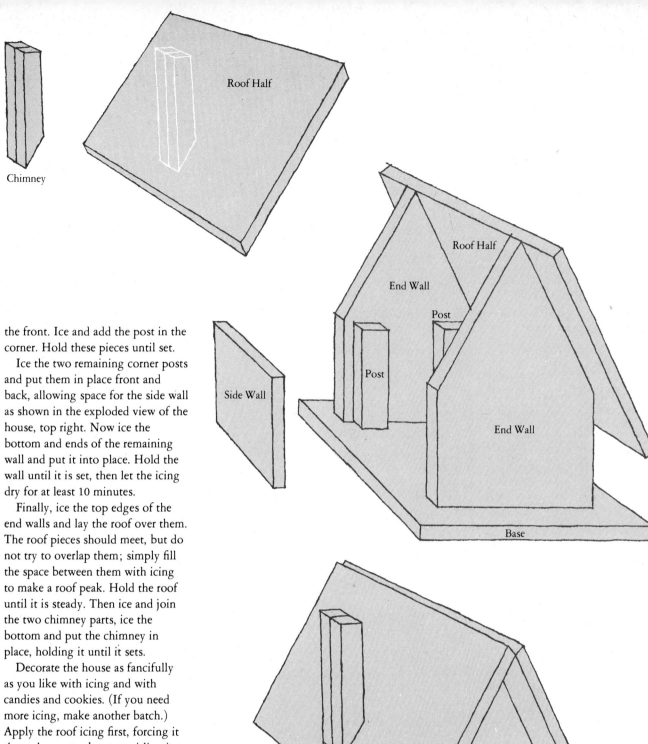

Chimney

Roof Half

Roof Half

End Wall

Post

Side Wall

Post

End Wall

Base

the front. Ice and add the post in the corner. Hold these pieces until set.

Ice the two remaining corner posts and put them in place front and back, allowing space for the side wall as shown in the exploded view of the house, top right. Now ice the bottom and ends of the remaining wall and put it into place. Hold the wall until it is set, then let the icing dry for at least 10 minutes.

Finally, ice the top edges of the end walls and lay the roof over them. The roof pieces should meet, but do not try to overlap them; simply fill the space between them with icing to make a roof peak. Hold the roof until it is steady. Then ice and join the two chimney parts, ice the bottom and put the chimney in place, holding it until it sets.

Decorate the house as fancifully as you like with icing and with candies and cookies. (If you need more icing, make another batch.) Apply the roof icing first, forcing it through a pastry bag or swirling it on with a small metal spatula. Don't forget a crown of icing snow for the chimney top. Spread the candies and cookies with icing and press them gently into place. When the house is done to your taste, sprinkle the roof and base with snowdrifts of sugar.

Fragile though it seems, the finished house can be a delight for many Christmases. Just cover it well with plastic wrap and store it in a cool dry place between seasons.

Glossary

ABENDBROT (AH-bent-broht): literally, "bread of the evening"; a light supper

ALTBIER (AHLT-beer): literally, "old beer"; a light, top-fermented beer

ANANAS (ah-nah-NAHS): pineapple

ANISKUCHEN (ah-NEES-koo-khen): cookies spiced with anisette

APFEL (AHP-fehl): apple

APFELMUS (AHP-fehl-moos): applesauce

APPELTATE (AHP-pel-tah-teh): a baked dessert of apples, almonds and raisins

APPELWOI (AHP-pel-voy): apple cider

AUSTERNSTUBE (OW-stern-shtoo-beh): an oyster bar

BAUMKUCHEN (BOWM-koo-khen): literally, "tree cake"; a traditional Christmas cake designed to resemble the trunk and bark of a tree

BEETENSUPPE (BEH-ten-zoop-peh): beet soup

BELEGTES BROT (beh-LAY'g-tess broht): literally, "covered bread"; a sandwich

BERLINER WEISSE (behr-LEE-nehr VICE-eh): literally, "Berlin white"; a pale, tart ale, which is traditionally served in a vast goblet

BIER (beer): beer

BIERHALLE (BEER-hahl'eh): beer hall

BIERLEICHEN (BEER-lye-khen): literally, "beer corpses"; people who pass out at Munich's Oktoberfest and have to be carted away

BIGOS (BEE-gohs): a hunter's stew eaten in Silesia and derived from Poland

BLATZ (blahtz): cookies of the Rhineland, consisting of crisp cones filled with whipped cream

BLINDHUHN (BLINT-hoon): literally, "blind hen"; a casserole of beans, fruit and vegetables

BLUMENKOHL (BLOO-men-kohl): cauliflower

BOHNENSALAT (BOHN-en-sah-laht): green bean salad

BOWLE (BOHV-leh): a festive drink generally made with wine and a flavoring of fruit, and served in a punch bowl

BRATEN (BRAH-ten): a roast generally cooked with a little liquid in a tightly covered pot on top of the stove

BRATHÄNDL (BRAHT-hendl): a spit-roasted chicken, often eaten at the Oktoberfest in Munich

BRATWURST (BRAHT-voorst): a type of sausage sold raw by the butcher. It must be pan-fried before eating

BROT (broht): bread

BROTZEIT (BROHT-ts'ite): the Munich expression for snack time. It includes such tidbits as beer, sausages, cheeses and radishes

BRÜHWURST (BREW-voorst): a type of sausage smoked and scalded by the butcher. It may be eaten as is, or heated by simmering

BÜCKLINGE (BEWK-leeng-eh): smoked herring

BUNTER TELLER (BOON-ter TELL-er): a brightly colored dish laden with fruits and cookies. It is a traditional part of the Christmas exchange of gifts

CHRISTKIND (KRISST-kint): Christ Child

DAMPFNUDELN (DAHMF-noo-deln): yeast dumplings

DELIKATE KLEINIGKEIT (deh-lee-KAH-teh KLINE-ikh-kite): literally, "a delicate little something"; a snack, as one that might be eaten after the theater

DREIKÖNIGSTAG (dry-KERN-igs-tahk): Epiphany

DUNKLES (DOONK-less): a dark-colored beer

EDELFRESSWELLE (EH-d'l-fress-vell-eh): literally, "exotic-food-devouring wave"; one of the temporary fashions that swept over Germany after World War II

EI (I): egg

EINTOPF (INE-tohpf): a one-dish meal, basic to German cooking

EISSALON (ICE-sah-lohn): an ice-cream parlor

ENTE (EHN-teh): duck

ERSTER WEIHNACHTSTAG (AIR-ster VYE-nakhts-tahk): Christmas Day

EXPORT BIER (EX-port beer): a type of strong bottom-fermented beer that is stored for two or three months so that it will not cloud up during shipment

FASAN (fa-ZAHN): pheasant

FASCHING (FA-shing): pre-Lenten carnival

FASTENFLEISCH (FAHS-ten-fly'sh): literally, "fast-day meat"; salt cod from northern Norway

FEINKOSTGESCHÄFT (FINE-kost-ghe-sheft): a delicatessen with gourmet foods

FORELLE (foh-REL-leh): a trout; **FORELLE BLAU** (foh-REL-leh bl'ow) is trout cooked *au bleu*

FRAU (fr'ow): a woman; Mrs.

FRÄULEIN (FROY-line): a young woman; Miss

FRESSGASSE (FRESS-gahs-seh): literally, "gorging street"; the Kleine Bockenheimer Strasse in Frankfurt, noted for its overwhelming number of gourmet delicatessens

FRESSWELLE (FRESS-vell-eh): literally, "devouring wave"; a phase of German life after World War II in which the populace indiscriminately ate huge quantities of food

FRÜHSTÜCK (FREW-shtewk): breakfast

FÜLLUNG (FEWL-loonk): a stuffing

GANS (gahns): goose

GÄNSEKLEIN (G'HEN-zeh-kline): giblets of goose, or a dish composed of them

GARKÜCHE (GAHR-kewkh-eh): an establishment in German cities in which food was cooked and sold during the Middle Ages

GASTHOF (GAHST-hohf): an inn

GEBILDBROTE (ghe-BEELT-broh-teh): literally, "picture breads"; types of German breads, first baked in the Middle Ages, characterized by elaborate shapes and superimposed designs

GEFÜLLT (ghe-FEWL't): filled

GEMÜTLICHKEIT (ghe-MEWT-leekh-kite): an atmosphere of warmth and fellowship

GESEGNETE MAHLZEIT (ghe-ZAY'g-neh-teh MAHL-ts'ite): literally, "blessed meal"; a phrase used, like *bon appétit* in French, to signify "enjoy your meal!"

GÖTTERTRUNK (GERT-ter-troonk): literally, "Drink of the Gods"; a punch consisting of port, brandy and black coffee

GRÜNKOHL (GREWN-kohl): kale

GURKE (GOOR-keh): cucumber

GUTES ESSEN (GOO-tess ESS'en): good eating or good food

GUT ESSEN GEHEN (goot ESS'en GAY'en): dining out well

GUTE STUBE (GOO-teh SHTOO-beh): the front parlor of a traditional German home

GUTSHERREN (GOOT's-hair'n): landed gentry

GUTSHOF (GOOT's-hohf): a farmyard, or the central yard of an estate

HACKEPETER (HAHK-eh-pay-ter): a dish popular in northern Germany consisting of ground meat (often pork or a mixture of beef and pork)

HALBES HELLES (HAHL-bess HELL-ess): a half liter (about a pint) of light beer

HAMMELFLEISCH (HAHM-mell-fly'sh): mutton

HANDSCHLAG (HAHNT-shlahk): literally, "a strike or blow of hands"; a traditional gesture used at an open-air market to close a deal

HAPPENPAPPEN (HAHP-en-pahp'en): a quick bite

HASE (HAH-zeh): a hare

HASELNUSS (HAH-zell-nooss): hazelnut

HASELNUSSMAKRONEN (HAH-zell-nooss-mah-KROHN-en): hazelnut macaroons

HASENPFEFFER (HAH-zen-pfehf'r): a spicy rabbit stew

HAUSFRAU (HOWSS-fr'ow): housewife

HAUSHERR (HOWSS-hehr): the master of a house

HEILBUTT (HILE-boot): halibut

HEILIGER ABEND (HI-lee-gher AH-bent): Christmas Eve

HEISS (hice): hot

HELLES (HELL-ess): a light-colored beer

HERR (hehr): sir; Mr.

HERRENABEND (HEHR-en-ah-bent): a social gathering of gentlemen; a stag party

HIMMEL UND ERDE (HIM-el oont AIR-deh): literally, "heaven and earth"; a dish of potatoes, apples, onion and bacon, popular in southern Germany

HIRSCH (heer'sh): a large stag

HONIGKUCHEN (HO-nik-koo-khen): honey cake

HONORATIOREN (HO-no-rah-TS'YOR-en): the gentry or men of influence in a village or small town

HOPPELPOPPEL (HO-pehl-pohp'l): a dish of fried potatoes mixed with eggs and bacon

HUHN (hoon): chicken

KAFFEE (KAH-fay): afternoon coffee which may be simple, with only a cup of coffee and a cookie, or elaborate, with a display of little sandwiches and cakes

KAFFEETISCH (kah-FAY-tish): a coffee table for displaying a variety of cakes and cookies

KALBSHAXE (KAHL'ps-ahx-eh): veal shanks

KALBSLEBER (KAHL'ps-lay-behr): calf's liver

KALBSROLLE (KAHL'ps-roll-eh): a stuffed and rolled breast of veal

KARTOFFEL (kar-TOH-fel): potato

KARTOFFELPUFFER (kar-TOH-fel-poof-er): potato pancakes

KARTOFFELSALAT (kar-TOH-fel-zah-laht): potato salad

KÄSE (KAY-zeh): cheese

KATEN (KAH-ten): peasants' huts where a type of ham was originally smoked

KATENSCHINKEN (KAH-ten-shin-ken): a type of ham originally smoked in peasants' wooden huts

KATERFRÜHSTÜCK (KAHT-er-frew-shtewk): a "hangover breakfast" consisting of herring and sausages

KATHRINCHEN (kaht-REEN-khen):

a type of spice cake originally baked in the German city of Thorn

KIPFEL (KIP-fel): a crescent roll

KLOPSE (KLOHP-seh): meatballs or hamburgers

KNEIPE (K'NYE-peh): a tavern

KNÖDEL or KNÖDL (k'nerd'l): dumplings

KOCHFRAU (KOH'kh-fr'ow): a free-lance cook often hired in earlier days for formal dinners

KOCHWURST (KOH'kh-voorst): a type of sausage, often smoked, that is cooked by the butcher. It includes the kinds of meats generally called cold cuts in the United States

KOHL (kohl): cabbage

KOMPOTT (kohm-POHT): a compote of stewed fruit

KONDITOREI (kohn-dee-toh-RYE): a pastry shop

KÖNIGINPASTETEN (KERN-ig-in-pah-shtet'en): literally, "queen's pastry"; puff-paste patties

KÖNIGSBERGER KLOPSE (KERN-igs-behrg-er KLOHP-seh): a poached meatball dish originating in the northeastern provinces of Germany

KREBSE (KREP-seh): crayfish or crab

KÜCHE (KEWKH-eh): a kitchen

KUCHEN (KOO-khen): a cake

LABSKAUS (LAHBS-kowss): seaman's dish, originally cooked aboard ship. It included onions and potatoes with fish, beef or both

LAGER (LAH-gher): literally, "to store"; a type of beer aged for about six weeks to clear and mellow it

LAUCH (l'ow'kh): leek

LEBER (LAY-behr): liver

LEBERKÄS (LAY-behr-kay'z): literally, "liver cheese"; a mixture of ground meats shaped into an oblong loaf, which may be eaten hot or cold

LEBKUCHEN (LAY'p-koo-khen): gingerbread

LINSENSUPPE (LIN-zen-zoop-peh): lentil soup

LOKAL (lo-KAHL): an eating and/or drinking establishment

MALZBIER (MAHL'ts-beer): a sweet, dark beer very low in alcoholic content

MANDELBREZELN (MAHN-del-bray-zehl'n): almond cookies

MANDELKERN (MAHN-del-kehrn): almond

MÄRZENBIER (MAIR-ts'en-beer): literally, "March beer"; a type of strong beer, between light and dark in color, brewed originally for spring consumption. It is popular at the Munich Oktoberfest

MARZIPAN (mahr-ts'ee-PAHN): a confection, popular in Germany since the Middle Ages, made of

sugar, almond paste and egg white

MILCHBAR (MILKH-bar): a milk bar or soda fountain

MITTAGESSEN (MIT-tahk-ess'en): a midday or early afternoon dinner

MOHNSTRIEZEL (MOHN-shtree-ts'el): a yeast loaf filled with poppy seeds, traditionally prepared at Christmastime

NACHTISCH (NAKH-tish): the final dessert course of the main midday meal, which may include bonbons, elaborate cookies, puddings or candied fruit

NIKOLASCHKA (nik-o-LA-shkah): a hangover cure consisting of brandy, topped with a slice of lemon and ground coffee

NUSS (nooss): nut

OBSTTORTEN (OHPST-tohr-ten): tarts varying in composition, but usually made with seasonal fruits

OKTOBERBIER (ohk-TOH-behr-beer): name sometimes used for *Märzenbier* (q.v.) because it is especially popular at the Munich Oktoberfest

OSTERHASE (OH-stehr-hah-zeh): Easter bunny

PFEFFERBROT (PFEHF-fer-broht): a type of spice cake, especially well known in the Köln version

PFEFFERKUCHEN (PFEHF-fer-koo-khen): a type of spice cake, especially well known in the Nürnberg version

PFEFFERSÄCKE (PFEHF-fer-zek-eh): literally, "pepper bags"; rich spice traders and merchants of the Middle Ages

PFIFFERLINGE (PFIF-fer-ling-eh): chanterelle—a type of wild mushroom

PFINGSTAUSFLUG (PFING'st-owss-flook): the traditional family outing held as part of the Whitsun festival to celebrate spring flowers

PFLAUMENKUCHEN (PFL'OW-men-koo-khen): plum tart

PICKERT (PICK-ert): bread made with wheat or potato flour; a Westphalian peasant food

PILSENER BIER (PEEL-zner beer): a light, bitterish beer

PILZE (PEEL-ts'eh): mushrooms

PINKEL (pink'l): a type of lightly smoked sausage

PLINSEN (PLEEN-zen): pancakes

POLTERABEND (POHL-ter-ah-bent): a traditional wedding-eve party

PREISELBEEREN (PRIZE-el-behr-en): lingonberries—small, tart berries that are used to make the German equivalent of cranberry sauce

PRINTEN (PRIN-ten): a type of spice cake, especially well known in the Aachen version

RADI (RAH-dee): dialect term for radish

RATSKELLER (RAHTS-kel-ler): an eating establishment

REH (reh): a small deer

ROHWURST (ROH-voorst): a type of sausage cured and smoked by the butcher, then eaten as is without further cooking

ROLLMÖPSE (ROLL-merp-seh): rolled herring fillets

ROSINE (roh-ZEE-neh): raisin

ROTWEIN (ROHT-vine): red wine

ROULADEN (roo-LA-den): rolled beef

SALAT (zah-LAHT): salad

SALZGEBÄCK (ZAHL'ts-ghe-bek): salted biscuit

SAUERBRATEN (ZOW-er-braht'en): marinated pot roast

SAUERKRAUT (ZOW-er-kraut): pickled cabbage

SAUER RAHM (ZOW-rehr rahm): sour cream

SCHAUESSEN (SH'OW-ess'en): literally, "foods for show"; dishes designed as much for their appearance as for their edibility

SCHINKEN (SHINK'en): ham

SCHLACHTFEST (SHLAHKHT-fest): literally, "slaughter feast"; a pig slaughtering followed by a feast

SCHMALZGEBACKENES (SHMAHL'ts-ghe-bah-ken-ess): any food fried in lard

SCHMANKERL (SHMAHN-kerl): in Munich, an untranslatable term applied to appealing little tidbits

SCHMARRN (shmahrn): egg-based pancakes

SCHMORGURKE (SHMOHR-goor-keh): cucumber braised in butter and dill

SCHNAPS (shnaps): clear brandy

SCHNELLIMBISS-STUBE (SHNELL-im-biss-shtoo-beh): a quick-lunch counter

SCHNELLKÜCHE (SHNELL-kewkh-eh): quick cookery

SCHNITZEL (SHNITS-sel): a very thin cut of meat prepared in various ways. It is traditionally veal, but may be pork or even beef

SCHOKOLADE (shoh-koh-LA-deh): chocolate

SCHÖN DECKEN (shern DEK'en): to set a table beautifully

SCHOPPENWEINE (SHOHP-pen-vine-eh): local open draft wines

SCHUNKELN (SHOONK-eln): to sway to and fro, often with linked arms; a common drinking custom

SCHUSS (shooss): literally, "a shot"; **BERLINER WEISSE MIT SCHUSS** is a glass of beer served with a shot of raspberry syrup

SEKTFRÜHSTÜCK (ZEKT-frew-shtewk): a champagne breakfast

SELLERIESALAT (SELL-er-EE-zah-laht): celery salad

SEMMEL (ZEHM-el): a white roll

SENF (zehnf): mustard

SOSSE (ZOHS-seh): sauce

SPÄTZLE (SHPEH-ts'leh): literally, "little sparrows"; tiny dumplings

SPECK (shpeck): bacon or lard

SPEKULATIUS (shpeh-koo-LA-ts'ee-ooss): a type of spice cake baked in the Rhineland

SPICKGANS (SHPIK-gahns): pickled and smoked breast of goose

SPRINGERLE (SHPRIN-girl-eh): molded anise-seed cookies

SPRITZGEBÄCK (SHPRITZ-ghe-bek): pressed hazelnut cookies

STAMMTISCH (SHTAHM-tish): the table in a village inn or restaurant reserved for regular and respected guests

STIFT (shtift): an endowed foundation for the elderly

STOLLEN (SHTOHL'en): fruit cakes, especially popular at Christmastime

STREUSELKUCHEN (SHTROY-zel-koo-khen): a yeast cake with a sugar-crumb topping

STRUDEL (SHTROO-d'l): a type of flaky pastry that is filled with apples, nuts or cheese, and baked

SÜLZE (ZEWL-ts'eh): head cheese

SÜSSE SPEISEN (ZEWS-seh SHPY-zen): sweet dishes

SÜSSGEBÄCK (ZEWS-ghe-bek): sweet baked goods

TOMATEN (toh-MAH-ten): tomatoes

TORTEN (TOHR-ten): tarts

VIEZ (feets): dry apple cider

VOLKSFEST (FOLKS-fest): a popular festival

VORSPEISEN (FOR-shpy-zen): appetizers

WEIHNACHTSBAUM (VINE-akhts-b'ow'm): Christmas tree

WEIHNACHTSMANN (VINE-akhts-mahn): Father Christmas

WEINGELEE (VINE-jeh-lay): wine jelly

WEINSTUBE (VINE-shtoob-eh): a restaurant specializing in wine

WEISSBIER (VICE-beer): literally, "white beer"; a type of weak beer

WEISSBROT (VICE-broht): white bread

WEISSWEIN (VICE-vine): white wine

WINZERFEST (VIN-ts'er-fest): local vintners' festival

WURST (voorst): sausage

ZELTEN (TS'EL-ten) plain flat cakes

ZWEITES FRÜHSTÜCK (ts'VITE-ess FREW-shtewk): second breakfast usually consisting of sandwiches or fruit, eaten between 9 and 10 o'clock

199

Recipe Index: English

NOTE: An R preceding a page refers to the Recipe Booklet. Size, weight and material are specified for pans in the recipes because they affect cooking results. A pan should be just large enough to hold its contents comfortably. Heavy pans heat slowly and cook food at a constant rate. Aluminum and cast iron conduct heat well but may discolor foods containing egg yolks, wine, vinegar or lemon. Enamelware is a fairly poor conductor of heat. Many recipes therefore recommend stainless steel or enameled cast iron, which do not have these faults.

Soups

Chicken giblet and barley soup		R2
Cream of cauliflower soup	60;	R6
Hot beer soup	81;	R4
Lentil soup	116;	R3
Potato soup with cucumber	137;	R5
Vegetable-beef soup with tiny dumplings	164;	R4

Fish

Fillet of walleyed pike with mustard butter		R7
"Fish for a hangover" with tomato sauce and pickles		R11
Halibut under a mountain of cream		R10
Rollmops	39;	R9
Walleyed pike baked in white wine		R8

Meat and Poultry

Beef in spiced sour-cream sauce	25;	R18
Beef short ribs with spiced lemon-and-caper sauce	140;	R12
Beefsteak Tartar	26;	R17
Berlin-style chicken fricassee		R40
Boiled beef with chive sauce		R15
Braised lamb shoulder with mustard and red wine sauce		R26
Braised stuffed beef rolls	63;	R13
Braised stuffed veal roll	40;	R22
Bratwurst in sweet-sour sauce		R34
Calf's liver with apples and onion rings	119;	R38
Corned beef hash with salt herring	122;	R37
Fresh ham, mock-boar style	26;	R32
Ham braised in burgundy	38;	R33
Lamb chops in onion sauce		R25
Marinated pot roast in sweet-and-sour sauce	22;	R16
Mixed meat and vegetable casserole	41;	R36
Poached meatballs in lemon-and-caper sauce	119;	R14
Pork chops in aspic	120;	R28
Pork chops with knockwurst and potatoes		R30
Roast duck with apple and bread stuffing	123;	R43
Roast goose with apple, raisin and nut stuffing		R38
Roasted smoked pork loin	140;	R31
Spareribs with pickle sauce		R35
Steamed bratwurst in sour-cream sauce	41;	R24
Veal roast stuffed with kidney		R24
Veal shanks in pickle sauce	165;	R19
Veal tongue, sweetbreads and mushrooms in white wine sauce		R20

Game

Braised rabbit in spiced red wine sauce	81;	R44
Game birds in burgundy	61;	R51
Pheasant in red wine		R52
Pheasant with giblet and crouton stuffing	83;	R53
Roast partridges with grapes	86;	R50
Roast saddle of venison with red wine sauce	84;	R47
Venison cutlets with mushrooms	60;	R45
Venison tenderloin in spiced brandy sauce		R49

Dumplings

Dessert dumplings with vanilla sauce	162;	R58
Farina dumplings	165;	R59
Potato dessert dumplings with prune-butter filling	139;	R57
Potato dumplings	137;	R56
Tiny dumplings	164;	R55
Yeast dumplings		R60

Vegetables

Baked kale with potatoes	136;	R66
Beans with fruit and vegetables	138;	R72
Brussels sprouts with ham and tomatoes		R70
Eggs with bacon, onions and potatoes	122;	R67
Endive baked with ham and cheese		R68
Green herb sauce		R73
Mushrooms with tomatoes and bacon	25;	R68
Pineapple sauerkraut	24;	R62
Potato pancakes with applesauce	118;	R65
Potatoes with apples	164;	R64
Red cabbage with apples	63;	R63
Sauerkraut with wine and grapes		R62
Sour potatoes		R64
Steamed spiced sauerkraut	24;	R61
Stewed cucumbers with sour cream and dill	117;	R69
Yellow pea purée with bacon	116;	R71

Salads

Celery root and apple salad	83;	R77
Green bean salad	43;	R74
Hot potato salad with bacon	42;	R76
Leek salad	61;	R78
Pickled-beet salad	42;	R75
Summer potato salad	136;	R76

Breads and Cookies

Almond crescent cookies	194;	R87
Brown butter cookies		R94
Chocolate pretzels	183;	R84
Dresden Christmas fruit bread	193;	R79
Gingerbread house	195;	R90
Hazelnut macaroons	182;	R82
Honey cake	181;	R88
Molded anise-seed cookies	182;	R86
Pressed hazelnut cookies	183;	R82
S-shaped butter cookies	194;	R83
Spice cookies	192;	R85
Spiced honey cookies		R89
White bread with caraway seeds	178;	R81

Cakes and Desserts

Almond layer cake		R102
Apple and pumpernickel crumb dessert	163;	R109
Apple and rum custard cake	64;	R108
Apple-filled pancakes	64;	R112
Black Forest cherry cake	160;	R98
Dried fruit compote	138;	R115
Farina layer cake with almonds		R103
"First frost" apple and cream dessert		R114
Hazelnut cream pudding	87;	R111
Layer cake with butter-cream filling and praline topping	180;	R96
Lemon cream dessert	43;	R113
Loaf cake with raisins, almonds and rum		R95
Mixed fruit tart	178;	R100
Poppy-seed cake		R104
Steamed chocolate pudding	65;	R110
Sugar-crumb cake	141;	R106
Wine jelly with fruit	123;	R114

Recipe Index: German

Soups

Blumenkohlsuppe 60; R6
Feine Kartoffelsuppe mit Gurken 137; R5
Gaisburger Marsch. 164; R4
Graupensuppe mit Hühnerklein. R2
Heisse Biersuppe. 81; R4
Linsensuppe 116; R3

Fish

Heilbutt unterm Sahneberg R10
Katerfisch R11
Rollmöpse 39; R9
Zander im Ofen gebacken mit Weisswein R8
Zander Schnitte mit Senfbutter R7

Meat and Poultry

Beefsteak Tartar 26; R17
Berliner Hühnerfrikassee. R40
Bratwurst mit saurer Sahnensosse 41; R34
Ente mit Äpfeln und Brot Füllung. 123; R43
Falscher Wildschweinbraten 26; R32
Gänsebraten mit Äpfeln, Rosinen und Nüssen R38
Gebratene Kalbsleber auf Berliner Art 119; R38
Hammel Koteletten mit Zwiebelsosse R25
Kalbshaxe mit Gewürzgurkensosse 165; R19
Kalbsnierenbraten. R24
Kalbsrolle 40; R22
Kasseler Rippenspeer 140; R31
Königsberger Klopse 119; R14
Labskaus 122; R37
Pichelsteiner Fleisch 41; R36
Piquante Hammelschulter R26
Ragoût fin R20
Rindfleisch mit Schnittlauchsosse R15
Rouladen 63; R13
Sauerbraten. 22; R16
Schinken in Burgunder. 38; R33
Schweinerippchen mit Gewürzgurkensosse R35
Schweinskoteletten mit Knackwurst und Kartoffeln . . . R30
Sülzkotelett 120; R28
Süss-saure Bratwurst. R34
Westfälischer Pfefferpotthast 140; R12
Würzfleisch 25; R18

Game

Fasan in Rotwein. R52
Gefüllter Fasan 83; R53
Hasenpfeffer. 81; R44
Piquante Rehfiletschnitten R49
Rebhühner mit Weintrauben 86; R50
Rehrücken mit Rotweinsosse 84; R47
Rehschnitzel mit Pilzen 60; R45
Wildgeflügel mit Burgunder. 61; R51

Dumplings

Dampfnudeln 162; R58
Griessklösse. 165; R59
Hefeklösse. R60
Kartoffelklösse 137; R56
Kartoffelklösse mit Pflaumenmus 139; R57
Spätzle 164; R59

Vegetables

Chicorée mit Schinken und Käse R68
Erbspüree 116; R71
Gedünstetes Sauerkraut 24; R61
Grüne Sosse R73
Grünkohl mit Kartoffeln 136; R66
Himmel und Erde. 164; R64
Hoppelpoppel. 122; R67
Kartoffelpuffer mit Apfelmus 118; R65
Pilze mit Tomaten und Speck 25; R68
Rosenkohl mit Schinken und Tomaten R70
Rotkohl mit Äpfeln 63; R63
Sauerkraut mit Ananas 24; R62
Saure Kartoffeln. R64
Schmorgurken mit saurem Rahm und Dill 117; R69
Weinkraut R62
Westfälisches Blindhuhn 138; R72

Salads

Bohnensalat 43; R74
Lauchsalat. 61; R78
Leichter Kartoffelsalat. 136; R76
Rote Rübensalat 42; R75
Selleriesalat mit Äpfeln 83; R77
Warmer Kartoffelsalat mit Speck 42; R76

Breads and Cookies

Dresdner Stollen 193; R79
Haselnussmakronen 182; R82
Heidesand R94
Honigkuchen 181; R88
Lebkuchen. R89
Lebkuchen Häuschen 195; R90
Mandel-Halbmonde 194; R87
Pfeffernüsse 192; R85
S-Gebäck 194; R83
Schokoladen Brezeln 183; R84
Springerle 182; R86
Spritzgebäck 183; R82
Weissbrot mit Kümmel 178; R81

Cakes and Desserts

Apfelbettelmann. 163; R109
Apfelkuchen 64; R108
Apfelpfannkuchen 64; R112
Backobstkompott 138; R115
Frankfurter Kranz. 180; R96
Griesstorte R103
Haselnusscreme 87; R111
Königskuchen R95
Mandeltorte R102
Mohnstriezel R104
Obsttorte 178; R100
Rauhreif. R114
Schokoladenpudding 65; R110
Schwarzwälder Kirschtorte 160; R98
Streuselkuchen 141; R106
Weingelee. 123; R114
Zitronencreme. 43; R113

General Index

Numerals in italics indicate a photograph or drawing of the subject mentioned.

Abendbrot, 29, 36
Adlon, Lorenz and Louis, 58
Advent calendar, *188*, 190
Albert, Prince, 130
Albrecht, Archbishop of Bremen, 91
Alsace-Lorraine, *map* 145
Altbier ("old beer"), 57
Anhalt, *map* 107
Antwerp, Belgium, 93
Apfelkuchen, 70
Appelwoi (hard apple cider), 127-129
Appetizers, 11
Apples, 14, 15, *104*; applesauce, 15, 36; baked with sour cherries and kirsch, 99; butter, 33; cake, 70; cider, 127, 128-129, 144; fritters; 91; *Himmel und Erde*, 14, 144; pudding, 35; stuffing for goose, 90
Apricots, 14
Architecture, Baroque, 96, 98, 130, 155; Westphalia, 125
Asparagus, 15, 45, 113, 155; with hollandaise, 47, 99, 155; soup, 11; South African, 54
Aspic, pork chops in, *121*
Augsburg: silver made in, 95
Austernstuben (oyster bars), 16

*B*ach, Johann Sebastian, 130
Bacon: with kraut, 98; for midday dinner, 36; smoked, 106, 126; soup, 105
Baden, 154-155; *map* 145
Bad Dürkheim, *145*; wine festival, *148-149*
Bad Godesberg, Haus Maternus restaurant, 45-46; Michaeli Stuben restaurant, 145
Bad Reinherz, *100*
Baking molds, 173
Baking powder, 169
Balkan foods, 58
Baltic Sea, 105, 107, 108; *map* 103
Baltic states, 75

Bananas, 58
Banquets, medieval, 91-92; Renaissance, 93-95
Barley: breads, 168; soup, 35
Baroque period, 96-98, 155; architecture, 130; Bavaria, 155
Baumkuchen (Christmas cakes), 115
Bavaria, *13*, *142*, 155-157; *map* 145
Bayreuth, Germany, 185
Beans: broad, 36, 126; green, *30-31*; white, *117*
Béarnaise sauce, 45
Beaver legs, preserved, 93
Beef: *Deutsches Beefsteak*, 35; ground, 12-13, 35; fillet of, 36; roast, 12, 35, 72, 99, over open fire, 90; roulade of, *62*; short-rib stew, 126-127; steak on toast with mushrooms, 37; stews, 13; Stroganoff, 46
Beefsteak Tartar (raw ground steak dish), *13*, *27*, 114, 129
Beer, *56-57;* Bavarian, 155, 156-157; Berlin, 115; Bernau, 95; Dortmund, 126; festivals, 185, *186-187;* medieval, 90; Munich, 156-157, *186-187;* soup, 93
Beerenauslese (wine), 47
Beetensuppe (borscht), 75
Belegtes Brot (sandwich), 32
Bergen, Norway, 93
Berlin, 70, 105, *107*, 114-115; Hardtke's restaurant, 45; Kranzler pastry shop, 37; porcelain manufacture, 98; Schlichter's restaurant, 32, 114; supermarkets, *10-11*
Berliner Pfannkuchen, 115
Berliner Riesenbratwurst mit Kartoffelsalat (large sausage with potato salad), 45
Berliner Weisse beer, *57*, 115
Bernard (French chef), 99
Bernau beer, 95
Bernkastel vineyards, *146*
Bernkasteler Doktor *Auslese* (wine), 54

Berries, 14, 15, *46*, 75
Beverages: apple cider, 127, 128-129; beer, *56-57*, 126; Berlin beers, 115; *Bowle* (wine beverage), 71; cocktails, 72; 18th Century, 96; hard liquors, 72; medieval, 90; mixed drinks, 74; Munich beers, 156-157, *186-187;* punch, 73-74; Rococo period, 98; *Schnaps*, 57, 72, 112, 113, 124, 126, 127, 134; Silesian liqueurs, 133; "Warsaw Death," *74;* wine, 71, 143, 144
Biedermeier period, 98
Bierhallen, 16
Bigos (Polish hunter's stew), 75, 131-132
Bismarck, Prince Otto von, 32, 73, 89, 102
Bismarck herring, 11, 108
Black puddings, 90
Blackberry liqueur, 133
Blindhuhn (bean casserole), *117*, 126
Blueberry preserves, 33
Boar, 14, 90, 93; marinated, 145; saddle of, 47, 106
Bock beer, 57, 156
Boj, Rudolf, 99
Bonbons, 35
Bonn, 145
Boppard, 185
Borscht, 75
Bouillon: with marrow, 35, 72; with pancake strips, 36
Bourbon whiskey, 72
Bowle (wine beverage), 71
Brägenwurst, 112
Brandenburg, *map* 107
Brandy, 72
Braten (roast), 12
Brathändl (spit-roasted chicken), *188*
Brathering (pickled herring), 108
Bratwurst, 55, 129, *152-153*, 155
Braunschweig (Brunswick), 112-114; *map* 107

Braunschweiger sausage, 112-113
Breads, 50, 167-169, *172;* for supper, 36; breakfast, 29; Christmas, 191; fruit, 173; sourdough, *170-171;* Westphalian, 127
Breakfast, 29-32
Brecht, Berthold, 114
Bremen, 105, *map* 107; *Ratskeller* restaurant, *52*
Bremer Kükenragout (chicken with ragoût sauce), 109
Brill, 108
Brillat-Savarin, 98
Bruehl, Count Heinrich von, 89
Bruges, Belgium, 93
Brühwurst, 55
Bücklinge (smoked herring), 108
Buffets, 66, 68-69
Bühl, 185
Butcher shops, 16
Butter, 35
Byk-Gulden Company of Konstanz, 99

*C*abbage, 15, 17, *18-19*, *20-21;* red, 35, *62*, 80, 106; soup, 105. *See also* Sauerkraut
Calf's liver, 144
Cakes, 59, *176-177;* apple, 70; *Baumkuchen*, 115; *Berliner Pfannkuchen*, 115; caraway, 75; cherry, *160-161;* chocolate, 70; Christmas, 191, *192;* honey, 174; at pastry shops, 37, *59; Punschtorte*, 114; Rococo period, 98; Saxony, 130; spice, 174-175
Candied fruits, 35
Candy shops, 173
Canned foods, 15-16
Capon, boned roast, 99; cooked with almonds, 98; stuffed with oysters, 98
Caraway cakes, 75
Carp, 12, 35, 90; boiled blue, 54; Christmas Eve dish, 131, 191
Carrot: cream soup, 35

Carving meat, 95; saddle of venison, *84-85*
Casseroles, 33; *Schlesisches Himmelreich* (pork with dried fruit), 133. *See also Eintopf* (one-pot dish)
Castle-Hotel Kronberg, *44*
Castles, 8
Catering, for entertaining, 68-69
Cauliflower, *30-31;* soup, 11, 35
Caviar, 32; Iranian, 16; Malassol, 54; with *Schnitzel à la Holstein,* 12
Celebrations: 185-191; confirmation, 72-73; engagement, 73; wedding, 73
Champagne, 32, 72-73
Champignon-Schnitte, 11
Chanterelle mushrooms, 46, *159*
Charlemagne, 90, 91
Charles IV, Emperor, 91, 175
Charles V of France, 91
Château Haut-Brion wine, 47
Cheeses, 16; Bavarian, 99, *142,* 157; at breakfast, 32; at midday dinner, 35; tarts, 75
Cherries, 15, 75, *160-161;* fritters, 91; tarts, 70, 75
Chicken, 13, 90; breaded fried boneless breasts, 99; *Bremer Kükenragout,* 109; fricassee, 114, 159; ragoût, 46; roast, 35; salad with Persian melon, 54; spit-roasted, 188; *Stubenküken,* 108-109
Children's festivals, 185
China (tableware), 88, 96, 98
Chocolate cake, 70
Chocolate pretzels, *183*
Chocolate pudding, 35
Chops, 12; pork in aspic, *121*
Christmas: celebrations, 189-190; gingerbread house, *196-197;* greens and decorations, *189, 190, 191; Stollen, 192*
Cider, 128-129, 144; in medieval diet, 90

Cities: Renaissance, 92-93
Coburg, 129-130
Cocktail parties, 71-72
Cod, salt, 90
Coffee, 29, 36-37, 69-70, *176-177*
Coffeecakes, 37
Coffeerooms, Rococo period, 98
Cold cuts: at breakfast, 32
Commerce: Hanseatic League, 92-93
Compotes, fruit, 14-15, *139;* with meat, 35
Confirmation ceremony celebration, 72-73
Consommés, 11, 99; with champagne breakfast, 32
Constantin of Bavaria, Prince, 73
Cookbooks, 12, 35; *Feste Feiern Wie Sie Fallen,* 67; *Geist der Kochkunst* (early 19th Century), 98; *Gesegnete Mahlzeit* (Silesian), 132; handwritten, 18th Century, 96; *Meine Kunst,* 47; *Praktisches Kochbuch,* 35; Renaissance, 95
Cookies, 35, 169, 173-174, *176-177;* Christmas, 191; Rhineland, 154; *Springerle, 166*
Cooks, for entertaining, 68-69
Corpus Christi Festival, 185
Cottage-cheese dessert, 36
Crabmeat cocktail, 72
Crabs, 11
Craft guilds, 93
Cranberry preserves, 36
Crayfish, 11, 16; bisque, 11; cooked in dill, 75; with *Schnitzel à la Holstein,* 12
Cream puffs, 70
Cream: with coffee, 37; in soups and gravies, 106
Cream of vanilla, 35
Cream sauce, with meats, 156
Cream soups, 35
Croissants, 168-169
Cucumbers, 114; garnish with beef Stroganoff, 46; salad, 35
Currants, 75; tarts, 75

Curried beef fillet, 46
Custards, egg, 15
Cutlets, 12; with cauliflower, 35

Danish influence on north German cooking, 105
Danzig, *map* 107
Davidis-Holle, Henriette, 35
Deidesheim, 185
Delicatessens, 16; foods, 36
Der Monat (magazine), 70
Desserts, 15; baked apples with sour cherries and kirsch, 99; cherry tarts, 75; cream cheese and peach, 46; 18th Century, 96; lemon cream, 72; marzipan, 93, *184;* medieval diet, 90-91; at midday dinner, 35, 36; rice pudding, 54; Silesian, 133; Westphalian, 127
Deutsches Beefsteak (hamburger), 12, 35
Dinkelsbühl, Germany, 185
Dinner, 29, 32-36; Christmas, 191; entertaining at, 72-73
Domino cocktail, 72
Dorpat, Estonia, 75
Dortmund beer, 126
Dresden, *103,* 130
Dresdner Stollen (Christmas cake), 130, *192*
Dried fruits, 14-15, *138*
Dubois (French chef), 99
Duck, 13-14; roast, 35, 105
Dumplings, 8, 10, *62,* 80, 99; fruit, 15; *Knödl,* 156; lobster, 99; potato, 129, *135;* Silesian, 132; *Spätzle,* 154-155
Dunkles beer, 56
Dürkheim Fair, *148-149,* 188
Düsseldorf, *map 103*
Dutch East India Company, 98
Dutch influence on north German cooking, 105

East Prussia, 67, 74, 75, 105, 106; *map* 107

East Germany, *map* 107
Easter celebrations, 188-189
Ebert, Frederick, 58
Éclairs, 36
Edelfresswelle, 55-58
Eel, 35, 105; *aux fines herbes,* 54; sautéed, 144; smoked, 107, *112-113*
Eggs: at breakfast, 29, 32; custards, 15; pickled hard-cooked, 115; shirred, 35; "egg cozies," 29, 32; scissors, 32
Einsiedler cocktail, 72
Eintopf (one-pot dish), 14, 33, *34, 143*
Eissalons, 16
Elbe River, 109; *map* 107
Elchkeule (leg of elk), 106
Elk, leg of, 106
Empire period, 98
Engagement, celebration of, 73
Epiphany, 190
Esslingen: marketplace, *9;* sauerkraut manufacture, *21*
Estonia, 75
Etiquette: Renaissance period, 95
Eutin, 108
Export beer, 57

Faïence manufacture, 96
Farm buildings, *104*
Fasching (pre-Lenten festival), 188
Feinkostgeschäft (delicatessen), 16, 36
Fish, 16; carp, boiled blue, 54; eel *aux fines herbes,* 54; *Forelle blau,* 47; herring, 11; *Labskaus,* 108; *Maränen,* 106; Mecklenburg and Pomeranian dishes, 107; medieval diet, 90; methods of preparation, 11-12; course for midday dinner, 35, 36; north German cuisine, 105; paprika, 36; pickled, 108; served in restaurants, 47; smoked, 108. *See also* Eel, Herring, etc.
Flaming dishes, 58

Flatfish, 90

Flensburg, *map* 107

Flounder, 11, 35, 105

Flower-growers: Hamburg area,
109; gift to hostess, 68, 72

Foie gras with aspic, 99; truffled,
105

Food fads, 55, 58

Food shortages, 55

Foreign restaurants, 16

Forelle blau, 47

Fowl, 90; wild, 76, 78-79, 86

Frankenthal: porcelain
manufacture, 98

Frankfurt: 127; Castle-Hotel
Kronberg, *44;* delicatessens, 16;
Frankfurter Stubb, 54;
Gutsschänke Neuhof restaurant,
50-51; Hotel Frankfurter Hof,
54; *Frankfurter Würstchen*, 127,
128

Frantzen, G. C., 77

Frederick the Great of Prussia, 98,
134

French influence, 96; in 18th
Century German life, 98; in 19th
Century German life, 99

Fresswelle, 55

Fritters, fruit, 91

Frühstück (breakfast), 29-32

Fruits: *94;* in *Bowlen* (wine
beverages), 71; breads, 173;
candied, 35; compote, 139; with
meat, 35, *139;* dried, 14, *138;*
dried, as sweeteners, 173; dried,
with meats, 105; dumplings, 15;
growing, *104;* jellies, 15; with
meat dishes, 14-15; pancakes, 15;
preserving, 75; in Saxonian
cuisine, 131; stewed, 35, 36, 99;
tarts, *59,* 70, 75, 129-130, *176-
177, 179;* tropical, 58. *See also*
Apples, Bananas, etc.

Fuel for cooking, 168

Fürst, Paul, 95

Fürstenberg, *map* 107; porcelain
manufacture, 98

Game meats, 14, 50, *76, 78-79,*
90, 96; boar, 47, 106; elk, 106;
partridge, 86; pâté with
Cumberland sauce, 54; rabbit
stew, *80;* in Rhineland cuisine,
145; venison, 46, 106; saddle of
venison, *82, 84-85*

Gänseklein, 107

Gasthöfe, 16, 126

Gebildbrote ("picture breads"), 168,
172

Gebratene Kalbsleber auf Berliner Art
(pan-fried liver), 114

Germany: in 1914, *map* 103

Getrüffelte Gänseleberwurst, 8

Gingerbread house: to make, *196-
197*

Godfrey of Bouillon, 91

Goose, 13-14, 90; Pomeranian,
106-107; roast, 35, 105; roast,
Christmas dish, 191; smoked
breast of, 54

Goose-fat spread, 66

Goose liver: pâté, 32; sausage, 8-
10

Gooseberries, 75; tarts, 35

Göttertrunk (port, brandy and
coffee), 74

Goulash, 36; soup, 32

Gourmets, 19th Century, 98

Grapes: in gelatin, 35; with
sauerkraut, 17

Graue Erbsen mit Speck (dried peas
with bacon), 106

Green sauce, Frankfurt, 54, 128

Grimm's fairy tales, 167

Ground meat, 12-13

Guilds, Renaissance, 93

Gutsschänke Neuhof restaurant,
50-51

Halibut, 105

Halle, *107*

Ham: at breakfast, 32; cooked with
onions and cream, 75; ways of
preparing, 12; Westphalian, *124,*
125, 126

Hamburg, *103;* Alsterpavillon, 37;
cuisine, 105; dinner parties, 72;
map 107; restaurants, 32, 108

Hamburg Hunting Association, 76-
77, *78-79*

Hamburger, 12, 35

Hameln, 112

Hanover, *103; map* 107; pastry
shop, *59*

Hanseatic League, 92-93, 109

Hare, 14, *76;* pie of, 96; ragoût,
35; roast, Christmas dish, 191;
stew, *80, 92*

Hart, 90

Hartshorn, 169

Harvest festivals, 75, 185

Hasenpfeffer (rabbit stew), *80, 92*

Haus Maternus restaurant, 45-46

Head cheese, 114

Heidschnucken (a breed of curly-
horned sheep), 109

Helles beer, 56

Henry II, King of France, 95

Herb sauce, green, 128

Herrenabend (gentlemen's evening),
73

Herring: 11, 105; for breakfast, 32;
for midday dinner, 35; pickled,
108; rolls, *38-39;* in Silesia, 131;
smoked, 108

Hesse, *map* 127

Himmel und Erde (potato and apple
dish), 14, 144

Hirsch venison, 46

Höchst, porcelain manufacture, 98

Hohenzollern, *map* 145

Holstein, Baron Friedrich von, 12

Honey, 173; in medieval cooking,
90-91

Honey cakes, spiced, 96, 173, 174

Hops, as a vegetable, 155

Hunting, 75, *76-77, 78-79,* 106

Hutzelbrot (fruit bread), 173

Ice cream, 35, 99; *Bombe*, 99;
nougat, 36

Industrialization, 99

Inns: signs, *48-49;* 58

Innsbruck, Austria, 95

Jaesrich, Hellmut, 70

Jägerschnitzel, 12

Jannings, Emil, 114

Jellies, 15

Johannistag festival, 185

Kaffee, 29, 36-37, 69-70, *176-
177*

Kalbsfilet Diplomaten Art (fillet of
veal), 46

Kalbshaxe (veal shanks), 156

Kalbsrolle (veal roll), *30-31*

Kardorff, Ursula von, *66, 67, 68-
69*

Karlsruhe, *103*

Kartoffelpuffer mit Apfelmus (potato
pancakes with applesauce), 114

Käseschnitzel, 12

Kasseler Rippenspeer (roasted smoked
pork loin), 12, 128

Katenschinken (smoked ham), 108

Katenwurst (smoked sausage), 108

Katerfrühstück ("hangover
breakfast"), 32

Keller, Gottfried, 174

Kidneys, 13; with onions and
raisins in wine sauce, 90

Kiel, *map* 107; 108

Kieler Sprotten (smoked herring),
108

Kipfel (crescent roll), 168-169

Kirsch (cherry brandy), *160-161*

Kitchen utensils, 94

Kitchens, 113-114

Klaren (*Schnaps*), 108

Knob-celery soup, 11

Knödl (dumplings), 156

Kochwurst, 55, 112

Köln, *map* 103; *Fasching*, 188

Kölsch (Rhenish beer), 57

Konditoreien (pastry shops), 37, *59,*
177

Konfirmation ceremony celebration,
72-73

Königinpasteten, 11
Königsberg, *maps* 103, 107
Königsberger Klopse (poached meatballs), 12, 102, 106, *118*
Korn. *See Schnaps*
Kraut: and bacon, 98. *See also* Sauerkraut
Krebse in Dill (crayfish cooked in dill), 75
Küchenmaysterey (15th Century cookbook), 95

L*abskaus* (seafood dishes), 108
Lager beer, 57
Lamb, stews, 13
Lämmerhüpfen, 75
Lamprey stew, 93
La Varenne (17th Century French chef), 96
Leberkäs, 13, 157
Lebkuchen (honey and spice cakes), *149,* 174-175, 189
Leeks, braised, *30-31*
Leftovers, 14
Leipzig, 131; trade fair, 130
Lemon cream, 72
Lemon juice, 106
Lentils: and peas, 98; soup, 11, 35, 36, *117*
Leo, Count Lanckoronski, 132
Leopold, Duke of Babenberg, 169
Lingonberries, stewed, 106
Lippe, *map* 107
Liqueurs: medieval, 90; Silesian, 133
Liver, 13; pan-fried, 114; in Saxonian cuisine, 131
Liverwurst, 112-113
Livestock markets, *110-111*
Lobsters, 11, 32; cocktail, 72; dumplings, 99; with dill mayonnaise, 99
Louis XIV, King of France, 96
Lübeck, *maps* 103, 107; marzipan manufacture, 175
Ludwig, Crown Prince of Bavaria, 188

Ludwigsburg, porcelain manufacture, 98
Lüneburg, *map* 107, 109
Luther, Martin, 130
Lüttje Lagen (Schnaps and beer), 112

M*agdenburg, map* 107
Malassol caviar, 32, 54
Malzbier, 57
Mangoes, 58
Maps: Germany-1914, 103; Central Belt, 127; Northern Belt, 107; Southern Belt, 145
Maränen, 106
Maria Laach church and abbey, 144
Marinades: for *Sauerbraten, 23;* for venison, 46
Marketplaces: 15-16; Esslingen, *9;* Osterholz-Scharmbeck, *110-111, 112;* Renaissance period, 93
Marrow dumplings, in soups, 11
Märzenbier, 57, 156
Marzipan, 93, 175, *184,* 191
Mastgeflügel (Vierlande-raised fowl), 108-109
Masurian Lakes district, 106; *map* 107
Matjes (pickled herring), 108
Maximilian I, King, 92
Meat shops, 16
Meat-filled pastries, 11
Meatballs: poached, 12, *118*
Meat: at breakfast, 32; at midday dinner, 35; pickled and smoked, 105. *See also* Beef, Pork, etc.
Mecklenburg province, 106; *map* 107
Medici, Catherine de', 95
Medici, Lorenzo de', 95
Mehlspeis, 156
Meissen, *103;* porcelain, *88,* 96, 98, 130, *176-177*
Menus: royal and court, *97, 99*
Mettingen, Germany, *170-171*
Michaeli Stuben, 145
Middle class and industrialization, 99

Milchbars, 16
Millet gruel, 93
Milt, 13
Mittagessen (midday dinner), 29, 32-36; Christmas, 191; entertaining at, 72-73
Molds for baking, 173
Monasteries, 90
Moor hen, 14
Mosel River Valley, 33, 143, 147
Moselle wines, 47, 54, 71
Müller, Beda von, 132
Munich: *map* 103; beers, 156-157; Café Glockenspiel, 37; Dallmayr's delicatessen, 16, 32; Franziskanerbräu, 47; Hofbräuhaus, 157; marketplace, Renaissance, 93; Oktoberfest, 57, 156-157, *186-187,* 188; Vier Jahreszeiten Hotel, 47; Walterspiel Restaurant, 47, 54
Münster Cathedral, *147, 150*
Mushrooms: 15, *158-159;* in appetizers, 11; in *ragoût fin,* 13; with *Schnitzel à la Holstein,* 12; soup, 36; with venison, 46
Music festivals, 185
Mussels, 11
Mutton: chops, 35; with kale, 93

N*achtisch,* 35
Nasi goreng, 46
Naturschnitzel, 12
Nikolaschka (a drink of brandy, lemon and coffee), 74
Noël (French chef), 98
North Sea: 105, *map* 103
Nougat ice cream, 36
Nürnberg: *103;* bread-baking, 168; Christmas toys and cakes, 189; spice and honey cakes, 174-175
Nymphenburg, porcelain manufacture, 98

O*bsttorten* (fruit tarts), 70, *176-177, 179*
Oder River, *map* 107

Oktoberfest, 156-157, *186-187,* 188
Oldenburg, *map* 107
Omelets, 37
Onions, 128
Osterholz-Scharmbeck marketplace, *110-111, 112*
Oxen, roast, over open fire, 90
Oxtail soup, 35, 46
Oysters: 99; Dutch, 54

P*ackaged foods,* 15-16
Paella valenciana, 46
Palatinate, *map* 145
Pancakes: fruit, 15; *Plinsen,* 130; potato, 33, 114, *135; Schmarrn,* 156
Pannhas (buckwheat mush with sausage), *126*
Papayas, 58
Paprika fish, 36
Paprikaspeck (smoked bacon), 126
Parfaits, *50*
Partridge: 14; breast of, 54; liver, 54; roast, *86,* 145; roast, with sauerkraut, 10, 35
Pastries: 37, *59, 170,* 173, *176-177;* cream puffs, 70; 18th Century, 96; puff-paste patties, meat-filled, 11; Silesian, 133
Pastry shops, 37, *59,* 98
Pâtés, game, with Cumberland sauce, 54
Peacock, 90
Peas: *30-31;* with lentils, 98; soup, 11, 36; yellow, *117;* soup with bacon, 99
Pears, 13, 14, 15, *82*
Perch, fillets of, 99
Pfalz, Liselotte von der, 190
Pfefferkuchen (spice cakes), 189
Pfefferpotthast (short-rib stew), 126-127
Pfifferlinge (chanterelle mushrooms), 46, *159*
Pflaumenkuchen (plum tarts), 70, 130
Pheasant, 14, *76,* 90; bouillon, 54; Rhenish, 145; soup, 99

Philip the Good of Burgundy, 91
Piccata napolitana, 46
Pichelsteiner Fleisch, 13, *34*
Pickled fish, 108
Pickled meats, 105, 108
Pied Piper of Hameln, 112
Pike: 12, 90; with dumplings, 35
Pilgrimages, 58
Pilsener beer, *57*
Pineapple, 58; with sauerkraut, *17*
Pinkel (lightly smoked sausage),
   109-112
Pinkus Müller's restaurant, *52*
Plaice, 11
Plums: 15; harvest festival, 185;
   tarts, 70
Poland, *map* 107
Polish influence on north German
   cooking, 105, 106
Polterabend (wedding-eve party), 73
Pomerania, 74, 106; *map* 107
Pommersfelden, Germany, 155
Poppy seeds, 131
Porcelain manufacture, 96, 98
Pork: barbecued, *149;* in Bavarian
   cuisine, 47, 156; "Beefsteak
   Tartar," 129; casseroles, 126;
   chop in aspic, 114, *121;* chops,
   grilled, 54; ground, 12; fillet of,
   145; fruit-stuffed roast, breast of,
   107; loin with applesauce, 35;
   loin of, 128; pickled, 108; roast,
   12; roast, with red cabbage, 36;
   roast leg of, 131; stews, 13; ways
   of preparing, 12; sausage-
   making, *151*
Posen province, 105; *map* 107
Pot roast, 12, 99
Potatoes: *134-135;* croquettes, 46;
   growing, *132-133;* home-fried,
   35; pancakes, *33*, 114; in
   Rhineland cuisine, 144; salad,
   45; soup, 11
Preiselbeeren (tart berries), 14, 15,
   46
Preiselbeerkompott (stewed
   lingonberries), 106

Pretzels: 169; chocolate, *183;*
   vanilla-flavored, 70
Prunes, 14, 15
Prussia, East. *See* East Prussia
Prussia, King of, 89
Puddings, 15, 35, 90
Pumpernickel bread, 124, 125-127
Punch: "Warsaw Death," 73-74
Pusztafeuer, 58

Quince ice cream, 35

Rabbit stew, *80*, 92
Ragoût fin: 13, 58; calf's head, 127;
   hare, 35
Rahmschnitzel, 12
Raspberries, 75
Rationing, food, 55
Ratskeller restaurants, 16, *52*
Räucherspeck (smoked bacon), 106
Reh venison, 46
Reis Trautmannsdorf (rice pudding),
   54
Religious festivals, 185-188
Restaurants: 16, 32, 37, 45-46, 54,
   114, 145, 157; service, 46-47
Rheingau *Cabinet* (wine), 86
Rhine River Valley, 143, 147
Rhine wines, 71
Rhineland: 143-154; *map* 145
Rice pudding, 15, 54
Risotto, 54
Roasts, 12
Rococo period, 98
Rohwurst, 55
Rollmops, 11, *38-39*
Rolls, breakfast, 29
Roman civilization, 89-90
Rose sugar, 98
Rostock, *map* 107
Rügenwaldermünde, 107
Ruhr mining district, 125
Rumohr, Karl-Friedrich von, 98
Rumpolt, Max, 95
Russian influence on north German
   cooking, 105, 106
Rye breads, 168

Salads: 15; hot potato, *135;* south
   German, 155
Salmon: 12; in Rhineland cuisine,
   144; smoked, 32, 99; with sauce,
   54; with *Schnitzel à la Holstein*,
   12
Salt pork, 90
Salzgebäck (salty biscuit), 71, 129
Sandtorte, 70
Sandwiches: for *Kaffee*, 37, 70;
   open-face, 37; for second
   breakfast, 32
Sauces: béarnaise, 45; Choron, 46;
   cream, with meats, 156; for fish,
   11-12; green herb sauce, 54, 128
Sauerbraten: 8, 10, *23;* Rhenish,
   144
Sauerkraut, 8, 10, *17, 18-19, 20-21*,
   99, 127-128
Sausages: 8, 16, 45, 55, 90, *94*, 112-
   113, *151, 152-153;* Bavarian, 155;
   for *Abendbrot*, 36; with
   pumpernickel, 32; Westphalian,
   99
Saxe-Coburg-Gotha family, 130
Saxony: *maps* 107, 127; cuisine,
   130-131
Schlachtfest, 126, 150
Schlesisches Himmelreich (pork and
   dried fruits), 14
Schleswig-Holstein: 108; *map* 107
Schloss Vollrads (wine), 144
Schmalzgebackenes (lard-fried
   pastries), 169
Schmand (sour cream), in soups and
   gravies, 106
Schmandschinken (ham cooked with
   onions and cream), 75
Schmarrn (egg pancakes), 156
Schnaps, *57*, 72, *113, 124*, 126, 127,
   134
Schnellimbiss-Stube, 16
Schnellküche (quick cookery), 33
Schnitzel, 12, 54, 55
Schnitzel à la Holstein, 12
Schoppenweine (local open wines),
   55

Schwärtelbraten (roast leg of pork),
   131
Schwarzsauer (goose giblet stew),
   14
Schwarzsauer von Gans, 107
Schwarzwälder Kirschtorte (cherry
   cake), *160-161*
Scotch whisky, 72
Sea-cucumber soup, 58
Sea perch, 108
Second breakfast, 29, 32
Sekt (German champagne), 72-73
Sektfrühstück (champagne
   breakfast), 32
Semolina soup, 155
Serbisches Reisfleish, 58
Shark's fin soup, 55-58
Shellfish, 11
Sherry, 72
Shrimp: bisque, 35; with dill sauce,
   46
Silesia: 74; cuisine, 131-133; *map*
   127
Silverware, Baroque period, 96
Slavic influence on north German
   cuisine, 105, 106
Smoked fish, 108
Smoked meat, 105
Snacks: 115; Munich cuisine, 157
Soest, Germany, 125
Sole, 11, 108; with sauce, 105
Soups: 11; barley, with prunes,
   114; beer, 93; *Beetensuppe*, 75;
   bouillon with marrow, 72; clear
   oxtail, 46; clear turtle, 46;
   consommé, 99; *consommé double*,
   46; cream, 35; *Kerbelsuppe*, 127;
   lentil, 36, *117;* for midday dinner,
   35; mushroom, 36; north
   German, 105; pea, 36; pea with
   bacon, 99; pheasant, 99;
   pheasant bouillon, 54; potato,
   135; sea-cucumber, 58; semolina,
   155; shark's fin, 55-58; Silesian,
   133; *suprême*, 99; turtle, 37, 55-
   58, 93

Sour cream: as a marinade, 46; in soups and gravies, 106
Spas, *100-101*
Spätlese (wine), 71
Spätzle (tiny dumplings), 36, 154-155
Speyer, Convocation of, 175
Spice cakes, 174-175
Spices, in medieval cooking, 90
Spickgans (goose cold cut), 106-107
Spinach soup, 11
Spitzkraut (savoy cabbage), *20*
Springerle (molded cookies), *166*, 173-174
Spritzkuchen (deep-fried crullers), 115
Squabs, served with salad, 96
Stammtisch, 58
Steaks: 12; tenderloin tips, 54; on toast with mushrooms, 37
Steinhäger: 72; (juniper-flavored *Schnaps*), 126
Stettin, *map* 107
Stews: 13, *34; Bigos* (Polish hunter's stew), 75, 131-132; *Eintopf*, 14; *Hasenpfeffer* (rabbit), *80, 92;* lamprey, 93; Silesian, 133
Stinnes, Hugo, 58
Stollen (fruit bread), 173, *192*
Strasbourg, 190
Streuselkuchen (sugar-crumb cake), 70
Strudel (filled pastry rolls), 156
Stubenküken (Vierlande chicken), 108-109
Stuffing: apple, for goose, 90; for boned breast of veal, *30-31*
Stuttgart: cabbage-growing, 17; Fünkturm Restaurant, 47
Suckling pig, *94*
Sugar, 173
Sugar beets, 130
Sugar cones, 74
Sülze (head cheese), 114

Sülzkotelett (pork chop in aspic), 114, *121*
Sunday meal menus, 35, 36
Supermarkets, *10-11*, 15-16
Supper, 29, 36
Süsse Speisen, 15
Swabia, 174
Swedish influence on north German cooking, 105
Sweet-and-sour dishes, 14
Sweet-and-sour sauces: for fish, 12; Saxonian cuisine, 131
Sweetbreads: 13; in *ragoût fin*, 13
Sweets: medieval diet, 90-91; Rococo period, 98; Silesian, 133

Table setting: 37, 95; Baroque period, 96
Tacitus, 89
Tails, 13
Tantenbesuche ("aunt-visiting"), 75
Tarts: cheese, 75; cherry, with custard, 75; currant, 75; fruit, *59, 70, 176-177*
Telgte, Westphalia, *124*
Tench, 108
Tettnang, 155
Teutonic Order of knights, 75
Thatched roofs, *104*
Thirty Years' War, 95-96
Thuringia: 129-130; *map* 127
Tomato cocktail, 36
Tongue, 13
Torten: 37, 59, 176-177; 18th Century, 96
Tournedos, 105
Trade, Hanseatic League, 93
Tragantfiguren (picture cookies), 174
Trier, Germany, 143, 144
Tripe, 13
Trockenbeerenauslese (wine), 71
Tropical fruits, 58
Trotters, 13
Trout: 12; *Forelle blau*, 47
Truffles: with boar, 47; with *Schnitzel à la Holstein*, 12

Tulaer Kirschkuchen (cherry tart with custard), 75
Turbot: 11, 35, 108; with hollandaise, 99; with sauce, 105
Turnip, 15
Turtle soup: 37, 55-58, 93; clear, 46

Udders, 13
Ungarische Rhapsodie, 58

Vaerst, Eugen Baron von, 98
Vanilla cream, 36, 70
Varat guidebooks, 55
Veal: in Bavarian cuisine, 156; boned breast of, *30-31;* fillet of, *28*, 46; ground, 12; kidney, 46; roast, 12, 35; with saffron, 93; sautéed scallop of, 47; *Schnitzel*, 54, 55; steaks, 47, sautéed, 45, with tropical fruit, 58; stews, 13; tongue, in *ragoût fin*, 13; stuffed sausages, 8
Vegetables: 15; Berlin cuisine, 114; Hessian cuisine, 128; in Saxonian cuisine, 131; with veal roll, *30-31*. See also Asparagus, Beans, etc.
Venison: 14, 46, 106; cutlets with cream sauce, 36; with red cabbage, 35; with red currants, 99; roast, 93; saddle of, *82, 84-85;* soufflé, 99; stews, 75, 96
Verlobung (engagement), 73
Victoria, Queen, 130
Vierlande district, 108-109
Vinegar, souring foods with, 106
Vineyards, 33; Rhineland, 143
Violet sugar, 98
Vistula River, *map* 107
Vorspeisen (appetizers), 11

Waffles, 75
Wagner, Richard, 130
Waldmeister (woodruff herb), 71
Walterspiel, Alfred, 7, 47, 54
Walzer, Albert, 173

"Warsaw Death," 74
Weddings: 73; feasts, Renaissance, 93-95
Weinstuben, 16
Weissbier ("white beer"), 57, *157*
Weissenfels, *map* 107
Weisswürste, 8, 157
Welsch Kochpuech verteutscht von Bartlme Scrappi (Renaissance cookbook), 95
Weser River, *map* 107
West Prussia: 105; *map* 107
Westphalia: *33, 124,* 125-127; *map* 127
Westphalian ham, 126
Whitsun Festival, 189
Wienerschnitzel, 12
Wildschweinrücken (saddle of wild boar), 106
Wilhelm I, Emperor, 99
Wilhelm II, Kaiser, 99
Windbeutel (cream puffs), 70
Wines: 46-47, 71; Bernkasteler Doktor *Auslese*, 54; festivals, *148-149*, 185; fairs, 188; German, 173; jellies, 15, 35, 36; making, *146, 147;* with meals, 73; medieval, 90; *Ratskeller* restaurant, *52;* Rheingau *Cabinet, 86; Schoppenweine*, 55; Schloss Vollrads, 144; with second breakfast, 32; soup, 35
Winzerfeste, 33, 148-149
Wismar, 93, *map* 107
Woodcock, 14
Woodruff (herb), 71
Wurst, 50, 55, 188; Bavarian, 155; making, *150-151;* types, *152-153,* 154
Würstchen (little sausages), 71
Württemberg, 155, *map* 145
Würzfleisch (spiced beef stew), 13

Yeast doughs, 169

Zweites Frühstück, 29, 32
Zwiebelkuchen (open tarts), 128

Credits and Acknowledgments

The sources for the illustrations in this book are shown below. Credits for the pictures from left to right are separated by commas, from top to bottom by dashes.

All photographs by Ralph Crane except: Cover—Fred Eng. 4—Monica Suder—Manuel Millan, Donald Hinkle. 13—German National Tourist Office. 17—Bill Helms. 23, 27, 30, 31, 34, 38, 39—Henry Groskinsky. 56, 57—George Haling. 62—Bill Helms. 66, 68, 69—Erich Lessing from Magnum. 70, 74—Drawings by Luciana Roselli. 76 through 79—Jochen H. Blume. 80—Henry Groskinsky. 82 —Bill Helms. 84, 85—Drawings by Matt Greene. 86— Henry Groskinsky. 88—Richard Meek. 92—Archiv für Kunst und Geschichte, Berlin. 94—From *Von Lucullus zu Escoffier* published by Interverlag Ag-Zurich. 97—Herbert Orth courtesy Walter Bickel, Gastronomical Academy of Germany, Berlin. 100—Culver Pictures. 103—Map base by Ginn and Company, Boston, Massachusetts; overlays by Lothar Roth. 107—Map by Lothar Roth. 117, 118—Bill Helms. 120—Drawing by Matt Greene. 121—Henry Groskinsky. 127—Map by Lothar Roth. 134, 135—Bill Helms. 138, 139—Clayton Price. 145—Map by Lothar Roth. 146—Horst Munzig. 147, 150—Werbe- und Verkehrsamt Münster. 152, 153—Bill Helms. 159—From "Kleine Pilzkunde," Herrenberger Verlag. 160, 161, 166— Henry Groskinsky. 169—From *Hausbuch der Landauerschen Zwölfbrüder Stiftung*, Stadtbibliothek, Nürnberg. 172—Will McBride. 176, 177—Henry Groskinsky. 179, 183— Clayton Price. 184—Henry Groskinsky. 188 through 191 —Drawings by Luciana Roselli. 192—Henry Groskinsky. 196, 197—Drawings by Matt Greene.

For their help in the production of this book the editors wish to thank the following: *in the United States,* Margaret Laun Afton; B. Altman & Co.; Antique Porcelain Co.; Baccarat Crystal; H. Baumann, Director of the German Tourist Office; Bonniers Inc.; Four Seasons Restaurant; Georg Jensen Inc.; Claus Glismann, Marketing Advisor to the German Food and Beverage Industry; Ingeborg Godenschweger of the German Information Center; Hammacher-Schlemmer; William Hellering; Hans Holterbosch, Inc.; Jean Silversmiths Inc.; Hanna Kiep of the German Embassy; M. Kumrow of the German Tourist Office; Lord & Taylor; Macy's; Norbert Muhlen; New York Beer Import Company; Norsk Inc.; The Pottery Barn; Hans Rathje, Public Relations, Lufthansa; Schaller and Weber; C. & J. Willenborg; *in Germany,* Altonaer Museum; Gisa von Barsewisch; I. K. H. Prinzessin Hella von Bayern; Dr. Karl Ludwig Bieser; Arthur Binder and family; Lilla von Brentano; Eduard and Aleke Brinkama; Shirley van Buiren; Anne-Marie Dieterici; Dominik Murr u. Sohn, in Munich; Gräfin Marion Dönhoff; Gerda Endler; Dr. Paul Engelmeier of Heimathaus, in Telgte; Landwirtschaftsdirektorin Feldmann of the Landwirtschaftskammer in Bonn; Martha Friedländer; Gaststätte Spieker; Anton Geiss; Christian Gellert and family; Alfons Graacher; Ulla Groth; Gutsschänke Neuhof; Ruth Hagen; W. Hartmann of the German Central Tourist Association; Firma Hengstenberg, in Esslingen; Ilse Hochhuth; Dr. Hellmut Jaesrich of *Der Monat;* E. Jung; Marcia Kahn; Ursula von Kardorff; M. Klase; Paul Klaus; Konditorei Kreipe, in Hanover; Ursula von Krosigk; O. A. Kunkel, in Berlin; Kur- und Verkehrsverein, in Bad Ems; die Landwirtschaftsschule of Bonn; Sigrid Lanzrath; Dr. Helga Leendertz of the Landwirtschaftskammer in Bonn; Graf Hans von Lehnsdorff; Else Marquart; Graf Matuschka-Greiffenclau; Pinkus Müller, in Münster; Camillo Noel of the Stadtverwaltung of Munich; Dr. Christa Pieske; Peter Range; the Ratskeller, in Bremen; Theodor W. Rautenstrauch; Klaus Ruestig; Schlosshotel Kronberg, the Taunus; Dr. Franz Schwarzenstein of the German Central Tourist Association, in Frankfurt; Rolf Schyle of the German Central Tourist Association, in Frankfurt; Franz Spelman; the Stadtverwaltung of Münster; Dr. Walter Stahl; Klara Strobel; Joseph and Georg Tafferthofer; Emmi Wahlbrodt; Steve Walleck; Karl-Adolf Willmann, Director of the Hotel Vier-Jahreszeiten, in Hamburg.

Sources consulted in the production of this book include: *German Cookery* by Hans Karl Adam; *Das schmeckt so gut in Deutschland* by Lilo Aureden; *Dr. Oetker German Home Cooking* by Dr. August Oetker, Bielefeld; *Dr. Oetker Kochbuch* by Dr. August Oetker, Bielefeld; *Deftige Hausmannskost* by Hans W. Blank; *Spezialitäten aus Deutschen Küchen* by Richard Boelke; *Doennigs Kochbuch* by Gertrud Brostowski; *Das neue grosse Kochbuch* by Roland Göock; *Leckerbissen aus deutschen Küchen* by Roland Göock; *Bayerisches Kochbuch* by Maria Hofmann; *Das neue Kiehnle Kochbuch* by Hermine Kiehnle; *Ostpreussische Spezialitäten* by Marion Lindt; *Die Kunst der heimatlichen Küche* by Ernst Marquardt; *Das grosse "Odette" Kochbuch* by Odette; *Schlesisches Kochbuch* by Henriette Pelz; *Spezialitäten Deutscher Lande* by Marianne Piepenstock; *Die Führung der Feinen und Bürgerlichen Küche* by M. Ridder; *German Cookery* by Elizabeth Schuler; *Mein Kochbuch* by Elizabeth Schuler; *The German Cookbook* by Mimi Sheraton; *Ich Helf Dir Kochen* by Hedwig Maria Stuber; *Das grosse 1 x 1 der guten Küche* by Gertrud Villforth.

x

PRODUCTION STAFF FOR TIME INCORPORATED

John L. Hallenbeck (Vice President and Director of Production), Robert E. Foy and Caroline Ferri. Text photocomposed under the direction of Albert J. Dunn